ABOUT THE AUTHOR

Janice Nix's journey is a remarkable story of someone with a criminal history transforming her life to become an award-winning Probation Service Officer. It embodies the transformative change that is possible for ex-offenders. Winning the probation service's Diversity and Engagement Award enabled her to believe in herself and extend that belief to others on similar journeys.

Janice lives to inspire and empower individuals and to be the best version of themselves that they can be. Her motto is 'Each one, teach one', and she truly believes that change is achievable, no matter who you are.

BREAKING OUT

JANICE NIX

WITH
ELIZABETH SHEPPARD

ONE PLACE. MANY STORIES

HQ
An imprint of HarperCollins*Publishers* Ltd
1 London Bridge Street
London SE1 9GF

www.harpercollins.co.uk

HarperCollins*Publishers*
1st Floor, Watermarque Building, Ringsend Road
Dublin 4, Ireland

This edition 2021

1
First published in Great Britain by
HQ, an imprint of HarperCollins*Publishers* Ltd 2021

ISBN: 978-0-00-838594-1

MIX
Paper from
responsible sources
FSC™ C007454

This book is produced from independently certified FSC™ paper
to ensure responsible forest management.

For more information visit: www.harpercollins.co.uk/green

Typeset in ITC Galliard by
Palimpsest Book Production Ltd, Falkirk, Stirlingshire

Printed and bound in Great Britain by
CPI Group (UK) Ltd, Croydon CR0 4YY

Janice
This book is dedicated to my daughter Nadia,
the real survivor

Elizabeth
For Edward and Alvin Shivmangal

CONTENTS

1: Fuck it bucket   1

2: Crisis centre   13

3: The year I took up badness   22

4: Aye aye, dick eye   44

5: Cops and robbers   77

6: If a woman runs the country – why can't we do this?   92

7: Murder on New Bond Street   108

8: You're a different cat, Mama J   136

9: Money talk, bullshit walk   169

10: Waiting like a loaded gun   194

11: In the dock in Gucci   224

12: Green channel   246

13: Alone time   276

14: Position of trust   301

15: Nine to five to nine   315

16: Clearing up a hurricane with a dustpan and brush   334

Acknowledgements   343

1

FUCK IT BUCKET

ISABELLE WAS BEAUTIFUL. GOLDEN hair, deep grey eyes, a high pale forehead. But I didn't gaze for long. The girl was a beautiful hot mess. My job was to keep her out of prison.

She was restless and supermodel thin. Smoking brown – heroin – had turned her into barely skin and bone. I knew she used white – cocaine – as well. *White takes yuh up, an' brown brings yuh down*. The angles of her face were filled with shadow and up close, I could see faint dried scabs where she'd been scratching. Craving for drugs makes you claw at your skin. Her dirty hair was full of tangles. The more details you noticed, the rougher this girl looked.

I was her engagement worker with London's proba-tion service. Izzie was a good girl underneath, I thought – she'd made it there each week since she'd been ordered to attend a support group with me. That Tuesday morning, for an hour and a half, she was one of ten women, all on probation, who'd come to report their progress. If they didn't engage with the service, and with me, they were likely to be going to prison.

Five weeks earlier, I'd set eyes on Izzie for the very first time. A probation officer colleague of mine had been trying to work with her. But Izzie didn't want to know. She'd been late to one meeting and missed a home visit entirely. She was one breach of probation away from the end of the line.

I quickly read her file. Involvement with gangs, drug dealing, prostitution. Arrested with forty other members of the ring – all the others received custodial sentences. But Izzie was put on three months' probation. A beautiful girl is often let off lightly by the courts. *And don't she just know it. Now she thinks that she can get away with anything.*

I looked her up and down. I saw a cute little wannabe smartarse – a chance-taker who badly overestimated how far her cuteness could go. She'd got a whole lot of attitude – but one look in her eyes and a scared little girl was staring back at me.

'Hello, Izzie,' I said. 'Your probation officer tells me that you're not engaging with her. What's wrong?'

I could see that she was taken aback by me, even a little intimidated. I'm tall and powerful-looking – I know how to make an impression. I've used that presence of mine to put the frighteners on far tougher customers than this girl. I watched her thinking, trying to decide how she could work this situation.

She decided to play it cute. She tried to flirt with me. She flipped her knotted hair and began a long spiel about all the problems she'd been having. How difficult it was to get to meetings with probation because the neighbours were noisy and kept her awake and the buses weren't reliable and she'd run out of money for her Oyster card and –

I cut right through her routine.

'Listen,' I said. 'This is fix-up time. It's your last chance.'

At least I'd got her attention.

'If you breach your probation order, they'll put you inside. It's very close to happening. Is that what you want?'

'Er – '

I looked her frankly up and down.

'You live far from the kitchen?' I asked her.

'Sorry – what?'

'It looks like you don't cook. Like you don't eat.'

When she understood, she tried to laugh it off.

'Oh, hahaha. Far from the kitchen. Yeah.'

'Izzie,' I said, 'I'm going to work with you, and together we are going to sort out this crap.'

She shuffled her feet.

'But before that – we're going out to lunch.'

I took her to a local eat-as-much-as-you-like Chinese buffet. She piled up her plate and I could tell that she was hungry. I let her dig in, and waited until she slowed down.

'Izzie.'

She raised her head. I noticed she looked better. The warm food had put a little colour in her face.

'We're going to start slow,' I said to her. 'Each day, we're going to set you a target. Something you have to get done. Maybe go out and buy some food. Do your laundry. Clean your place.'

'Okay.'

I knew she was only playing me along. She was still using drugs, so I wouldn't get a whole lot of co-operation. Still, we had to start somewhere.

'We're going to keep in touch by phone as well. I want to hear how things are going.'

'Okay.'

'Three times a week,' I told her. 'I'll call you at ten in the morning, on Monday and Wednesday and Friday.'

I could see straightaway she was not too happy with that.

'Do you think that's too early?' I asked.

'Uh – well, Janice, look. Quite often I'm still in bed then.'

'It's good for you to get up in the morning. It might be hard at first, but you'll get used to it.'

She stared down at the table.

'And I'll see you next week, in the office, for our meeting. On time. I don't accept excuses for lateness.'

She looked at me wide-eyed, and then she nodded. She didn't try to argue again.

Back at my desk, I read her file in full. Artistic parents – her father was a musician – but their marriage broke down while their daughter was a very small child. Her mother had been diagnosed with bipolar depression. After the split with Izzie's dad, she found another guy quite quickly. But Izzie and her stepfather didn't get along. The older she got, the nastier their arguments became. Eventually the fighting at home got physical. Then, when Izzie was thirteen, she found a boyfriend. That was when the real trouble started.

Jake was a messed-up eighteen-year-old who carried a knife to feel more manly. He beat up his girlfriends if he thought they had stepped out of line. To Izzie, he seemed sophisticated, handsome and cool. By now she had been taken into care because of her stepfather's violence, but no one from children's services could keep tabs on her. Soon she was sleeping in a football club storeroom with Jake. One moment he was kind and supportive, the next he was accusing her of sleeping with his friends. She was dragged into his world of mental control.

When she turned sixteen, social services arranged for her to move into a flat of her own. One day Jake came round to visit and found a man's sock. It belonged to the boyfriend of a friend, but he blew his top with paranoid jealousy. He beat Izzie up so badly that she ended up in hospital. Then he disappeared. She was too scared to press charges, just in case he didn't get a prison sentence and came looking for her.

A friend of a friend introduced her to the crack pipe. Izzie found a way she could blot out all the misery and mess of a life that was going off the rails. Pretty quickly she was hooked. She had a new boyfriend, and the two of them started robbing dealers. They'd ring up and say that they wanted to buy a large amount. The local dealers used younger boys as runners, so when the runner arrived with the drugs, the new boyfriend beat the lads up and took their stuff.

Then Izzie was recruited as a runner herself. By now the drugs ring had been infiltrated by police. She'd not been working long when she tried to score with a user who was really an undercover cop. That was how she was arrested.

The women's group met in the conference room at Brixton probation office. It was spare and plain, with three off-white walls and the fourth painted deep swampy green. The paint needed retouching. We pushed the small tables up to one end and made a circle of chairs in the middle, our backs to the clamour of notices pinned on the walls. Those sheets of A4 paper signalled all the chaos in the lives of the people who were sitting in those chairs.

WORRIED ABOUT DOMESTIC VIOLENCE?

HAVE YOU BEEN SEXUALLY ABUSED?

PROBLEMS WITH BENEFIT CLAIMS?

**WE'LL FIND THE RIGHT COURSE
FOR THE RIGHT JOB!**

STAND UP FOR YOUR RIGHTS!

In the middle of the circle, I placed the fuck it bucket. It's not a real bucket, but we all imagined it together. I told the women to sling their rubbish in.

'Chuck it in there, ladies. Doesn't matter what it is. Doesn't matter if it's messy. Maybe you screwed up. Maybe you made a decision in a panic, then found out it isn't working. If it hurts or doesn't work or it's gone all wrong – in it goes. We'll get these problems out and take a look at them, one at a time. We'll think together, and we'll all try to help.'

As the bucket filled up, I felt the room grow calmer. When women talk, I know that things can change.

I looked around. I could see that Izzie wasn't listening to the talk in the group – just the same as the last three weeks that she'd been there. She was distracted, glancing at her watch, then looking again, easing up the cuff of her sweatshirt very slowly so that maybe I wouldn't notice what she was doing. She looked at the clock on the wall and fidgeted, wondering if her watch might be slow. She was attending the meeting, doing as she was told – but she wasn't really there.

Who you waitin' for, girl?

Again I spotted her swift furtive glance towards the window.

Who you waitin' for, Izzie?

I thought I knew the answer, but I needed to be certain, so I walked to the window and peered through its vertical white bars into the street. Just as I looked outside, a silver BMW 5 Series rolled round the corner and parked right opposite. I'd seen it before, each

Tuesday for the previous three weeks. It got me wondering – same driver, same car. He was a black man, West Indian. *A bredda*, I thought to myself.

We had fifteen minutes until the group was over. I'd done all I could to help the other women that day. I looked again at the still shape of the man waiting in the car. I was pretty sure by then what he was doing here, and what he'd come to do. Bit by bit, line by line, he'd come to destroy Izzie's life.

Whatever it took, I decided that I was going to stop him.

'Can you please start clearing up?' I said to the group. 'I have to see to something.'

I walked along the building's winding corridors, then pressed the buzzer which released the final outer door. It was an early summer day – a sharp breeze still blew, but I could feel the warmth of the sun. I crossed the road and tapped on the BMW's window.

The man in the driving seat looked up. Nice car, but he was still dressed rough. I suspected that he was a shotter – selling drugs on the street. That's why he wasn't flash. He didn't want to draw attention to himself.

I know what you're doing here. Yuh can't tek mi fi fool.

When he met my eyes, I rotated my hand, telling him to wind down the window. He was so surprised that he did it.

'Good morning, young man. You waitin' for Izzie?' I asked.

He didn't answer – just stared up at me without blinking.

Slowly, through pursed lips, he exhaled.

'I am from probation.' I touched the ID badge that hung around my neck. *'Mi nah waa see yuh yah again.'*

The dealer shrugged. I spoke more firmly.

'Leave Izzie alone. If I see you here again, I will call the police.'

Now he looked straight at me. At first he was surprised, but I could see I'd made him angry. Eye to eye for a moment, we both held our ground.

'Don' make mi spin two time an see yuh out here,' I said to him. My words were a warning.

Still holding my gaze, he wound the window back up. Then he started the engine, and the car slid forwards. I watched as he drove around the corner into Stockwell Road, and vanished from sight.

Back in the conference room, the group was breaking up. The women were chatting, but Izzie wasn't joining in. She was pulling up her leggings and flipping back her hair. She went over to the pile of coats and jackets on a table in the corner and searched for her own.

'Izzie?' I said.

'Yes?' She half turned towards me, threw me that distracted, lovely smile.

'Can I have a word, when the others have gone?'

'Errrr – '

She thought she was in a hurry for her date with her dealer.

'You got time, Izzie. Nobody's waiting outside.'

'But – '

I was her engagement worker, which meant she couldn't argue with me. She pressed her lips shut and looked confused.

'Your man in the BMW,' I said to her. 'The guy waiting outside. What's the deal with him?'

'Markie? He's a – friend. He picks me up here and takes me back home.'

She knew I didn't believe her.

'So what's the real deal with Markie?' I asked.

She shrugged and didn't answer.

'Let's sit down,' I said. 'Let's talk. You've not said anything today. We need a catch-up.'

'Yeah, yeah – sure. But Janice – I need to meet Markie right now.'

I looked her straight in the eye.

'You don't need to meet Markie now. Or ever. I told you, no one's waiting. He's gone.'

She gasped.

'Why?'

'Because I told him to go away and leave you alone.'

Her face clouded over. 'Why did you – ?' Then she remembered again that I work for probation. She stopped speaking and folded her arms. As she gathered her sweatshirt back against her body, I noticed again how painfully thin she really was.

'Will you do something for me?' I said to her. She nodded, but I knew she was angry.

'Izzie, I want you to look in the mirror. For five

minutes, every evening, before you go to bed.' I put on a southern belle-style accent, pursed my lips up and gave a sexy little wiggle. 'Really look in dat mirror, girl, an' see just how damn gawjus you are.'

She gave me a small, uncertain smile. She shifted from foot to foot.

'Uh – '

I knew I'd be taking a big chance, but I thought I could reach her.

'And then,' I went on firmly, 'when you've realised that – realise something else. Izzie – you're a walking commodity. Shall I tell you why?'

Now she was staring at the floor.

'Izzie – if I was a certain type of criminal, a man with intentions, I'd entertain you. I'd wine you and I'd dine you. I'd get you seen in all the right places. Put you in a flat in Mayfair. Do you know how much escorts make up there? You'd be my prize girl.'

She didn't lift her eyes.

'Or maybe I'd put you on a plane. Get you working as a drugs mule. Just look at you,' I went on. 'What a useful commodity you'd be.'

A moment before, she'd heard something that caught her attention. I could tell she was listening now.

'If you was a certain type of criminal, Janice?' she said. 'What's that mean?'

'Let's just say – before probation, I led a pretty colourful life.'

She was silent, weighing me up.

'That shit you buy from Markie changes everything,'

I said to her. 'Smoke that crap, and the people who really care about you will feel like the bad guys. Your drug friends become your whole new world. But in that world, everybody feeds off everybody. I want to stop them feeding off you, Izzie.'

'But how can you?' she asked me softly.

'It's going to take a while,' I said to her. 'But Izzie – *tek yeh pussy off yeh forehead, girl.*'

She burst out laughing. I'd never heard her laughter before. I'd never seen her face without the little hooks of strain dragging down her eyes and her mouth.

'Izzie,' I said to her, 'we're going to change all this. We're going to make you a new life. You won't be a walking commodity no more.'

2

CRISIS CENTRE

PROBATION IS A LIFELINE.

I looked at the pile of client case files on my desk. Every file held a life. It was the story of a human being in desperate trouble, struggling to cope with the issues they were facing.

I knew that some offenders were never going to listen. They didn't want to work with me. They were people who hadn't accepted they needed change in their lives. But mostly what I faced day by day was different kinds of crisis. Some crises are slow-burning, and some are immediate and violent and dreadful.

My job is to keep offenders out of prison. To help them to make changes before it's too late. To support them as they try to turn things round. A client on probation sees his or her officer or engagement worker weekly. We check that the client is doing the community work ordered by the court and advise them on looking for a job, housing problems, benefit applications, child-care or domestic issues. The client can ask us for support with anything else they might be worried about.

But far too often, the lifeline is pulled tight. It's close to breaking. Then a probation meeting becomes a frantic attempt to grab hold of someone who's teetering on the edge of a cliff. I have one last chance to catch them before they topple backwards and vanish from sight.

A new client, Becca, was in serious trouble for breaching the terms of her probation. I reached court early, dressed in the smart black clothes my job required. I wanted to make sure I spoke to Becca before her appearance.

Breach court was where the people who had fallen through the system ended up. They were there because they'd failed to keep the terms of their probation, which usually meant they'd failed to fulfil a community work order. Now they were in breach of the instructions of the court. They were sent back before the judge. Sometimes the court would accept that there were reasons why the problems had happened. But for others, this was the last stop on the line. If you breach the terms of your probation, it usually means prison.

In the entrance hall, security staff checked everyone who came into the building for weapons and drugs. The guard on duty smiled and said good morning. I went through checks and bag searches and headed to the first floor. I was hoping I'd find Becca in the waiting room for court number two, although I wasn't confident she'd even make it to the hearing. But to my surprise, she'd got there before me. What didn't surprise me was the misery, confusion and defeat in her face.

She hunched forward in her seat, arms tightly wrapped around her chest, rocking backwards and forwards. Her coat was bristly with dog hairs. Her dark hair was greasy and uncombed. Her face was very pale. I could see she was completely exhausted.

'Good morning,' I said. Her eyes flicked towards me when I spoke, but she made no reply.

'Becca, come with me for a minute. Let's go and sit in the consultation room where it's private.'

I held the door open and watched her shuffle slowly along the wide corridor. The consultation room was tiny and windowless, painted a chilly pale blue. She sat down heavily in one of the wooden chairs. I closed the door behind us.

It was three weeks since my colleague Ros had handed me her bulging case file with a worried frown.

'One for you, Jan. She's breaching and things are getting serious. Any chance you can talk to her?'

The case file told a wretched story. Becca was a gentle, kind-hearted woman. She loved her twelve-year-old son Jack, and Martin, her husband, very much, though she couldn't always manage to take care of them. She had learning difficulties and her mental health was up and down. Her GP kept on trying to ease her mood swings and depression with medication, but it wasn't so easy for someone like Becca to follow a routine. From time to time, she'd forget to take her tablets and things would go pear-shaped – but at least the family was together. As a unit, they were coping. Then one June day, Becca found Martin dead in their kitchen. He'd had a heart attack, out of the blue.

Martin had done everything at home. He was Becca's carer, he looked after Jack and he kept the household running. Without him, things quickly fell apart. Becca didn't know how the bills got paid or how the light-bulbs got changed or how the heating got fixed. She didn't understand that the housing benefit covered the rent, or how to make sure it stayed that way.

So she did nothing to keep her life in order. She'd no idea at all what to do. She failed to contact anyone she needed to. More confused and scared every day, she simply froze. She spent all the money in her bank account, and when the cash ran out, she started stealing food. Letters from the council and benefit forms from the Department for Work and Pensions landed on the doormat, but Becca just ignored them. As the writing in the letters turned red, she shut the DWP and the council from her mind.

When a man she knew offered her a chance to earn some money, she believed he was her friend. He spent time with her at home, which she thought was nice because since Martin died, she'd often been lonely. Then her friend invited other friends to hang out there as well. Five or six strangers took over Becca's living room until the small hours of the morning, drinking and smoking weed. The job her friend gave her was to take a bunch of credit cards and go out and buy watches. Pretty soon, she'd been arrested for credit card fraud.

By now it was November. Her heating wasn't working and the house was freezing cold, but her landlord refused to do repairs while the rent was in arrears. The unopened letters in the kitchen were all final demands for unpaid bills, and Becca and Jack were in danger of eviction from their home. When her fraud case went to court, the judge put Becca on probation. She didn't keep the appointments. She'd never been able to get organised without Martin. But by breaching the terms of her probation, she was at risk of being sent to prison.

I remembered our first meeting. At the best of times she was easily confused, and by that stage her thinking had almost completely shut down. All she could say when I'd asked about any situation in her life was 'my husband did it'. A few days after we first met, she and her daughter were evicted. Jack was put into emergency foster care by the local council. Forced to sleep in the open, alone and terrified, Becca thought the park near Iceland seemed a safe and quiet place. But late at night she was attacked there by two men. Both of them raped her.

I had to find a way to get her off the street. She was in terrible danger, and with every day that passed, the weather grew colder. Her homelessness endangered her life. But my power was limited. As an engagement worker, I couldn't give her all the help and support she needed. She needed to go to a crisis centre, so that her name could be added to the list for emergency housing. I'd tried to explain this in a way which wouldn't overwhelm her. But as I'd searched for the words, I could see she wasn't taking it in. She'd just kept shaking her head.

It was filling out forms that was the problem, I realised. She'd anxiously questioned me about it. 'Forms. Will they have forms?' Even when I told her I'd go with her, it didn't seem to help. That's when I'd suddenly understood how all of this had gone so wrong. Gently, I'd asked Becca whether she could read. She answered in a whisper: 'No. My husband did it.'

All those letters from the council piling up. Those final demands for bills she hadn't paid. Those notifications of arrears. She hadn't understood a single one of them. For Becca, being asked to fill out forms was almost as humiliating as having nowhere to sleep.

Now she sat in the court's consultation room, arms folded tightly, just rocking. I glanced at my watch. In a few minutes, she must face the judge. A paralysing panic had her in its grip. I knew I must break through it. I looked for a way to help her trust me.

'Becca, I understand how you feel.'

She made no response.

'If I told you something, something about me, would you believe me?'

For a moment she looked up. Her eyes met mine.

'So,' I went on, 'I was on probation once. Just like you. It was a long time ago. And I breached, and they sent me to prison.'

Her expression didn't change. She was so stressed and overwhelmed that I wasn't sure she'd heard me.

'So I know what this is like,' I continued. 'It's scary when you have to face the judge. But I promise you that I am here to support you.'

'You were sent to prison?' she whispered.

'Yes. Yes, I was. I know how scared you are. I hope the judge is sensible today and doesn't send you down. I think that's what will happen. So as soon as we're done here, we'll go and get you something to eat.'

Two tears had trickled down her cheeks. She quickly wiped them away.

'Okay,' she whispered.

'How about we get a sausage roll? Is that a deal?'

When she heard the words 'sausage roll', she looked up at me at last.

'Deal,' said Becca. I reached over and gently squeezed her hand.

SEPTEMBER 1985

I was driven to Holloway prison in a crowded van – the squeeze box. I saw the two stern stone griffins on the gateway as it opened with a harsh metallic scrape. Night had fallen on the way, and tears streamed down my face in the darkness of the van.

The first thing I noticed inside was the stench. Even breathing the air made me feel dirty. We were put into a gloomy room to wait to be processed. Every new arrival had a number, and after each was called, there was a long, long wait for the next.

A girl was sitting in the waiting area with a plate on

her knee, eating a small cake filled with custard. I had no idea where the cake could have come from. As she tried to raise the spoon from the plate to her mouth, she kept missing, smearing custard on her cheeks. Each time, her head dipped lower. Her hair began to trail in the mess on the plate. Everyone looked away.

'Can I help you?' I asked.

'She gouchin',' someone muttered. That means she was so far out on heroin that she was helpless. No one else spoke. The girl toppled forwards. Her face slowly sank into the broken leaky cake.

With good behaviour, I would have to serve twelve weeks. But suddenly, an hour seemed an endless stretch of time. I was very close to panic. Waves of nausea and fear spread through my body.

I was all alone. I didn't know how I would get through it. I didn't know if I could.

'Becca, I have a suggestion,' I said. 'You don't have to decide now, but just hear me out. Then you can think about it.'

'Okay.'

She was sitting in a coffee shop with me. She'd had some warm food. She was calmer. Her court hearing had gone well, with a sensible judge. He saw she had no chance of keeping to her terms of probation right now. She was lost in fear and grief and chaos. The court had requested a PSR – a pre-sentencing report – on her, along with a mental health assessment.

Now we had a little bit of time – time to take her

to the council and help her get started with the process of applying for housing benefit. If she could find a stable home and attend her probation meetings, there was a chance that Jack could live with her again. There might be a way to get her life back on track.

'At probation,' I said, 'we run a group for women. There are two staff there – well, usually two. I'm one of them. It started a few months ago and quite a few people come along.'

She sipped her coffee slowly.

'We talk. We listen to each other and we try to find solutions to the problems we face every day. All the women there are on probation, so they understand how difficult things can be – including me. Nobody thinks badly of anyone.'

'Talking to strangers?' said Becca suspiciously.

'You don't have to say anything. You can just come along and listen. We have tea and coffee and sandwiches.'

'I'm not sure.'

'Okay. Just take your time. I'll be seeing you next week at your appointment. If you'd like to join the group, we'll sort it out then. But a lot of the people who come – they find it helps.'

Becca lost her way. When her husband died, she was vulnerable. She'd trusted the wrong person. She took just one wrong turning. And now, to find her way back to safety seemed a nearly impossible task. I understood how quickly this could happen. I knew it all too well. Because a long time ago, I took a wrong turning too.

3

THE YEAR I TOOK UP BADNESS

ON A COLD NIGHT in March 1976, I left my mother's house and caught the last train to London. I didn't tell her I was leaving. I knew it would only cause a fight.

I couldn't pay for a ticket. But in those days, the stations had no barriers, and no one on the journey came to check. When I reached Euston, it was late and the place was deserted. I was scared, but I knew I had to hide it. I took a deep breath, and set out across the huge empty concourse all alone. I'd come to lose myself in the noise and confusion of the city. I was looking for a way to disappear.

And Sugarlips helped me do it. I met her straight-away, right outside Euston station. It was almost as if she had been waiting for me there. I saw her from the corner of my eye, leaning against the high black wall of one of the big modern offices just outside. She was slight with dark pageboy-style hair, dressed in bell-bottomed jeans with frayed hems. A big leather bag swung from her arm.

'Where you comin' from, chuck?' she called out. She had a northern accent.

'Leicester.'

'What's your name?'

'Janice.'

'How old are you?'

'Twenty,' I lied.

'Where you goin'?'

I didn't know. I'd left Leicester in a panic. Then, on the train, I'd thought about Daddy. I knew he lived in Ealing, but I hadn't heard a word from him in months. Perhaps I could find him and ask him for help.

'Er – my dad lives down here.' I was trying to remember his address. 'I'm going to his house.'

'Anyone know you've come?'

'Um – no. Not really.'

'Will your dad help you?'

'Uh – yeah. Yeah, I think so. But – um – I'm not sure where he lives. He might have moved.'

She waited for a moment, then she asked me, 'Are you hungry?'

Just hearing the word 'hungry' made my stomach rumble.

'Oh, yes.'

'Would you like a chip butty?'

'Yes please!'

She was the turning in my path. And before I even knew it, I had travelled far away.

*

Sugarlips lived at the YWCA in Central London. She told me I could stay with her that night if I wanted. I didn't understand why she wanted to be friends, but at least it was somewhere to sleep. Her tiny room smelled of weed. She had a sink, two single beds, a bashed-up portable telly and a scrappy little curtain nailed in place across the window.

I'd brought almost nothing with me, so I decided to wash my underwear in the sink with Sugarlips' bar of White Windsor soap. At least then I'd have something for tomorrow that was clean.

'What are you doing?'

'Washing my knickers.'

Sugarlips burst out laughing.

'Don't bother – we can get you some new ones!'

'I don't have much money,' I said nervously.

She smiled.

'Don't worry, Janice – we can always get things!'

Next morning, I found out what she meant.

We went shopping, but we didn't buy anything. Instead we just wandered the whole length of Oxford Street, looking in the big department stores. Sugarlips kept picking up one thing then another and asking if I liked them. Back at the YWCA, she reached into her bag. She said simply: 'There you are, these are yours!' and tossed a pack of M&S knickers onto my knee.

'Did you nick them?'

Sugarlips rolled her eyes.

'Where else you think they come from?' she said.

*

Shoplifting was her business. She worked to order and looked after a group of other girls who did the same. I had no money and no home. So when she asked me if I wanted to join them, I decided that I did.

'You're green as grass, Janice,' she told me, but she said it in a friendly sort of way. A fresh face like mine was an advantage – no one in the stores where Sugarlips and her crew went to work would know who I was. Still, because I was a black girl, she told me bluntly, I must be extra careful. Security would watch me very closely.

In her tiny room, she taught me how to steal. My first lesson was arming. She showed me how to slide an item that I'd taken right up under my arm between my jacket and my bag. Do it in a second, so that people barely notice. Then carry on strolling, browsing the racks, never fiddling with your arm or your shoulder because that just draws attention. Don't rush, don't look round, just admire a few more items then walk right on.

My second lesson was crotching: how to roll an item tightly then shove it right up between your legs. The fabric of your skirt can make a difference – nothing smooth or clingy that reveals what you're carrying underneath. Once the item's in position, walk calmly and slowly. Never touch the item, or try to adjust it.

To conceal stolen goods, Sugarlips said, you need a store carrier bag – one that's new and fresh-looking, as though you only just paid for what's inside it. It's easy to get them – just go into a shop with your hands full and act flustered. The assistants are helpful and will give you a big store bag to help you out. We kept our bags in a cupboard, crisp and flat, ready for our next expedition.

Some days, we'd meet the team of girls Sugarlips managed and all go for coffee or for lunch. On other days, the men who paid her came to visit, collected their goods and gave us our new orders. They were detailed and specific on the brands and styles they wanted – and off we went to source them for our clients.

Sugarlips was friendly, but as the weeks went by I still knew almost nothing about her. We lived so close together, but she was always secretive and quiet. She was all alone in the city, just as I was. She never talked about herself or asked me any questions – why I'd run away, or where my family lived. But she noticed when I was feeling sad. '*You and me against the world, chuck,*' she'd say with a quick little smile.

She noticed that I knew my way around, and I explained that although I'd run away from Leicester, I grew up in London. I told her a bit about my past. She frowned as she heard about my parents' one-roomed flat in Notting Hill, which was a poor and working class area then.

'Daddy came here to work,' I explained. 'Not on the *Windrush* – you know, the famous boat that came over, but not long after. He had friends who came as well. This country needed workers – it was after the war – and there were opportunities here. But then –

you know, the way they got treated, it was like they weren't welcome after all. People put signs up in the guest houses – no blacks, no Irish.'

Sugarlips shook her head. We were taking a break in a coffee shop in Selfridges.

'What job did your dad get?' she asked me.

'The Walls factory first, then Nestlé in west London. He used to do the night shifts, and when we came home from school we had to be quiet because he was sleeping. That was later, though, when we'd moved to Southall. We had a house by then.'

'He must have worked hard.'

'He did. They both did. And long hours. They'd change his shifts sometimes, right at the last minute. That's why he was tired – it made him lose his finger.'

'What d'you mean – lose his finger?'

'He caught his hand in some machinery – it should have been covered, but it wasn't. It tore the top two joints off.'

I saw Sugarlips shudder.

'We had a paraffin stove to do the cooking, and Mummy made us sit on the bed to make sure we didn't touch it, but one day she went outside – it was only for a minute, and Terry – that's my little brother – climbed down and tried to put his hand in the pot. He nearly tipped it over – all the liquid poured out and it was hissing and smoking. Daddy got back home just at that minute and saw the smoke out the window. He was really shouting, but I think it was because he was scared. After that we moved.'

I hoped that if I talked, she might do the same and let me get to know her. But Sugarlips would never drop her guard. She wouldn't even tell me her real name. I wanted to find out how she'd started to live her strange life. She was quick-witted and observant – I remembered how she'd spotted me at Euston – so surely, I thought, there must be other ways apart from crime that she could earn a living. One day, I asked her nervously why she didn't get an ordinary job.

'D'you think I have qualifications, Jan?' she answered abruptly.

'You're smart,' I told her. It was true.

'No, I'm not. Not like that, anyway. I didn't pass exams.'

Now I was worried I'd upset her. 'Sugarlips, I didn't mean to – '

'So what else can I do? I can't go back to Bradford, not after – '

Sugarlips stopped speaking. I felt a jolt of darkness in the room. It was as though the lights had flickered.

'Is that where you come from – Bradford?' I asked.

But she'd said too much already. She pressed her lips together and turned her head away. She quickly forgave me, though, offering a smile and a packet of Jaffa cakes.

Sugarlips didn't want to remember her past. I understood how she felt because in Leicester, before I ran away, things happened that I didn't want to think about either. Things that made me feel dirty. A friend of my uncle's quite often came to visit. He'd come upstairs to find me when I was on my own. It made me feel sick when he'd put his hot, dry hand on my knee. I didn't dare ask him to stop. The only escape was to pretend to hear my mother calling for me. I'd shout, 'Yes, Mummy?' then jump up and quickly leave the room.

I felt glad to be in London with Sugarlips to look after me. I was better off in charge of my own life, no matter what. I was never going home, I decided. No matter how many risks we were taking, it was safer for me here.

One day in D H Evans on Oxford Street, I crotched four bottles of expensive aftershave. They were safely up my skirt and I wanted to leave, but I noticed a detective who was working the floor. She was suspicious and extremely persistent, her eyes on me wherever I walked. I hung around, pretending to browse while I watched her reflection in the shiny displays. If I tried to step outside, I knew that she would pounce.

After half an hour, I gave up. Today's take would have to go back on the shelves. I returned to the perfume hall, stooped to examine something on a lower shelf, slid my bottles of aftershave carefully out of their hiding place and left them there. Completely clean and carrying nothing, I approached the exit to Oxford Street.

'Excuse me, madam. Could you step back into the store, please?'

'Of course. Is there a problem?'

'I'd just like to ask you a few questions.'

'Sure. Certainly.'

'I believe that you put something in your bag.'

'I beg your pardon?'

'If you don't mind, madam, I would like to take a look.'

'In my bag? Well, of course.'

We were standing next to a glass perfumery counter. With a clatter, I started to pile up my possessions on its surface.

'Please tell me if there's anything belonging to you here,' I said to her. There wasn't. By the time the bag was empty, she was getting annoyed.

'Would you step into the office for a moment?'

She was joined by a male colleague. I thought quickly.

'Do you want to search me?' I asked them.

They frowned at each other. I took off my jacket, then started to unbutton my blouse.

'Madam, there's no need . . . '

I slid the blouse off my shoulders and reached for the zipper on my trousers. Now there was consternation.

'Madam! I assure you, you don't – '

'But I'm happy to be searched,' I announced.

'No – ah – no, no, that really won't be necessary.'

My attempted striptease flummoxed them completely. They banned me from the store, but they'd found nothing on me. There wasn't any action they could take. When I told Sugarlips about my quick thinking, she hooted with laughter.

'Good for you, chuck!' she said. 'That's the way to do it!'

We were a team now. *You an' me against the world*. I knew that there was no going back, even if I'd wanted to.

I heard a rough screech of brakes and a shout of 'Hey! Watch out there!'

The bumper of a car came to a halt just inches from my arm. Although I jumped with fright, I made sure I kept my legs pressed tightly together. I had to, with a stolen Dior handbag firmly crotched between my thighs.

I'd left Bourne & Hollingsworth in a hurry with the bag well in place, right up inside my skirt. Then I noticed the security guy on the door. His eyes seemed just too careful as he studied me, then studied me again. He was suspicious. Once I was out in the open, I needed to move quickly away. In the dazzling morning sunlight, the car seemed to come out of nowhere.

The driver wound down the window, but before he could say anything, the back seat passenger leaned out. I saw a dark-haired man with a familiar thin face and a short black beard. It was Paul McCartney, the world famous member of the Beatles and Wings.

'Are you alright there?' he shouted, with a worried expression. I couldn't believe it was really him. But my real concern was that the Dior bag had slipped down as I jumped with fright. To hold it in place, I had to clamp all my muscles so tightly that it made it hard to speak.

'I'm – ah – oh! I'm fine! I'm okay!'

'Good!' He looked relieved. 'You take care now!' Paul McCartney ducked back inside the car.

I gave him a bright and cheery wave and wobbled on, with my stolen Dior handbag still firmly lodged in place.

'Jan, did you notice the furs?'

Sugarlips and I sat in her room eating Jaffa cakes. I'd certainly noticed that the furs in Harrods weren't well secured on their rails.

'Well, yeah, but . . . '

'The boss wants us to get more like the ones you got last week. I think that fur room's pretty easy.'

'What about all the staff?'

'They're old ladies! They're sweet, but they won't be on the ball.'

She was right. We found that the best time to hit the fur room in Harrods was early in the morning. While the ladies were distracted, trotting back and forth across the shop floor setting up for the day, we could take whatever we wanted. There was a security camera – the first one I'd ever seen in Knightsbridge – but only one, right over the main door. Once the goods were crotched, we could safely walk right underneath it.

But a few weeks after that, we discovered a new problem. Someone had been working on security, and suddenly the furs had all been wired – connected together with electrical alarm cables running over to the department's main desk. 'Dammit,' said Sugarlips when she saw them. We went to get ice-creams in the sundae bar downstairs while we decided what to do. I glanced across at her as we sat at the high counter, and noticed how determined she looked.

'Janice,' she said, 'we need pliers.'

'Seriously?' I asked her. 'You think we should cut the coats out?'

'Why not?'

'As soon as we do that, the buzzers will go off. Then won't security come?'

'Not straight away. When they hear the alarm, the old dears will all get into a tizzy. They won't be looking at us. We'll have a couple of minutes before anyone comes. We can lift our stuff and then get clear.'

We got some pliers and headed back to work. One quick snip, the buzzer sounded, and the fur ladies rushed about the floor. In all the fuss and confusion, I stepped behind the counter and grabbed as many green plastic bags as I could reach from the pile on a shelf below the till. Once we had those, all we needed to do was take our goods into the changing rooms and get them into the bags. A brand new store carrier bag was never examined. We packed up our goods and strolled freely out of Harrods.

I started to hang out with Sugarlips' team of lifters. I was amazed and impressed by the luxuries they all seemed to have – beautiful possessions and fashionable clothes by Dior, Gucci and Louis Vuitton. Babs's flat in Brixton Hill was crammed from floor to ceiling with expensive cosmetics. In Patsy's house, a television set hung from the ceiling and the drinks were kept inside a painted globe with a top that lifted up. Their lifestyle was worlds away from anything I'd ever seen before, and so much nicer than the cramped little room I shared with Sugarlips. As the long hot summer ended, I decided it was time to move on from the YWCA.

When Babs had a baby – a gorgeous little girl called Aaliyah – she asked me to live with her and help. Instead of paying rent, I tidied up and minded the baby. Babs gave me presents to make sure I stayed around. I liked being part of their gang. The only thing I didn't enjoy was their teasing – *Janice – you're not ready for the road!*' they would say to me. They talked as though as I was an innocent, still unaware of the realities of life. *'You're just a country girl – you've still got an accent from Leicester!'*

I tried to smile and shrug it off. After all, I was new to the group. I still had a lot of things to learn. I didn't understand at first how useful my innocence was. When we'd meet up after working in Oxford Street or Regent Street or Knightsbridge, the others passed their bags of hot merchandise straight into my hands.

'Can you carry for us, babe?' they'd ask. *'Janice – you're the best!'* *'Thank you, darlin'! How did we manage all this stuff before we had you around?'* I wanted to belong, to be helpful, to fit in. But I was holding everything that everyone had taken. The way they were working it, the risk of being caught fell entirely on me.

Slowly I realised that my new friends were using me. If anything went wrong, it was the country girl who'd carry the can.

SEPTEMBER 1977

Out clubbing with my friends, I met a guy called Emmanuel. He worked as a chauffeur for the High Commission of Trinidad and Tobago. He was street-wise and he knew what I did for a living, but he was following the straight life now – working his hours at the job then heading home each evening to his house in south London. He was divorced but very close to Nicholas and Alicia, his young son and daughter.

Emmanuel asked me for my number. A few days after we met, he picked me up and took me out to dinner. Then he invited me back to his place and played me his jazz music – before offering me a lift home. He really was a gentleman. He asked me out again, and then again. I was starting to like him.

As we got to know each other, I told him how I'd run away from home and never heard from my family. My story seemed to upset him. He asked me to make contact with my mother.

'I don't know,' I said. 'Things weren't good in Leicester.' I wasn't sure how to tell him just how bad they'd really been.

'But she's still your mum, Janice! She must miss you. And she'll be worried. Everybody will be.'

He wouldn't take no for an answer. As I got to

know him better, I learned that this would always be his choice – the peaceful life, the family. It made him happy, and he wanted the same happiness for me. He was trying to be kind and I was grateful, even though he'd never understand just how complicated family can be.

I let him drive me up, and he waited in the car while I knocked on Mummy's door. When she answered, the two of us went in. She seemed happy to see me and pleased to meet my boyfriend, but she didn't ask me anything – not why I'd left home or even where I'd been all this time. We didn't really talk. We never had, and now it seemed too difficult to start.

For me, the best part of the day was seeing my little brother Terry – except he wasn't little any more. He gave me a great big hug the moment I walked in. Within minutes we were talking just as though I had never been away.

As he drove me home again, Emmanuel was smiling.

'See, Jan, she was made up. That's much better – having peace with your mum.' He hadn't noticed the tension in the air.

He was close to Ida, his mother, and she was very proud to be a grandmother, visiting his house and always bringing presents for her grandchildren. When Ida looked at them, I could tell that she was bursting with pride. I found myself wishing that I'd had a childhood like that, and memories of someone who was proud of me in the way that she was.

BREAKING OUT

1966 – SOUTHALL

'Mummy,' I said, 'I'm going to be a singer and sing like Sandy Shaw.'

I'd seen her on the telly and I really, really liked her. I pulled a pair of tights onto my head so that the empty legs would whirl about like hair, and danced around pretending to perform with a hairbrush for a microphone.

'Janice, Sandy Shaw is white and barefoot,' was all my mother answered. I didn't understand what she meant. She was telling me that white girls can sometimes break the rules. But that's because the rules were made for them in the first place. Black girls couldn't ever do that. Black girls got picked on in school. No one expected them to have important jobs, or be successful in the world. So I mustn't hope to do what Sandy Shaw could do. Nobody would even let me try.

Mummy said I was an ugly little girl. She was trying to keep me in my lane, in my place, not believing in myself too much, or holding high hopes for my life. She didn't want me to be hurt by disappointment. If I had no hopes in the first place, then she thought that I would always be safe.

So when Emmanuel told me I was beautiful, I found I could hardly bear to listen. I still heard my mother's voice telling me I was an ugly little girl. I didn't trust his words and I turned my head away.

Ida welcomed me warmly to her family. I started to look forward to our chats and our trips out to play bingo. I noticed there was lots and lots of money in her house – sometimes thousands of pounds. She ran pardners – saving schemes for her and her friends. Each week, every person in a pardner put in a cash contribution, then they each took turns to benefit. Ida was the pardners' banker because everybody trusted her. But I hadn't realised yet just how shrewd she really was.

'You wear lovely clothes, Janice,' she said to me one day. We were cooking together in Emmanuel's kitchen. 'And jewellery. Always such nice things.'

'Thank you, Mums.'

'I don't think Emmanuel buys them for you.' I realised she was watching me carefully.

'Er – no, well – sometimes he gives me presents. But – uh – most of this is mine.'

'Get them from your own family, do you?'

'Uh – sometimes.'

She turned to face me, putting her hands on her hips. She smiled, but I could see it was a serious smile.

'Oh, Janice – what are we going to do with you?'

'What do you mean, Mums?'

'When are you going to stop this lifestyle?'

'Uh – '

'I'm not a fool, Janice. I know you're up to some-thing illegal. I'm glad that Emmanuel is in a good job and able to support you. He's never got into any serious trouble. He wouldn't risk it – Nicholas and Alicia are far too important to him. His kids are his world.'

'Um . . . ' I was extremely taken aback.

'There's some kind of anger in you, Janice,' Ida said. 'I don't think you recognise how angry you are. Anger can eat you up for years. It can do things you can't even imagine.'

'Look, Mums – '

'All I'll say is this. If you need help, come to me. Between us, whatever it is, we'll fix it. Don't talk to Emmanuel. Come and talk to me.'

'I don't talk to him about everything.'

'That's good. He doesn't want to know. He's had a bad experience already.'

'What kind of bad experience?'

'With a woman. It doesn't matter now. The past is over. Just remember what I say.'

I was beginning to feel part of Emmanuel's family. They were lovely people, always generous and kind. Ida had a very good friend whom we called Auntie Beatrice, and Beatrice's daughter Sabrina became the best friend I'd ever had.

Sabrina shared my birthday – not just the date, but the same year as well. We joked that we were secretly twins, but then, as time went by, it stopped feeling like a joke. I told her everything about me – and I knew she loved me just as I was.

'You're brave, you know, Janice. I don't know how you get the nerve to go out shoplifting,' she said.

'I'm not brave really,' I said. 'It's just a job.'

'No way!' She rolled her eyes. 'I'd be so frightened! Aren't you scared they're going to catch you?'

'Naaah!'

But I couldn't lie to Sab – she saw right through me.

'Yes you are, JanJan. I can see it. You're scared sometimes.'

She was right. But my excitement was stronger than my fear. I was hooked on the danger of lifting. Nothing else could give me that buzz.

'It's just the way it is,' I told her. 'I took up badness. There's no way back now.'

For a moment, the two of us were silent. And then Sabrina smiled.

'Well now – we're sisters for life, so I guess I have to take all this bullshit of yours and put up with it!'

Then one of the gang disappeared. Patsy was caught while she was working, and sentenced to prison. We used to hang out down at her place quite often – but once she was gone, no one mentioned her name. It was as though she had never existed. It scared me badly. What had happened to her could just as easily happen to me. If it did, would I vanish just like she had?

That was when Emmanuel asked me to move in with him. He said he thought that we should be together all the time – then he could look after me. I knew what he really meant was that I should stop shoplifting. I decided he was right. When I thought about Patsy, all alone in prison, my stomach churned with fear. The buzz just wasn't worth it. I decided I was going to start again – and this time lead a different kind of life.

I'd put those risks and dangers behind me. The past would be forgotten. I felt sure that Emmanuel and I would make each other happy for always.

Emmanuel, Nicholas and Alicia were my ready-made family. The children often spent the night, and came around to see him at weekends. I didn't mind at all – I liked looking after them. When their mum picked them up, she and Emmanuel seemed friendly. Whatever had happened in the past, both of them put the children first.

Life was quiet, uneventful. As the months went by, I noticed that the days were starting to seem long. I missed the excitement of working up West. And the more I tried to ignore that feeling, the more the feeling grew.

A glamorous woman rang the doorbell late one afternoon. I was watching TV in the kitchen while I rinsed out the children's lunchboxes. She was a few years older than I was, and beautifully dressed. She made me feel quite awestruck.

'Hi – you must be Janice? Nice to meet you. I've come to pick up the kids. I'm Lucy – I'm a friend of their mum's. She's been delayed at work.'

'Uh – well, I'm sorry, but nobody told me. Can you wait while I phone up and check?'

She smiled at me. 'Of course,' she said, 'that's absolutely fine. I'm glad you're careful.'

We chatted. I liked her, and she seemed very interested in everything I said. A few days later, she came round again. This time, the children weren't there. Soon she was visiting quite often, always when Emmanuel was working. She sometimes brought me presents – lovely new clothes, shoes and perfume. She didn't explain where they came from. Then one day she asked me if I'd like to come shopping with her. The nervous expression on my face made her laugh.

'Would Emmanuel be angry if you went out by yourself?' she asked me.

'No!' I said quickly. 'No, of course not. He just – he likes it when I stay around the house.'

'Well – I won't tell your old man if you don't! And I think you're a bit young to stay at home all day and be a housewife, don't you?'

I didn't like the thought of lying to Emmanuel. But Lucy was right. I was nineteen – and he was 34. His kids were lovely, I felt safe and secure . . . but hanging round the house all the time was a drag. Patsy's arrest had been months ago, and the shock of it had faded.

Lucy was watching me carefully. When I said, 'Okay, then,' she gave a little smile.

'That's my girl, Janice.'

She took me back to my old workplace – Oxford Street and Bond Street. We wandered through the shops, stopped for coffee, then wandered some more. But I still wasn't sure just what Lucy was up to. Then, in the late afternoon when we were having a drink, I noticed her handbag. It was different from the one she'd been carrying that morning. Glancing inside it as she searched for her purse, I saw the shiny clasps of two other, smaller bags tucked down inside.

Instantly a tingle of excitement sped through my body. I'd missed the thrill of danger. Although I'd tried the straight life, I realised that it wasn't for me.

'Are you lifting?' I said to her. She answered with a smile.

'Sort of.'

'What do you mean, sort of?'

'Well – my game is slightly different. I'm a dipper. Sometimes the best bargains aren't hanging on the rails. And the people I'm taking from don't employ security guards.'

As Lucy explained, I looked around at the affluent shoppers in the café with their bags of designer shopping, their bulging purses. Everywhere, I saw the gleam of money for the taking.

'So – are you in?' she asked me.

'Oh yes,' I said to her. 'Yes, Lucy. I'm in.'

4

AYE AYE, DICK EYE

SEPTEMBER 2014

'SO HOW YOU DOING now, Izzie?'

It was a week since I'd last seen her. She sat opposite me in the coffee shop, skinny, crumpled and hunched over. She was even paler than before and looked completely exhausted.

'I'm okay.' Her voice was a whisper. Taking crack heightens sensitivity to sound, so people who are using the drug often speak very quietly. But Izzie sounded even more subdued than she usually did.

'You don't seem okay to me,' I told her gently.

She shivered and wrapped her arms more tightly round her chest.

'You not feeling so good?'

Withdrawal is a terrible experience. You wake up every day feeling sick to your bones. Your body aches as though you're getting 'flu. You shiver, then the next minute you're burning up, soaked through with sweat. Your brain is jammed with anxiety and fear. And your first thought, your only thought, circling round your head with no escape, is – how am I going to get some money? Once you have an answer, you feel a bit better. Now you know for sure that you'll have your drugs today, whatever you might have to do to get them.

I fetched us both hot drinks, and put a warm panini on a plate down in front of her. She took no notice of the food, but she did pick up the drink and take a sip.

'I'm glad you came,' I said to her. 'When you missed our phone call yesterday I was worried about you.'

The phone calls were part of the structure I was building in her life. Setting little goals to shape her empty days, to help her remember that she really existed. To clean up her room. To go out and buy herself some food. As well as our meetings at probation, I phoned her three times a week. Each time she picked up, I could tell if she'd been using. She would stutter and jump around from subject to subject, struggling to focus and making little sense. But the most important thing was just to make the calls and speak – to show her that somebody was there for her, no matter what.

'Izzie? Did something happen?'

She closed her eyes tightly.

'Yeah,' she muttered. 'Yeah – I – I – ' Then the words seemed to freeze in her mouth.

'J-Janice – I need a cigarette.'

'Okay. You go outside and have one. But when you get back, I want to see you eat your sandwich.'

I watched her through the window as she leaned against a lamp post, smoking in rapid, shaky puffs. From a distance, she always had that angular, super-model loveliness. From here you didn't notice the rough, tattered edges or the terror in her eyes.

When she sat back down again at the table, she picked up the panini and obediently ate a few bites. A part of her was always trying to co-operate – I noticed it again and again. It was the part that wanted something different, a life that was so much better than all this. If I stayed next to this girl, she could get out of the shit that she was in – I was sure of it.

'I need you to level with me, Izzie,' I said. 'Something bad happened – didn't it?'

Slowly the tears started running down her face.

'Baby, what is it?'

'It was K-Karim. You know – the g-guy who lives upstairs. He – he – '

She stopped and squeezed her eyes tight shut.

'Izzie,' I said, 'whatever this man did, it's a reflection of him not a reflection of you. Please tell me.'

'Okay.' Her words came out in a stumbling rush. 'It was three days ago. Karim – '

Izzie lived in a rented bedsit – a downstairs room with a tiny little kitchen in the corner. The house was packed full of tenants – far too many for their welfare. Their unscrupulous landlord only wanted to make money and wasn't much concerned if they were safe. A few weeks earlier, a large group of men had moved in, sharing the room right above Izzie's. They slept in a row across the floor. They'd not been in the house a day before they started harassing her. Not all of them had keys and they were ringing on the doorbell all hours of the day and night, grabbing at her hair and her clothes when she came to let them in.

'Karim s-said let's do a deal, and – '

'The same deal he did with you before?' I asked her quietly.

'Yeah.' Her voice was a whisper. 'Fifteen quid for a blowjob. Look – I know what you said – I know you told me not – '

'That's okay, Izzie. Just tell me what happened.'

'S-so I said alright, and we did that – '

When Karim had finished, he'd usually throw the money on the floor.

'But this time he said he wasn't done, and n-now he wanted to – to – but I said no, that wasn't what you said – '

Her hands were shaking uncontrollably.

'Izzie,' I said, 'baby, it's okay. Just take a breath for a minute.'

She began sobbing really hard, rocking backwards and forwards.

'So he kept trying – but he couldn't get it up, because he'd just – so he went all – all animalistic – really rough, like he was wanting to find a way so he could – oh God, Jan. Oh God.'

I laid my hand gently on her arm, controlling my anger at the horror that she was describing.

'I th-thought he might kill me.'

'Did he manage to do anything?' I asked her.

'No. He couldn't. Oh my God, he was so angry. He was yelling like it was my fault. In the end he just gave up, and then he threw a fiver on the floor – '

She covered her face with her hands. I could barely catch her words.

'S-so I s-said that we'd agreed on £15 and then he hit me. And after that he went upstairs.'

This was the first time she'd really opened up. I was appalled by what she'd told me. I would have to report her situation to the rest of the team. Her accommodation was very unsafe. But underneath all the mess, I felt a burst of hope. If she could trust me and talk to me like this, there had to be a chance.

'So baby, you've had an awful shock. Nothing that happened was your fault. Karim tried to rape you. That's a serious crime.'

'But Jan – you know what's worse?' she whispered.

'What was worse?'

'I heard them later on, a whole bunch of them. They banged on my door and they were laughing really loudly. He's told them something. So now when they see me, they always keep on laughing, every time.'

JUNE 1978

Lucy was a clever, skilful thief. Just as I'd learned from Sugarlips two years earlier, now I started learning from her.

She was a great actress too, carefully performing her

role. Out shopping, she'd hold up a jacket or a dress as though she was checking on the length or the size. Then she'd turn and show it to me, talking excitedly and draping it to and fro across her body – *'Do you like this one, Jan? How d'you think it suits me?'* But her movements and her chatter were all a big pretend. While she waved the clothes around, admired the fabric and examined the buttons, she was creating a distraction. Then she softly slid her hand into the bag of her chosen victim close beside her.

So many West End shoppers were wealthy, international people – and yet they seemed completely unaware. They'd leave their handbags gaping open or dangling behind them, then wander around, oblivious to danger. They were inviting us to pounce.

I watched in amazement as a woman in a Salvatore Ferragamo dress left her bag unattended in the open, on the top of a huge pile of her shopping. Once she'd wandered away, there was plenty of time for Lucy to lift the bag, take the money from her purse, check for other valuables then lay the bag right back at the top of the pile. Its owner was so busy admiring a rack of fur coats, she never even noticed it was missing.

'Is it always this easy?' I asked Lucy.

'Not always quite as easy as that one!' She gave a wide grin. 'But this is Harvey Nicks! The place is full of money, and the people with the money – they really aren't so careful.'

At the end of our first day working together, as we were heading home, Lucy gently touched my arm.

'Here you are, Janice. This is just for you – to buy anything you might need.' She placed £100 – five £20 notes, the ones we called Shakespeares – into my hand.

I'd never had cash of my own before. Sugarlips had bought me anything I needed, and Emmanuel paid for everything now. But this was really mine, and I was pleased. I couldn't explain to anyone at home where the money had come from, so I hid it in the bottom of the spare bedroom wardrobe.

In the squad, our working technique was dip and cover. The thieves go out in pairs. One provides the cover while the dipper does the take. I started out as cover to Lucy, the boss of the team. Then she introduced me to the others. All three of them were older, and all of them had kids. There was Gill, who smoked so much weed that her voice was a deep throaty growl. There was smart, sarcastic Suzi Q, and bright, funny Pepper whose husband Scorcher was a well-known south London street drug dealer. He was in and out of prison, while she looked after their children on her own.

'I just wish she'd leave him,' muttered Gill with a roll of her eyes whenever Scorcher's name was mentioned. 'That girl's far too loyal for her own good.'

Dressing up was a big part of our game. To stay a step ahead of store security, the squad chopped and changed our appearances with wigs and clothes and glasses. Sometimes I would copy the West End's super-rich Nigerians in their hair wraps and long patterned dresses. I loved the way it always brought the shop assistants rushing towards me. *'How can I help you, madam? Is there anything that madam requires?'* On other days, I'd dress in more subtle, understated wealth – a tasteful Windsmoor jacket, an Aquascutum coat.

I felt myself falling in love with the game. I loved the beautiful clothes, I loved the glamour, I loved the crazy highs, the tension and excitement. It made me feel alive. Best of all, I loved the look in people's eyes when they saw the possessions that I had. It made me feel like somebody. A person to be treated with respect.

A working crew would never walk together. We strung out across the shop floor, waiting until someone gave the signal to move in on our target. 'Aye aye, dick eye,' we'd say, when we knew we'd made a spot.

'Aye aye, dick eye?' I asked Lucy. 'What's that mean, then?'

'It means "Heads up! Look over there."'

'It does? How come?'

'Don't know. It's kind of slang. It reminds us to never use our names when we're working.'

Pretty soon, I became the sharpest spotter on the team. The others questioned me at first. *'Why her, Jan? Nah – this one's looking better.'* Then they noticed just how good my spotting was.

It was more than just the little tells of wealth – the shoes and handbags, the soft designer jeans, the drape and swing of expensively cut hair. Real money is a shine a person has on the inside. It's in the way they walk and how they hold their head. It's a certain air of distance – as though they don't quite notice the world.

To me, that signal always flashed out loud and clear.

'You're so tall, girl!' Gill said. She laughed. 'You're like a lamp-post!'

And that was the nickname they gave me. My height and the width of my shoulders were a help because they blocked the victim's sight. But they made me stand out too, so I worked extra hard to blend in, always careful to play the role of the shopper, examining the goods, admiring and selecting, never glancing around to check on how the dip was going. Staring down at the action only draws the eyes of the mark. I also learned never to speak – conversation is dangerous. It gives the mark too much about you to remember.

Our most important rule was to keep a £10 note at the ready. That meant we could jump straight in a black cab as soon as we got outside. The West End cabbies had been warned by the police to look for dippers, so the cover always sat in the pull-down seat with her back to the driver. She would block his view while the taker counted profits and we made our escape.

'You going to be a cover all your life, Lamp-post?'

Of all Lucy's squad, I liked Pepper the best. I loved her fiery streak of independence. She didn't like to answer to anyone.

'You should start dipping for yourself,' she said to me. 'I mean it. I could teach you.'

'Okay,' I muttered. Secretly, the thought made me nervous.

'Do your thing!' she told me. 'Be your own boss. Don't be depending on Lucy so much.'

'Don't you trust her? I thought you were friends.'

'Oh yes,' said Pepper lightly, 'we're friends for sure. But sometimes you'll find Lucy . . . plays games.'

'What kind of games?'

'Look – it's nothing. She's cool.'

'It doesn't sound cool to me.'

Pepper frowned. 'Look – just be warned – that's all I'm saying. Think about working for yourself. Get ready for the day you have to tell her you won't take it anymore.'

'Aye aye, dick eye.' But this time, Suzi Q didn't look so sure.

Carnaby Street was packed with Christmas shoppers. Night was falling and the festive lights were sparkling overhead. On the corner of Ganton Street, a knot of people crowded round a glass-blowing display, ooh-ing and aah-ing at the dazzling torch and the craftsman's skill and thinking about Christmas presents. And while they were doing all of that, they weren't paying attention to their valuables. I felt a stir of excitement in my belly.

Half an hour before, we'd finished work and gone strolling, admiring the West End's festive decorations. The crowds made lifting easier than usual, and my find of the day had been a pair of beautiful Bruno Magli shoes, in my size as well – nines, a rarity. I was tired and my feet hurt – but I still wanted one more take for the road.

I spotted a Chinese man watching the display, arm in arm with his wife. From his free hand swung a bulging leather pouch. I caught Q's eye, then nodded very slowly towards him.

Pepper had been teaching me to dip just liked she'd promised, and here was a chance for me to test out my new skill. Dipping felt intimate – edging in so close that I could hear a person breathe and almost touch them skin-to-skin, judging the moment to distract their attention just before the strike. If my heart was racing, I'd noticed that the mark could sense an agitation in the air. So I'd learned to slow my breathing to their rhythm – in and out, in and out, slow and easy, making my presence calm, staying in control. Sometimes the rise and fall of terror then relief made me dizzy. But the rush of excitement was still the feeling I loved best.

'You check?' I murmured softly.

She gave the Chinese man a swift glance. Q could assess a strike in seconds.

'Yeah, he's nice. But it's late now. Let's just leave it.'

I could see why she was worried. There were many eyes out here. How would I know if I was being spotted? But then I looked again at the man. The pouch swung temptingly. He and his wife were pushing forward, enthralled by the glass blowing. I couldn't bear to let this one go.

'Nah, I like him,' I told Q. 'I'll do it.' She pulled a face, but we were a team. She moved in to cover me.

I edged into the crowd and eased myself close up

behind my victim, keeping my eyes fixed on the glow of the glassblower's torch. I knew I'd have to work by touch alone, and make sure that I never once glanced down. My reaching fingers quickly made contact with the strap of the pouch. I knew better than to take its weight – even though its owner was distracted, he'd notice any change in the pressure on his arm. I eased my fingers carefully just inside the flap – and there was a bulging roll of banknotes. I felt a surge of triumph – I'd known I was right! I gently stretched further. Right next to it – a second roll was nestling. But still – to rush the lift now could be fatal. I carefully pulled back.

'I'm going to make the take,' I told Q softly.

She still looked uneasy.

'We're in the open! Anyone could see.'

'Don't worry! I just need a big distraction.'

She pulled a face.

'Okay then.'

Q went into action like the pro she was. She eased her way right to the front of the crowd. Then she leaned forward and asked the salesman just how much his goods cost. 'Is that for just one goblet? Is there a discount if I want to buy a set? Do they come in a box?'

Controlling my breathing, I lifted up the flap of the Chinese man's pouch. Very slowly, I closed my hand around the first bundle of money. I eased it out, and pushed it deep into the pocket of my coat. One down and one to go. The glass-blower's torch gave a flare and a hiss. The crowd swayed around me. 'Don't you have a bigger box?' Q was loudly demanding. I inched my fingers back inside the pouch.

Suddenly the Chinese man jerked his head around. He looked straight up at me and roughly grabbed my arm.

'You!' he shouted.

I froze. My heart jumped into my throat.

'Pah!' I said scornfully. I pushed past him through the crowd. 'What? What you mean?'

'You!' he bellowed at me. 'You!'

He said something to his wife in a different language. She widened her eyes and started pointing at me. *They don't speak English,* I realised. *They know what's going on, but they can't tell anyone.* Still, now that both of them were shouting, the crowd was going to catch on pretty fast.

I backed hastily away, then turned and started striding – not fast in case I drew too much attention. Ganton Street was narrow and cobbled. From the corner of my eye, I saw Suzi Q following me and the Chinese man behind her in pursuit. He was pulling his wife by the arm and still shouting, 'You!' He prodded other shoppers, pointing at me, trying to draw everyone's attention.

'Money!' he cried. 'Money!' I took a lightning glance behind. I saw a sea of puzzled faces. More and more people were starting to look where he was pointing and trying to explain.

'What's going on?'

'What's he saying?'

It was too late now to worry about not being conspicuous – I needed to run. I shot down Ganton Street as fast as I could go on the damp, slippery stones. Soho was dark between the pools of light that spilled out from doorways. The streets were crammed and I kept colliding with shoppers and people walking in the opposite direction. My bag with the Bruno Magli shoes in their gorgeous box was banging against my legs. Q had vanished – she must have slipped away up a side street.

Swinging wildly from my hand, my sharp-edged shoebox hit a very small dog on a lead. The dog let out a yelp and its owner bellowed furiously. Close to panic, I tried to push around them. But my shoe bag was slowing me down – it was going to have to go. With a pang of regret, I shoved my beautiful size nine Bruno Maglis underneath a parked car.

I zigzagged down a narrow red-light alley, where men loitered outside strip joints, dashing past the Soho punters with a confused straggle of pursuers on my tail. Lucy had friends in a cab office in Rupert Street. They knew our game, and if we turned up wanting a car right away, they'd oblige. Just opposite their office was a door where a fellow would charge £100 to anyone who wanted to wait until the high-class hooker upstairs was ready to see her next customer. Men eagerly paid and stood there waiting, but they waited a long time because the whole thing was a scam. When I went to get a cab I used to see them loitering, excited at first, then disappointed and furious.

When I reached the cab office door, the pavement was so packed that no one saw me darting inside. I hurtled through the front office and dashed into the back where I was instantly hidden from view. My gang of angry pursuers must have wondered how I'd vanished.

As I leaned against the wall and gasped for breath, I realised that understanding my limits was a skill I badly needed to learn. Q had been switched on – she'd warned me to leave the job alone. This was a reality check – and a lesson I knew I must remember.

Our first mark of the afternoon in Evans was young with long blonde hair and an expensive-looking blue patterned jacket. Her air of assurance told me straight away that she had money.

I moved up on the woman's left-hand side, then created a distraction by picking up a coat from the railing and peering at the pockets. I bumped the woman slightly as I did so, then gave her a quick apologetic smile. Her attention was now fully to her left. To her right, Lucy swooped. Down went her hand. It was a smooth and easy take. She turned away.

But as I stepped back, the blonde woman grabbed me.

'You've got my purse!' she said accusingly.

'No I don't!' I said indignantly. 'I don't know what you're talking about.'

'You took it!' she said firmly. She was very upper class and sounded confident – a person who knew that whatever she said would be treated as important. 'It was you – you were standing right next to me.'

Indignantly, I opened my bag wide.

'Call somebody!' I told her. 'You can search me.'

She flushed dark red with anger.

'Security!'

'This woman has accused me of stealing her purse,' I told the security guard. 'But I've no idea at all what she means.'

As I held out my bag to be searched, she was growing less certain. 'I was robbed just now,' she muttered. 'I know it was you.'

Store security summoned the police. Lucy was long gone by now. A policeman searched my bag and found nothing. I stayed calm, knowing that my smart, well-dressed appearance was helping me. I could tell that the policeman had noticed it. My height and lovely clothes could often make a positive impression. Meanwhile, the woman whose purse had been stolen grew more and more frustrated and angry.

'Will this take long?' I asked the officer. 'My husband is waiting to meet me. He works at the Trinidad High Commission.'

The policeman looked up sharply. 'High Commission?'

'Yes.' I'd thought they might treat me differently if I had a husband whose job sounded important. But just the words 'High Commission' were like a magic spell. I quickly followed up.

'Er – would it be possible for me to make a phone call to the High Commission? I'm sure my husband will ring his office if I don't turn up. He'll be terribly worried.'

'Like an embassy. Diplomatic rules,' the policeman muttered to the guard. 'Immunity. We have to let her go.'

'Madam,' said the security guard to the long-haired woman. 'I'm afraid there is no evidence at all that this lady took anything from you.'

She looked furious.

'But I've been robbed in broad daylight! Is there nothing at all that you can do?'

'I'm sorry,' the policeman said, to me and not to her. 'There must have been some mistake.'

I smiled graciously and accepted his apology. But I was sweating and shaking inside. It seemed to take forever before I was safely outside the store. Now I knew what it would really feel like to be caught.

Lucy and I had a meeting place – the Shakespeare pub in Victoria station. But by the time I got there, she was gone. I sat on the bar stool and ordered a straight brandy. I closed my eyes and downed it in one. Gradually, the tremors in my body began to die away. I'd got away with it – this time. But it had been a very close call.

When I got home, I still felt shaky. I tried to busy myself cleaning and tidying the house, hoping that ordinary jobs might help me calm my mind. But the jitters wouldn't leave me. Eventually, I made my way upstairs. I pulled the secret shoebox out of the bottom of the wardrobe. This money was worth it, I reminded myself. This money kept me safe. Slowly and dreamily, I started to count.

One hundred pounds . . . two hundred pounds . . . three hundred . . . four . . .

Even as a little girl, I'd drawn attention – never just been able to fade into the background. But it wasn't attention in a good way. I remembered the school playground and three girls dancing round me, singing and giggling. One started pulling at my skirt. I slapped her hand away furiously.

'Janice has a ta-ail! Janice has a ta-ail!'

'No, I don't!' I shouted. 'Don't be so stupid!'

'Yeah, you do! My mum said!'

'Then your mum's a big idiot!'

'Mum said you're like a monkey with a tail!'

I was angry, but my eyes had started filling up with tears. How could I make them stop?

'Well,' I said, 'so she's stupid too!'

'You got to show us! Show us!'

'Show you what?'

'Your tail!'

'I haven't got a tail!'

'Bet you do really!' And they ran away laughing.

Five hundred pounds . . . six hundred . . . seven hundred . . . eight . . .

*

Daddy always worked long hours. But recently, he'd started to go missing more and more, even when he wasn't working. Mummy asked him where he'd been, but he would never answer. Lying awake in bed at night, I heard their raised voices through the wall.

'Where I bin? I don' know, Rita! Out!'

'Wha' you mean – you bin out?'

'I jus' bin out! Maybe walkin!'

Mummy sounded angry and suspicious.

'Mi know what you doin'!' she would say. *'You gettin' Westernised! Sittin' in pub! You followin' de white people dem!'*

'Ri-ta! Leave mi alone!'

After that, Mummy always cried.

Nine hundred pounds . . . a thousand pounds . . . one thousand one . . .

Miss Crosby was a teacher at my infant school in Southall. She had gold-framed spectacles, and pointy black shoes just like a witch might wear. All the children were scared of Miss Crosby.

'The boys and girls whose names I call out will come to the front of the class!' she shouted. 'Janice, Jaswinder, Lynne and Paul!'

Jaswinder was Asian. Lynne was Nigerian. Paul's parents had come over from Ireland. We did as we were told and stood all in a line. She walked very slowly past us, and walked back again. She peered down into our faces.

BREAKING OUT

'I don't know which one of you it is,' said Miss Crosby to the class, 'but one of you children *smells*.'

The English girls and boys burst into giggles. The four of us looked at each other. My face grew hot with shame. Was something wrong with me? Was I the one who smelled? Humiliated, not quite knowing why our teacher was doing this, none of us could think of what to say.

One thousand two hundred pounds, one thousand three . . . one thousand four . . .

I remembered the day I went out stealing sweets with my schoolfriends. Susan and Jill distracted Tom, who owned the local newsagents, while I shovelled as many sherbets and pink shrimps as I could into my satchel. Tom gave no sign that he'd seen what I was doing. Walking down the road with my bag of stolen sweets, my stomach churned with angry satisfaction.

When I got home that afternoon, Mummy was upstairs. As I shut the front door behind me, she shouted out my name. I could hear the menace in her voice.

'Janice!'

'Yes, Mummy?'

She came down into the hall and stood in front of me.

'Do you stop anywhere this morning?'

'No, Mummy, I just went to school.'

From the expression on her face, already I knew that

she knew. I felt an awful surge of shame, mixed up with disappointment. I hadn't got away with it after all.

'Janice – where did you stop?'

'Oh – we went into Tom's shop.'

'Come with me,' she said – and took me straight back there.

She asked him straightaway: 'Tom – what happen this morning?'

When he'd finished speaking, Mummy looked at me.

'So, Janice – Tom is lying?' was all she said.

I whispered: 'No, Mummy.'

She made me apologise to Tom. She was very, very angry. But she never once asked me why I stole. Even if she had, I couldn't find the words for my anger and confusion.

I don't think I could ever have explained.

One thousand five hundred pounds, one thousand six, one thousand seven . . . .

Daddy worked at the Nestlé factory in west London. Every year, the workers and their families were all invited to the big staff Christmas party. The year that I was ten and Terry almost eight, we went to the party just with Daddy, because Mummy was at work.

He stayed for a while to watch us play party games with the others. But a few minutes later, when I looked around, he was gone. I told Terry I would find out where he was. I wandered to the far end of the ballroom, and there I saw a door with two round glass panes in it, like portholes. Curiously, I pressed my nose right up against the glass – and to my surprise I saw Daddy straight away. He was standing in a gloomy, half-lit hallway, close to a white lady in a short sleeveless dress. The portholes let two long bars of daylight fall across the floor. In the bright stripes, the lady's pale arms gleamed. I saw that she was kissing Daddy.

I stood and stared. I couldn't keep this secret on my own. I ran to find Terry.

'*Terry – Daddy has a girlfriend!*'

He wanted to see, so I quickly led him back to the porthole door and lifted him up. He stared for a moment, then said that he was going to tell.

'Tell who?' I demanded.

'Mummy, of course!'

'You can't!'

He stuck out his lower lip determinedly.

'But Terry,' I told him, 'you mustn't! They'll have another argument!'

But it wasn't Terry who told Mummy – it was me. For days the awful secret squirmed inside me until I couldn't hold it in any longer. *Why does Daddy like white girls better than Mummy?*

It burst out of me one evening in the kitchen. She was cooking at the stove. It seemed easier to tell her when her back was turned.

'Mummy,' I said, 'at the Christmas party I saw Daddy kiss a lady. She was white!'

Mummy stood absolutely still.

'Janice – wha' you jus' say?' She sounded as if I must be making it up.

'Terry saw too!' I cried indignantly. 'Terry saw too!'

In the New Year, Mummy told us that we were leaving England. We were going home with her, to Antigua. We would have a house and go to school, and when everything was ready, Daddy would come and live with us. When we got there, we waited months and months. Every day, we expected her to tell us when Daddy would arrive. But he was never coming. My parents had split up and now they were getting a divorce. No one told us anything about it. I had to work it out for myself.

From the moment we landed in the dark at V. C. Bird International airport and stepped from the plane into the warmth of the night, I loved Antigua. All I'd known up until then was the city. Here there was open space around us. The windows stood open and we felt the soft wind stir instead of huddling indoors. In spite of my parents' separation, life was good. It quickly felt like home. I decided I was never going back, not *ever*.

So when Mummy told us we were moving back to England, I was furious. As usual, she didn't tell us why. Why did no one explain or give a reason for anything? Why did my opinion never matter? Why did I have to return to that cold and wretched place?

This time, we went to live in Leicester. We had relatives there who helped us out for a while. But by now I was so angry with Mummy that we could barely speak without getting in a fight. I hated everything and everyone. I loathed the bitter English winter and the dull brown Midlands city under dull brown clouds and rain. When I saw the girls who stood around selling sex at the end of our street, I felt embarrassed and ashamed. In the cramped house my family shared for months on end, there seemed to be no air at all to breathe. Worst of all were the times when my uncle's friend tried to stroke my knee with his hot, dry hand and push himself against me when nobody else was around. But there was no one I could tell – and if I had, I knew they wouldn't believe me.

The local school didn't have a place for me. My education ended, but no one seemed to care. If I had hopes for my future, they didn't notice. I went to work at Woolworth's in Gallowtree Gate.

Two thousand one hundred pounds . . . two thousand two . . . two thousand three . . . two thousand four . . .

Then one day, it all blew up. It was March of 1976. Our neighbour offered me a lift to the shops. His name was Talbot and he'd always seemed friendly up until then. But as soon I got into his car, without a word of warning he drove me all the way to Manchester. He parked outside a semi in the suburbs and told me to come inside with him. I was puzzled, but not yet really frightened because Talbot was a friend of my mother.

A smiling woman opened the door, said hello and asked me my age. Then she and Talbot left without a word. The moment they were gone, I realised that the front door was deadlocked. I was trapped in the house. Dusk was falling. Nobody knew that I was there. I thought of the street girls back in Leicester – and into my head came the wild idea that this was all a plot. Talbot had kidnapped me and brought me here to work as a prostitute.

Frightened and muddled, I panicked. I ran upstairs, climbed out of the bathroom window, scrambled across the kitchen roof and jumped down into the garden. I was breathless with fright, still thinking that Talbot or the lady would come back and stop me leaving. The gate at the side of the house was half open. Sobbing with relief, I ran away as fast as I could and found my way to the station.

I got back to Leicester very late. I hadn't eaten for hours. I had no idea what had just happened. I felt dizzy with anxiety and shock. Bewildered and stammering, I tried to explain to Mummy what Talbot had done. But she was far too angry to listen. She started a tremendous argument about where I had been. Both of us were screaming and shouting. She threw a flowerpot at me. I picked up the pot and threw it back. Everything and everyone seemed crazy. There was no one in the world that I could trust.

A few days later, I packed a little bag and made my way to the station. This time, I caught the London train. No matter what – I was determined I wasn't going back.

As I looked at the bundles of money I had hidden in Emmanuel's house, I wondered how much more I would need before I got that secret shine – the one I always saw in the West End. The glow that came from people who knew that they belonged in the world. How much would it take? When could I put on that armour – the kind that you wear on the inside? That was what I wanted most of all – the unshakeable protection of wealth.

Oh my God – where is it? Where has it gone?

The next time I went to count, I thought at first I'd made a mistake. Maybe I'd moved the money myself then forgotten where I'd put it. Frantically, I opened drawers and cupboards. I lay flat on the floor and peered into the dust under the spare bed. I scrabbled through the heap of scuffed-up objects in the bottom of the wardrobe – old winter boots and shoes, scarves that had slid from their hangers up above, old jazz records, a biscuit tin full of family photos. Nothing. My money had vanished. Maybe the house had been burgled, I thought wildly. But what sort of burglar breaks in, ignores everything else and just opens the spare bedroom wardrobe?

It had to be Emmanuel who'd taken it. But how had he found out that it was there? Why hadn't he said anything? What would he do next? My mind was in a whirl. When he came home, he seemed quite normal. I didn't dare say a word. The longer I wondered and waited for him to speak, the more worried and confused I became.

Next day, Lucy dropped round for a visit – just a friendly call to catch up and make some social plans. I made us tea in the kitchen and tried to keep things casual, hoping she wouldn't notice how distracted I was.

Then I heard the crunch of Emmanuel's key turning in the front door – two hours before he normally came home. The moment I saw his expression, I knew that this was trouble.

'She's here, isn't she?' he asked me. 'Lucy is here?'

'Uh . . . '

'She's been visiting, hasn't she?' His face was grim. 'I should have known she'd try to make friends.'

'She's upstairs,' I told him.

'And how long has this been going on?'

'Has what been going on?'

'Don't play games, Janice!'

'Please don't be angry!' I said to him. 'She's not – '

'Don't you tell me about her!' Emmanuel said to me. 'You don't know anything! You've no idea at all what she's like!'

None of this was making any sense. But before I could think how to reply, Lucy appeared at the top of the stairs. She stepped slowly down towards us.

'What d'you think you're doing here?' Emmanuel demanded. His voice was tight with anger.

'Getting to know Janice.'

'Well – Janice doesn't want to know you!'

'I think that's Janice's decision, not yours.'

'I told you already – you're not welcome in my house.'

'Well now, Janice said I was welcome.'

'Look – what's going on?' I asked them both. 'Do you two – I mean – uh . . . '

Emmanuel ignored me. His eyes were fixed on Lucy.

'Janice doesn't know what she's doing!' he said.

'Don't treat her like a child. She can make friends with who she likes.'

'Just get out of this house,' he said to her. 'Get out!' I'd never heard him speak that way before, in such a low, cold voice.

Lucy just shrugged. She didn't seem too bothered.

'I need to get home. Catch you soon, Jan.'

She lifted her jacket from the hook on the wall by the front door. 'Bye, babe,' she said to me lightly. When she was gone, Emmanuel let out a sigh and walked straight past me, into the kitchen. He sat heavily down at the table with his head in his hands. Nervously I followed him, not sure what he was going to say.

'D'you think I'm a fool, Janice?'

But I had some questions of my own.

'I don't understand what's going on! How exactly do you know Lucy?' I demanded.

'D'you think I wouldn't notice this behaviour?' Emmanuel replied. 'Your dodgy movements? And the money?'

I flinched. So he knew.

'Maybe now you're going to say you've got a job but you just forgot to tell me!' he said.

'I – um – '

'Why did you lie, Janice?' Then suddenly I saw that he was very close to crying.

'I'm sorry. Em, I'm so sorry. Lucy said – '

'*Lucy said?* Lucy said *bloodclart what?*' He sounded weary now. He pushed back his chair and stood up, shaking his head. Again he muttered, '*Bloodclart Lucy.*'

Only one explanation made sense. I remembered what Ida had told me. *Emmanuel had a bad experience with a woman.* I'd never thought that the woman might still be close at hand.

'Did you used to go out with Lucy?' I asked him.

'Yes. It was a long time ago. Before the children. Back then, I really thought – oh – I was a fool. Until I found out what she got up to. How she was out *tiefin'* while I was out at work, trying to do the best I could.'

I didn't know what to say.

'And now you!' Emmanuel shouted. 'You too! Doin' crime! Mashin' up our lives! I thought you wouldn't do it anymore!'

'Look,' I said, 'you know what I do to make a living. You knew it when you met me.'

'But I thought – I thought – ' Emmanuel shook his head despairingly. 'Janice! I would never put you wrong. Why won't you listen? *Are you not aware of what Lucy is?*'

'It's like she said,' I told him. 'I'll make up my own mind about how to live my life.'

'What can I say to you?' he cried. '*I don't want to lose another woman, Janice!*'

*

72

I acted tough, but I was terribly upset by our fight. Emmanuel's words rang in my head for days. I was so tense and on edge that I got into a fight in Thornton Heath. A woman shoved a shop door open and it slammed right into me. Instead of keeping calm and accepting her apology, I lost my temper and slapped her. I was taken to court for assault.

Afterwards, I truly felt ashamed. My temper was fiery, but I knew how important it was to always stay in control. And I remembered what Ida had said to me. *Anger can eat you up.*

She was right. Even when life's bullshit was bad, I was determined to master my anger.

13 November 1978, Croydon Magistrates' Court.
Threatening behaviour and assault occasioning actual bodily harm. Bound over for 12 months and fined £50.00.

DECEMBER 1978

I felt a sharp tap on my shoulder. A cop was right alongside me.

'You are under arrest on suspicion of intent to steal from persons unknown.'

Suzi Q and I had been working in New Bond Street, but she vanished like a shadow when she saw him moving in. He showed me his badge. Most West End dippers got picked up from time to time under SUS laws – stop and search. We would carefully check out the area before we went to work, spotting the formations the police used on patrol, usually a triangle of one in the front and two behind. Picking out the coppers wasn't difficult in those days, when all of them had crew cuts. I'd started to recognise the guys who worked this patch, Shane and Willis. Willis was the one I liked the least – tall and skinny with his salt and pepper hair and a crooked broken nose.

This gruesome twosome was based in Marylebone police station in Seymour Street, just behind Selfridges. From there, they patrolled along Oxford Street, Bond Street and the tangles of wealth in between. Today, though, somehow we'd missed them. Dammit. I kept myself carefully disguised at all times, always changing my appearance. But I knew I was distinctive as a tall, black woman. I had started to recognise the boys, and the danger was growing that they had also started spotting me.

'Name? Date of birth?' asked Willis.

The police radio crackled as the information was relayed to the station. I knew that when my name came back with a criminal record, I was going to be arrested. When he got the word on me, Willis gave a smile of satisfaction. I was nicked.

'We have reason to believe that you are part of a shoplifting ring. You are under arrest.'

They radioed for the van and took me to Seymour Street station. I was held in a cell until the shops shut – standard procedure. If you get nicked up West on late opening night, you won't be back on the pavement until well after midnight. But as the evening wore on, they had no evidence against me. They had to let me go.

As I signed the release form, I stole a quick glance at Willis. He wasn't happy at all to see me walking free. Somewhere down the line, I thought, this copper is going to be a problem.

'Lamp-post – you were brilliant today!' said Lucy.

In the back of a cab in Charing Cross Road, I sat blocking the driver's view as usual while she counted our takings.

'Thanks,' I replied. I was watching her closely.

'Can you count these?' She handed me a bundle of travellers' cheques.

Inside her big leather bag, Lucy had a small Gucci clutch and two purses. She opened the clutch and began transferring its contents. Her hands were out of sight.

'How much travellers, Jan?'

'Hold on. Eight hundred pounds.'

Lucy went on busying herself inside the bag. She started to chat, but I didn't want to listen.

She's creating a distraction, I thought. *What's really going on inside that bag?*

'Jan – can you count these as well?'

She passed me a second bunch of travellers' cheques.

She's making me count so that I don't pay attention. What is she doing with the money?

I glanced into her bag. I saw a bundle of notes as Lucy moved them from one purse to another.

'This clutch is lovely!' she continued, with a smile. 'I think I'll keep this.' I realised I had no idea now how much money was inside it, or how the takings were being shared between us.

I'm getting less than she is, I thought, despite the risks I've run. *She thinks I haven't noticed.*

It wouldn't matter in a law court who was dip and who was bloody cover. We'd all be going to jail. I took exactly the same chances as she did, but Lucy was cheating me. I thought of Emmanuel's words: *Are you not aware of what she is?*

For now, I'll let it go. But if Lucy believe she ah go tek mi fi eediot, time longa dan rope.

She was going to learn that I was nobody's fool.

5

COPS AND ROBBERS

JUNE 2017

THE YOUNG MAN LOOKED frightened. He was still in his teens – gangly and slight, not very tall. I wondered how a baby like him could have got himself into this much trouble already.

Today was the first day of a new project for offenders on probation. Their community payback was to work at a nature garden in south London, tidying, digging and planting. The garden was a mini-oasis in a quiet suburban street, a green and tranquil place with two small ponds and wooden seats beneath the trees. I was there to work with the group, along with the project's gardening manager who would teach them the skills they would need.

This lad still had a soft, boyish face. At least it looked that way from the tiny part of it that I could see. He sat hunched in his chair at the back of the hall, dressed all in black, hood up, baseball cap right down, hands thrust out of sight, deep into the pockets of his hoodie.

We were hoping that some of the offenders might enjoy working in the garden. It's a creative thing to do and it can be relaxing too. But this boy couldn't have been further from relaxed. As I watched him growing more agitated, I realised that he had a problem. He didn't want to be there. He was terrified someone was going to recognise him.

I stood up to introduce myself and the gardening manager, then explained the rules.

'It's your responsibility to attend your project on time every week,' I told them. 'Any absences must be evidenced by a medical certificate or letter of appointment. If you fail to attend, you will be issued with a breach notice. You must contact your probation officer and explain. Should you fail to comply, you will be returned to court where your work order could be revoked and you could be re-sentenced.'

The service users listened in silence. Whilst I talked, I observed the boy in black. He wasn't just avoiding eye contact with me. He wouldn't look around the hall at all. He slumped lower and lower in his chair, raising his hand to the side of his face to shield him from view.

'A bottle of water would be a good idea when the weather's warm, like now, but only water is allowed,' I continued. 'We practise zero tolerance for any kind of drugs. One hundred and twenty hours of community service means seven hours work, one day a week. So most of you will finish in three months. That's if you turn up every session and do your work consistently.'

To them, I knew three months seemed a very long time. To me, it was a tiny window of opportunity to reach them.

'Before you leave today, I'll have a word with each of you. That's your chance to ask me questions and make sure that everything is clear to you.'

There was an unimpressed silence. Nobody wanted to be there. As they got to their feet and shuffled outside with the gardening manager, I picked the lad in black out first of all.

'What's your name?' I asked him.

'Harrison.' He mumbled his reply from below the brim of his cap.

'So, Harrison!' I raised my voice, startling him. 'Are we awake under there?'

'What do you mean, miss?' I liked his gentle London accent.

'I can barely see you in that cap.'

'Oh. Uh – '

He adjusted his cap by a fraction of one degree.

'That's not much difference! I still can't see you.'

He didn't reply.

'So, Harrison, something's worrying you.'

'No, miss.'

'From you step in the place, you're moving dodgy. Come on, man. What's going on?'

He hesitated.

'Miss,' he said suddenly, 'I shouldn't be here. I can't come round these sides.'

'And that's because of gangs, is it? You involved?'

'Uhhh . . . ' He rubbed his face nervously. 'Look, miss, you don't understand. This is serious.'

'I take it very seriously,' I said, 'but you'll have to tell me more if you want me to help you.'

'My mother,' he muttered. 'She lives across the road. I crept up here last week late to see her. I was only there a few minutes. When she rang me up and told me, she was screaming, miss. They'd shot up her place.'

'Who shot up her place?'

'The SLRs. They run these sides, miss. Someone must have seen me.'

'The SLRs?'

'South London Rebels,' Harrison muttered.

'A gang? What exactly did they do?'

'I told you, miss. They shot up her house. Fired a load of bullets in her wall. Mum's terrified to open the front door.'

'Did you report this?'

'You're not serious, miss. Call the feds? Nah.' He shook his head slowly. 'Now on top of that, probation telling man to come here.'

'You do have to come here.'

'If anything happens to me, miss, you lot responsible, you know.'

I thought quickly.

'Harrison,' I said, 'just go and chill. Let me speak to the project supervisor.'

I asked Harrison to tell me his mother's address. That made him jump to his feet in alarm. I reassured him that we needed to record what was happening for his safety and for ours. We understood how dangerous the situation was. Then the supervisor and I went to find the house in the little estate across the road.

The sun was peeping out from behind a pile of cloud. As we approached, a sunbathing cat jumped up and scampered away along the paved path between the houses. Harrison's mother must like gardening – she'd dug out two flower beds in the small patch in front of her place and planted them. Soft green stems were starting to push through the soil.

But right across the front wall of the house was a spattering of holes. It looked as though a giant's finger-nail had dragged along the building. Bullets had torn into the brickwork, leaving a long uneven scar. One or two had caught the downstairs front window frame, taking little bites out of the paint. Long splinters had been ripped from the fence at the side by ricocheting bullets. Gang life is real, and it's frightening. We stood there and stared.

'My God,' the supervisor whispered. 'When exactly did this happen?'

'Eight days ago, he says. On Sunday night – well, early Monday morning.'

'Did she call the police?'

'No.'

'Did anyone?'

'Yes, but it's not clear what happened.'

I thought of the deafening burst of noise in the silence of the small, sleeping hours. The flashes in the dark as the bullets bounced away. Whoever fired didn't care about where those shots might go. Harrison's mother must have woken in terror. So must all her neighbours. This had been a clear and brutal warning.

'So – he can't do his community service round here.'

'He certainly can't.'

We went back across the road. Harrison was pacing up and down inside the hall. When I told him that we would send him home, and arrange his community service at a project in a different part of London, I saw his relief. Sending him further away would mean bigger travel expenses. The service was already financially stretched. But after what I'd seen, there was no doubt in my mind that it was vital.

The morning had grown hot. As we waited for the cab to arrive, he took his cap off at last and eased his hood back very slightly. There was a skull and cross-bones tattoo up the side of his neck, and more patterns on his knuckles and the backs of his hands. I was pretty sure these markings were the signs of the gang he was involved with.

'Harrison,' I said, 'can you tell me what happened? Why are they out for you?'

'It's my little brother,' he told me.

Harrison's brother was fourteen. The SLRs wanted him to join, and they were putting on the pressure. For boys, gang recruitment is often by fear and intimidation – the threat of harm to family members leaves no option but to get involved. That might mean carrying drugs, holding stolen goods, even taking part in intimidation. Girls are controlled a different way –

by rape and sexual abuse, which is recorded. The video can then be used to silence her. Harrison had tried to keep his brother away from the gang. But they had made it clear who was in control. This was a warning to stay out of their business.

We gave him a receipt for three hours' induction at the nature garden. That time would count as part of his community service. We hoped his future travels in these dangerous streets would be safe. There was very little else that we could do for Harrison and his family.

When I pictured his gentle, anxious face, I was flooded with anger. There was real good in the boy. I thought of how upset he was about what happened to his mother, and how he'd tried to stop his brother going down the path of gang involvement. He was out there on the streets, making bad decisions – decisions that might cost him his life – with no one around him who could help.

I wanted to give him so much more. If only he could talk, decide what he wanted, think about another kind of future and how to make it happen. Instead, all I was doing was tinkering round the edges. I had headed off a crisis – for now. But next time, I wasn't going to be there – and what would happen then?

JANUARY 1979

Face to face with Willis again. He and Shane must have spotted me early in the morning going into Fenwick's on Bond Street. They waited, then as soon as I came out, they were onto me. Suzi Q, twenty steps behind, had time to spot them and swerve away. In my bag I had three wallets. I felt sick. I was going to be done.

Willis gave me a grin.

'So, Janice – what are you up to today?'

He frisked me down, then went through my handbag. A few passers-by had a nice long stare.

'How much is in here, Janice?' Willis asked.

I didn't answer.

On his belt, his radio crackled. He didn't respond.

He took a coil of notes out of my bag. The two cops looked at each other. The radio crackled again.

Something's not right with this, I thought.

'You not calling the van?' I enquired.

Willis riffled through the notes, divided the bundle in two, then held out one half to Shane. Shane took it and slipped it in his pocket. Then, with a grin, Willis did the same.

'What the fuck?' I demanded.

'Janice!' said Willis mockingly. 'That's not very ladylike!'

They both laughed.

'Anyway, Janice – it's a pleasure to see you as always. Let's call this an early Christmas bonus, eh? On your way.'

Just like me, these guys were on the hustle. What a crazy game of cops and robbers it was. Willis turned on his heel and continued his patrol along Brook Street, maintaining law and order for the citizens of W1.

One afternoon a few weeks later, I came out of C&A with Pepper just behind me. I had a big fat take in my bag – three wallets and a bundle of travellers. We knew our routine well: separate at once, get out of the store and then away. But as we emerged into the daylight, dead opposite me outside Evans, there they were again, Shane and Willis.

Willis was looking in my direction. I turned my back and faced into C&A's window. I stood there holding my breath.

A few seconds later, Pepper came outside. Unfortunately, she wasn't following procedure. Instead of walking on, she stopped.

'Keep on walking!' I muttered to her frantically. 'Cross the road!' I could feel two pairs of police eyes raking over us. 'Pepper!' I hissed. *'Mi say crass de road!'*

'What's wrong, Lamp-post?' she asked. 'Why are you – ?'

'Police!' I muttered.

I fumbled in my bulging handbag, keeping my head down, managing to find my sunglasses. I was already disguised in a wig, but once I'd shoved my Versaces on my nose, I felt a little bit safer. But as I watched the policemen's reflections in C&A's window, Willis's stare was chilling. Had he recognised us? We four were frozen in position, like a couple of cats staring out two mice.

'Do they know it's us?' whispered Pepper.

'I don't know. But if that fucker Willis holds onto me now, I'm going to jail.'

'Lamp-post – it's okay. If they were sure, they wouldn't wait. They'd come over here.'

I realised she was right. The law said that before they could approach us, they had to have reasonable grounds for suspicion.

No point standing waiting while they make up their minds. We need to make a move. What's the very last thing the police would expect us to do?

Suddenly I knew.

'Pepper – come!'

I pulled her by the arm. We crossed Oxford Street together and headed up a side street. Shane and Willis moved too. They tracked us past the Annunciation church. But when we turned the corner into Seymour Street, Pepper realised where we were going.

'Uh – Lamp-post – we're not – ?'

I didn't reply. I walked up the steps of Marylebone police station and calmly pushed open the door.

'What are you doing?' hissed Pepper. 'We can't go in there!'

Inside the station, a queue of people waited at the desk to see the duty sergeant. I joined the line, with Pepper alongside me. She kept on nervously rubbing her nose with the back of her hand as a disguise. We stood there for several minutes, but the progress of the queue was very slow. After a while I wandered back to the entrance. I glanced outside as someone else came in.

Shane and Willis were deep in conversation on the far side of the road. There seemed to be some sort of disagreement going on. Then Shane threw his hands in the air – and they both walked away. They couldn't believe that the two of us would dare to come in here. We'd outwitted them! I drew a deep breath of relief.

Pepper and I stood in the line for five more minutes. We still hadn't got to the desk. No one was paying us attention – so with no fuss or bother, we could leave.

'My God, Lamp-post – you've got a nerve! We could have gone to jail!' hissed Pepper as soon as we were far enough away from the station to speak. I looked at her and grinned.

'No jail today, baby,' I answered her. 'Not this girl.'

When I found out I was pregnant, I was overjoyed. Sabrina had two little daughters already, and she was happy for me too. We sat in her back garden one spring day, watching her children run around. Soon, I thought, I'll be bringing my new baby here to play.

'You're quiet today, JanJan. Something on your mind?' Sabrina said.

'Yeah,' I said. 'Yeah – there is. I've got problems, Sab. Bad problems. I don't know what to do.'

'What's the matter?'

I took a deep breath.

'It's Emmanuel.'

'Isn't he pleased about the baby?'

'Oh – he is. He really is. But – the baby won't fix it.'

'Won't fix what?'

'Won't fix anything! It doesn't work anymore with me and him.'

'Are you sure?'

'Yeah. I'm sure. We're walking round on eggshells all the time. We don't argue – but that's because we never really talk.'

'Is it about – you know – your business?'

'Yes. He won't accept it. Ever. He hates how I work.' Sabrina sighed.

'Don't tell me to stop,' I said her. 'I'm not ready to do that. And anyway – what else would I do?'

'I'm not going to tell you anything, JanJan.'

'It's over between us.' I felt tears fill my eyes. 'The baby doesn't change that. I have to decide what to do.'

Sabrina squeezed my hand.

'Maybe you don't,' she said. 'Not just yet. Maybe for now you can just wait. This isn't a good time to decide. See what it's like when the baby comes.'

'And there's something else,' I told her. 'There's a problem with Lucy.'

'Lucy? What did she do?'

'When we're out working, you know, she doesn't share the money out right.'

'What d'you mean – she doesn't share it right?'

'She doesn't split it equally. First she hides half of it, and then she shares the rest.'

'How come she can do that?'

'When we split the take, it's always very quick. It's on the move – in a cab, in a bus. She tries to distract me. The first few times, it worked. She still thinks I've not noticed. But she definitely doesn't share it right.'

Sabrina's eyes narrowed.

'That's not fair, Jan.'

'No, it's not. She treats me like a kid. She doesn't show me respect.'

Sabrina gently laid her hand on my arm.

'Perhaps she won't respect you,' she told me very quietly, 'until you don't give her any choice.'

It was autumn, close to the time that my baby was due. Lucy and I were up West. Already the shops were extra-crowded with Christmas shoppers. My pregnancy was perfect for cover.

But that day, things went badly. Twice in a row we lined up a take and I was ready – then the mark moved away. It happened sometimes – their instincts kicked in and all at once they were on guard. The first was an elderly man who was suddenly joined by his wife. She glared at me suspiciously, and guided her husband out of the department. I was sure that I'd given her no cause for alarm.

Twenty minutes later, I was shadowing a woman on the first floor, in one of the designer rooms. I got close enough to check out the contents of her lush leather handbag. 'Aye aye, dick eye' – and Lucy and I were set to go. Then all at once the woman seemed to grow more alert. She looked around. She spotted that her handbag was wide open. Looking puzzled, she closed the clasp hastily and left.

Frustrated, we headed down the escalators into the perfume halls, then out into the clatter and jostle of Oxford Street. We didn't speak till we were fifty yards away – and then Lucy started to cuss me.

'What's wrong with you today, Jan? That was twice in a row you fucked things up!'

Enough already, I thought. *I'm not listening to this.*

'Hey!' I said to her. 'Just stop right there! Why're you blaming me?'

Lucy looked startled. I'd never talked back to her before.

'Because you set her off! She was onto you!' she said angrily.

'No, I didn't. I don't know what set her off.'

'Same with the old guy's wife – you set her off too. What's wrong with you today?'

I thought of what Pepper had once told me. *Just be warned. Get ready for the day you have to tell her you won't take it anymore.*

I stopped and turned to face her.

'That's right, Lucy,' I said sarcastically. '*Blame the bloodclart cover.*'

'I'm blaming the cover because it was your fault! Today's a total waste of time. If you want money – do your job properly.'

She talkin' to me like she's the boss. Time to unzip my lip.

'Money, Lucy?' My voice was level. 'You want to talk about money?'

She instantly flushed guilty bright red. I'd never seen her flustered before.

'You sure you want to go there?' I asked.

But she was one tough cookie. In seconds she'd pulled herself together.

'The only place I'm going is back to work!' she said sharply. 'And if you don't mind, I'd like some decent fucking cover.'

But I'd seen that guilty smear across her cheeks when I'd mentioned the money. *She knows I know.*

'So let's talk about the share-out,' I said to her. 'I'm not sure "share" is the right word to use. What do you think?'

She looked as though I'd put my foot up her arse.

'Do you think I'm blind?' I demanded. 'You think I never noticed you put half the take away for yourself? You've got me risking my freedom – and you're cheating me!'

We looked each other straight in the eye. I remembered that no matter how angry I was feeling, or how much pressure I was under, I must never let my anger go wild.

'Understand me now.' I spoke in a calm and steady voice. 'When I work with you – when I run risk – I will get an equal share.'

There was a very long silence. She gave a little nod, then drew a breath as though she wanted to start speaking. I put my finger to my lips.

Dis gyal ah tek mi fi fool. Not nuh more.

'Lucy,' I said to her, '*mi done talk.* Let's go back to work.'

I pointed down the road, back to the bright lights of Selfridges shining through the early autumn twilight.

6

IF A WOMAN RUNS THE COUNTRY – WHY CAN'T WE DO THIS?

MARCH 2015

IZZIE'S DOCTOR HAD PUT her on methadone. It would help, but it wasn't a fix for her problems.

She had to take her prescription every day, picking it up from the medical centre and drinking it right there in front of the staff. It's a dark green sticky drink that tastes cloyingly sweet. She grumbled about how embarrassing it was to have to drink it in public.

Methadone wouldn't stop her wanting to use. Until she'd filled the space in her life where using had been, the craving was going to stick around. But at least it would ease the daily sickness when she didn't take drugs, and help her feel more normal.

Some days she was full of bravado. 'I've got it under control, Jan – I have,' she would say to me. When she said this, I'd just listen, knowing she had no kind of control. Underneath, she was a girl in a void. Her life had been hollowed out by drugs.

BREAKING OUT

The only purpose of her day – every day – was to get herself a fix. She told me once it was a feeling of doom hanging over her. The doom only lifted when she'd managed to work out where each day's score would come from. Perhaps it would be shoplifting alcohol from a supermarket, then selling it. Perhaps it would be people she knew – not friends, because she had none, just addicts with the same kinds of problems – pooling their cash then gathering together round the pipe, watching each other's every movement with suspicion in case anyone did better than anybody else. Afterwards they'd sit there for hours, smoking endless rollies. No one had anywhere to go. Or perhaps she'd do a blowjob for Karim. All these things left her numb – but they all got her the money she needed. The only happiness she knew how to feel was when the drugs were on the way.

She was hanging around with a scary group of men, and sleeping with them all. Leroy, Mr B and Jay were Yardies – the leaders of a gang that had south London on lock. The guys were smart and slick, always dressed for business, especially Leroy, who was clearly the leader of the pack. All of them were married with kids, but they came round to her place to do their deals and then get sex. They told her she was beautiful and cool and important while they used her in any way they wanted. Mr B even said that he'd fallen in love with her – this very handsome man with deep dark eyes and long dreads knew exactly what to say. But his sweet talk was just grooming. Her thinking was too clouded to see what was really going on.

I understood these men. They had great power, but no empathy and no sense of consequence. If they cost Izzie her life, to them that was street business. In their eyes, she was replaceable – another pretty crackhead who made terrible decisions.

'Uh . . . Jan,' Izzie said to me at one of our meetings in the office. 'If I can't make it here next week – is that a problem?'

'Yes,' I said. 'It is. It's most definitely a problem.'

'But if I'm out of the country . . . '

Now my alarm bells were ringing loud and clear.

'And why would you be out of the country?'

'Um . . . well. It's B. He's sending me on holiday.' She gave me her very cutest smile.

'Holiday?' I questioned her. I knew this script already. 'Holiday where, exactly?'

'Mexico!' She sounded excited. 'Three days in a resort. It's really posh. It's got pools and – '

'Mexico?'

'It's going to be a blast, B says.'

'And what do you have to do, to get this trip?'

'Uh – well.' Her smile was fading. 'Um. Just a parcel. I have to bring a parcel back to London.'

There are so many drug mules inside – women who believed their lives of poverty would change if they worked for the smugglers. They desperately wanted a way out of misery – that's what made them easy to manipulate. A couple of thousand pounds seemed like a win on the lottery. *You just have to carry this package. It's going to be fine . . . '*

'Izzie. Just listen for a moment. Let me tell you something about your Mr B.'

'Janice – ' She started to protest. She didn't want to hear.

'No. You listen. You know why B is doing this. He doesn't care what happens to you. He isn't even paying you. He thinks you'll risk ten years of your life to spend a few nights in a fancy hotel.'

She looked deflated and lost.

'Izzie – you know this. He says he cares. He doesn't. So – no. Don't go to Mexico. Don't ever go anywhere they send you. And I want you here next week, on time for our meeting. No ifs, no buts, no arguments. We've got work to do.'

NOVEMBER 1979

I named my daughter Nadia. Her backflips in my belly made me think of the famous Romanian gymnast, Nadia Comãneci, star of the 1976 Olympic Games. She'd been on every TV screen, all around the world – tiny, dark-eyed and fierce. Just like my little Nadia was.

I want you to be proud of who you are, baby girl.

When I was a child, I felt so lost, so confused. Now I set out to show Nadia that anything was possible. I wanted to be big and bold and boss for her – to take on the world. Sometimes the thought of staying safe at home – like Emmanuel wanted – would tempt me. He still hoped Nadia might keep me in the house. But the quiet life, the peaceful life – I knew they weren't for me.

Luckily my girlfriends were happy to help me with the baby. Sabrina's daughters adored little Nadia and constantly asked to take care of her. Ida begged to have her to stay. When she was with them, I knew that she was always loved and cared for.

As the months went by, Emmanuel and I drifted further and further apart. He stopped asking where I'd been when I went out. Now only Nadia's giggles filled the silences between us. Although my daughter made me happy, the sadness and emptiness at home were weighing me down.

The phone rang early one evening. It was Pepper.

'Lamp-post? Fancy coming round to Bagga's? I've got a surprise for you.'

'What kind of surprise?'

'I thought we'd drink that cognac. The one from Harrods.'

'Mmm – *mmm.*'

Bagga was a friend of hers – a fun party guy I'd met a couple of times before. And the cognac was a beauty. Baby Nadia was sleeping. I decided I would go. Emmanuel was watching TV. He looked up when the phone rang, but didn't say a word as he watched me fetch my coat. Ten minutes later, I was knocking on Bagga's door.

When Pepper answered, I greeted her with a hug, laughing and joking just like normal. But she softly laid her finger on her lips and beckoned me inside. Bagga was sitting at the dining table. The curtains were drawn. The lights were low. It took a second or two before I realised what he was doing.

In front of Bagga was his gear. I saw the glass pipe on the mirror, the glint of the Stanley knife, the bright lines of pinkish white powder marked with fine grooves. This was the first time I had ever seen cocaine.

'Babe – ' I whispered to Pepper. 'I didn't know you – '

'JanJan – this is good. Don't you worry. You'll like it.'

I watched Bagga in the half-light as he scooped a heap of crystal grains onto the filter then gently applied the flame of a lighter. Then he put the mouthpiece to his lips and softly drew. Ribbons of smooth creamy smoke filled the globe of the pipe. To me it was mesmerising, beautiful, seductive. A part of me loved to break the rules. Now this was a whole new level. The drug seemed to call to me. I was fascinated, curious, a little bit afraid. I pushed through my fear.

Bagga put the pipe down.

'Would you like to try some?'

'Yes, please.'

He put another scoop of grains on the filter.

'Not so much,' Pepper murmured. 'She's not done it before.'

'Don't worry.' Bagga's voice was very soft. 'I'll look after JanJan. Take your time now. Pull gently.' Again he warmed up the grains. Tentatively, I sucked at the pipe. I felt nothing.

'You're pulling too quick,' Bagga told me. 'You need to slow it down. But not too much or you'll make water come through.'

I tried another puff. Still nothing.

'Try again,' said Bagga. 'You need to relax. And stand up – you'll breathe more deeply.'

I did as he said, and pulled again. This time it was different.

A storm of white smoke began to swirl. My ears popped, as though there'd been a change in air pressure. The bubbling thud of the pump in Bagga's fish tank seemed to vibrate through the walls. My hands grew warm and heavy while the rest of me was joyfully floating. Somewhere I could hear a bird singing.

This feels fuckin' amazin'.

Slowly, I passed the pipe to Bagga. My scattered hearing came back together.

'You good?' Bagga asked me. 'You alright?'

Oh, man. Oh, dis shit is bad.

Pepper said to me: 'It's sweet, isn't it, Jan?'

'Yes,' I said at last, still feeling that my lips weren't quite my own. 'Oh, yes.'

After my argument with Lucy, I'd turned to Pepper more and more. Soon we had become close friends. We both had troubles at home – mine with Emmanuel, and Pepper's husband Scorcher was cheating – again. We felt lonely and confused, uncertain of our futures. It helped to have someone who understood. The two of us began to share a quiet pipe at the end of a working day up West.

Cocaine is a beautiful drug. It could make us forget about our problems and our worries and our fears. It calmed the rush of adrenalin we lived on. While we smoked, the past didn't matter and the future with its tangle of concerns just slipped away.

And Bagga was a very good chemist. Although he didn't like me asking questions, I learned from him by watching. He knew how to wash cocaine, turning the powder into solid form – crack – for smoking in a pipe. I stared in fascination as he added the bicarb and water to the powder in a test tube, then heated it. The water bubbled and the oil dropped to the bottom. As the test tube cooled, a stone began to form. Bagga would gently twirl the tube, trickling cold water down the outside, until we heard the chink of the stone. The crystal was most often white or cream. But pink was the real sign of quality – a promise of the highest high of all, and of a great deal of money.

Working up West, I'd seen how customers – some customers – would pay to get the best. It wasn't just the goods that they were buying – it was everything. The way that they were treated. The beautiful surroundings. The quality of all the things they saw and smelled and touched. I saw how the shop assistants rushed to help a person who had serious money to spend. It's what good customer service looked like.

This was very different. As I spent time with Bagga, watching how he did his trades, who he dealt with, I grew more and more dissatisfied with how the business worked. He had a couple of dealers he knew well, and a regular party crowd that he would sell to. Even though the customers had money, they did an awful lot of hanging about. And when the dealer did turn up, he'd have an attitude – even though his buyers were putting the cash into his pocket. *Awful customer service*, I thought to myself.

I knew why it happened. The business ran on fear. Underneath their bravado, the dealers were afraid. Alone on the road with their product, there was always the chance of being caught by the feds. Then there were opportunists and chancers who might try to rob them. And I noticed the same fear in the party smokers' eyes as they opened their gleaming front doors in their desirable postcodes to buy from Bagga. No mistake – they liked their taste of danger and excitement. But underneath, these wealthy customers were wondering just who their dealer was. Could they really trust him?

White is very powerful, I realised. They were risking their beautiful, safe lives – just so they could get it. They wanted it that much.

One evening, we went round to Annie's. Annie was a lovely girl, a good friend of Pepper's, but that night, all I could see was that Annie was a mess. She used to have a job, Pepper said, and keep her place real nice – but not anymore. Now it was a crack house, and anyone could knock her door all hours for a smoke. Her dealer was pretty often round there – he used the place to sell. And I could see he had another reason for visiting.

'Why's she acting like there's something going on

with her and him?' I asked Pepper. 'Everybody knows he has a girlfriend.'

'They have an arrangement.'

'What kind of arrangement?'

Pepper rolled her eyes. 'What kind d'you think?'

'For a twenty-pound stone?' I asked her.

'She's been smoking, so she's hardly going to stop him.'

Now I saw a whole different side to the business. The pipe relaxes you. Your judgement gets clouded. How men are aware of this. They seize the opportunity to violate. A woman might not like it – but she isn't letting go of the pipe. He's a predator, and she is easy prey.

Then, a few weeks later, I went along with Bagga to sell in a crack house down in Peckham. That place was full of scary shit. It was pitch black and stinking, empty fridge, dirty plates in the sink, bins overflowing, chaos everywhere. I did a few more errands like that. Each time, I hated what I saw. Smokers would sit peeping out of their window for hours because they thought the house was being watched. They crawled round on the carpet in a fingertip search for some little crumb of crack that might have fallen from the pipe. I watched a smoker picking at a white woollen sweater – she thought that the pattern might be crystals. Any guy who wanted a blowjob in a place like that could get one – sometimes for a smoke, other times just because.

Sometimes smokers stole from each other. They'd

try any trick at all – hiding splinters of rock under their fingernails just so they could have a little bit more. They were too mashed up to care if they'd eaten, or if their children had. Their messy stinky babies ran around in wet nappies and they didn't even see. These people were helpless.

Because cocaine is an ugly drug too. It can cost you every single thing you have – your self-respect, your friends, your family, your life. And you'll still pay whatever it takes to get more, because you can't face a day when you don't have it.

JULY 1980

'Bagga? Is everything okay?'

He was standing in his front room, staring out into the street. He was usually a chill kind of guy, but when I said his name, he jumped and looked around.

'Janice!'

'What is it?'

'See dat?'

Bagga pointed out of the window. It was early in the evening. Everything outside was quiet. A man with a briefcase walked briskly along on the opposite pavement. Somewhere I could hear a dog barking.

'See what?'

'Dat pigeon!'

'What pigeon, Bags?'

'DERE!' he hissed at me. 'Sittin' on dat branch!'

'No,' I said. 'I can't see a pigeon.'

'It's juss gaan. It did a hide!'

'Did a what?'

'Ah polis, Jan – dem train dem fi watch people!'

'Police pigeon? What are you talking about?'

Sometimes smokers would realise how crazy they were acting, and nervously laugh at themselves. But Bagga wasn't laughing. He was deadly serious.

He's proper prang, I thought. *Outta his tree. Paranoid. Imaginin' all kinds of nonsense.*

'Look, Bagga – '

'Di polis! Dey train dem to watch! Dey got di pigeons watchin' dis house!'

'I can't see any pigeons, Bagga, and neither can you.'

'Mi tell you – it's becos dey hidin' now!'

'I think they're just nesting somewhere.'

'No!' He seemed really annoyed that I didn't believe him. 'Trained pigeons, Janice!'

'Man,' I said, 'you've been blazing. You're prang. Smoking too much shit.'

'Janice! You need to tek dis seriously!'

I couldn't persuade him that south London's streets weren't patrolled by teams of specially trained police pigeons. I didn't like this kind of madness at all. And I had to admit it – the crap was getting harder to ignore.

A few days later, I lay back in the bath, cigarette in my hand. I let out a long lungful of smoke. The pale blue plume rose, then dwindled in the clouds of warm steam. I wanted to chill out, but I couldn't. I was asking some very tough questions of myself.

Las' night, mi spent seven hundred pounds on the pipe. Yes, mi have money, but that's an awful lot to puff away. What the fuck mi doin' with mi life?

I watched the curls of nothingness winding round the cigarette's glowing tip.

Every day I chance my freedom for that money. And here I am, burning it. Risking my future, just for stolen handbags and smoke.

Even when you sleep, the pipe keeps calling you. *'You want me,'* it whispers, *'you want me, you know you want one more.'* It's an addiction of the mind. It takes all your will to control it.

Well – it's not having me. This has gone far enough. I took a long deep breath.

Nah. From today, no more. I will control *yuh,* not yuh control *me. I'm goin' to be my own boss. That's the way it's goin' to be.*

'Hey, Lamp-post,' asked Pepper, 'where've you been? I've not seen you for ages.'

I'd been at home, going through a whole lot of stuff in my head. The phone had rung plenty of times, but I'd ignored it. I needed space to think.

'Sorry, Pep. How's things?'

I noticed straightaway she seemed distracted and unhappy.

'Not so good. I got problems with Scorch.'

'You've not let him move back in?'

'No. Not yet.'

But I knew that she would. Her husband Scorcher

was a bad boy with a bad reputation. But to Pepper he was just boo – he was sweet, he was funny, he was charming. It was his cheating that drove her insane. When it got too painful, she would tell him to leave. Once he got tired of his latest toy, he came running home. She would always take him back. That was who she was. For the sake of the children, she kept the family together. She was strong. A man like Scorcher knew how to use her strength against her.

'Girl – don't be a fool.' I always said it, though I knew she'd never listen. 'He's never going to change.'

'I know he isn't, JanJan.' My tough, good-humoured Pepper seemed very down. I wanted to distract her from her thoughts.

'So . . . what if we didn't need to bother with these men?' I asked her.

'Huh?'

'What if we didn't need to have these guys around? If we were independent?'

'Oh.' She gave a wistful little smile. 'Yeah. I think that would be nice.'

'Well, I've got an idea.'

'Okay.'

I told her what it was, and she stared at me in shock.

'JanJan – have you lost your mind?'

'Why shouldn't we?'

'It's dangerous! And anyway – we don't know what to do!'

'Yeah, we do. I've been watching. I've made contacts. I've been learning how it's done.'

She slowly shook her head.

'Jan – you must be crazy. We can't. Dealing drugs is a game for men.'

'Look,' I said to her, 'stop saying that we can't and just listen for a minute. 'Cos I'm going to tell you how we can. You and me – we should think about the future. This is a bigger game than dipping. This would mean real money. We could change our lives for good – yours and mine, the kids.'

'Well, maybe so, but . . . '

'Check these dealers, Pep. Look how they are with their customers. You ring them. You say you want to buy. They say they're coming round in ten minutes. You wait an hour, then you ring again. And you get the attitude thing – like they're doing something for free.'

She was laughing reluctantly, and shaking her head.

'It's true, Janice. Them dealers always take the piss.'

'They keep you waiting on purpose. They know what they're doing. It's a mind game.'

'God, Jan, you're right.'

'So – we'll treat our customers much better.'

She started to smile.

'Our customers?'

'Yes, Pepper. It'd be – market forces. Like she says – the Prime Minister. Maggie T. Leave it up to the markets.'

'Be serious! It's risky!'

'I am serious. We'll start off really small. Just locally. Business will come if we're reliable.'

I could see that she was starting to think about it.

'Word spreads quickly when you have good gear,' I

went on. 'We'll turn up on time, not mess customers around. Give them what they want to buy.'

Pepper grinned.

'Just like Mrs Thatcher says!'

'Yeah – like Maggie!'

'You wanna lead like the Iron Lady?'

I threw my head back and laughed.

But Pepper looked suddenly uneasy.

'But look,' she said, 'you're going too fast. How do we store these drugs? How do we keep the money safe? How do we bank it? My God, Janice, no. No, we can't do this.'

'It's cool, Pepper. It's cool. I've thought about that too. I could ask Ida – you know, Emmanuel's mum. She holds the money for the pardners. She once told me I could ask her if I ever needed help. One really good thing about Mums – no matter what, she's not talking.'

'Well now, Mama J – I am impressed. You have thought this out!'

Mama J. I liked how that name sounded.

'By the time we're fifty,' I told her, 'we'll be driving Rolls-Royces!'

Pepper looked like she was making up her mind. She just had one more question.

'But would you really feel safe?' she asked me. 'As a woman – out there selling, driving round at night with the work?'

'Our Prime Minister's a woman,' I said to her, 'and she can run the whole damn country. Why can't we do this?'

7

MURDER ON NEW BOND STREET

NOVEMBER 2016

IT WASN'T LATE, BUT already winter darkness had fallen. Inside the probation office, there was the usual deeply misleading silence.

Upstairs, most of the team sat at their desks in a hush of concentration, tackling the constant backlog of form-filling and report-writing which followed our appointments with clients. Downstairs, although many of the interview rooms were occupied, the maze of quiet corridors made the place feel empty. Each room was well sound-proofed and equipped with CCTV. But we couldn't be sure that the monitors were always watched, so we also carried personal panic alarms, just in case an incident kicked off and someone needed assistance fast. Like the rest of my colleagues, I felt vulnerable working at times. If an angry client decided to take his frustration out on me, help would come – but possibly not quickly enough.

I was waiting for Nathan, my 4.30 appointment. It

was only the second time I'd seen him since a colleague had asked me to step in. His process of engagement wasn't working. He was missing appointments, and when he showed up he was hostile and withdrawn, refusing to respond no matter what was said. The call came through and I made my way down to the waiting room to fetch him.

The waiting room opened off the street, and when clients came in, they reported to the reception desk then waited for their officer to meet them. The receptionist sat behind a window made of toughened glass. All our security could make the place forbidding. I was very much aware of this, and also of the message of suspicion and distrust it sent out. But there was no other choice. Service users could be troubled and angry. All of them were under heavy stress. Aggression could flare up, and mental health issues meant that people's reactions could sometimes be extreme. When I met a client, I always did a quick evaluation – a chat as we walked to the interview room, trying to work out how this person was doing and how the session was likely to go. But my instincts couldn't always be accurate. However off-putting, the security equipment was vital for protection.

For Nathan, I could see that the location was part of the problem. He bitterly resented these appointments. They offended his dignity. He felt monitored, controlled, and he hated that feeling. I'd looked through his notes with a real pang of sadness – 22 years old and already a veteran of prison with time served in Belmarsh and Brixton. Three weeks before, he'd been released on licence. At our first meeting, I hadn't pushed too hard. I could see he wasn't ready to talk. My questions about his private life came across to him as interfering and intrusive. By showing him that I was there to listen and giving him time to get to know me, I hoped we might get past this and make progress.

His first two sentences had been for possession of drugs with intent to supply. Intent can be a tricky thing to prove. Up to seven grams of weed is regarded as being for personal usage – unless it's divided into bags for sale which makes clear that the owner is dealing. Of course, a person who had a smaller block might be dealing too – but if they were employed, the usual rule was to treat their drugs as personal use too. When someone with no job has a block of weed in their pocket, however, it's probably their income. Prosecution is likely to follow.

But Nathan's third offence was motoring-related. If he liked cars, perhaps we could use his interest to help him to engage. I could be a source of guidance for clients like him to whom the whole system seemed remote and bureaucratic. I wanted to take their side, sharing their frustration at how hard it could be to get a quick response. But for Nathan right now, it seemed as though the world was against him. Nobody cared. I was just another face of an authority he hated and despised.

'Hey, Nathan. Nice to see you. Come this way.'

He clearly didn't think that it was nice to see me. I led him in silence through the corridors, down to the interview room I'd booked for our meeting. The room seemed smaller after dark than in daylight. Its windows were barred. It was sparsely furnished, with just a table and two chairs.

I asked him how things were at home. He was living at his mother's. She had three other much younger children. His notes were full of complaints about the lack of privacy, noise and disruption caused by his sisters and brother. But he'd lost his own flat due to being in prison for more than twelve weeks. After that, his housing benefit had ceased and he had been evicted for arrears whilst he was still inside.

Nathan didn't answer. He was sitting on the edge of his seat, drumming his fingers on the table. There was a thin line of sweat across his upper lip. I noticed the tension in his body.

'Why do I have to come here?' he demanded abruptly.

He was looking for conflict. I understood his anger, but right now there was a process that he must follow or face the consequences. My goal was to help him to co-operate and move forward.

'These appointments are the terms of your probation, Nathan. They are instead of prison. I hope you will find that when you come here, we can help you and support you.'

'Support me? You mean lecture me?'

'I don't think I'm lecturing you. I'd like you to tell me how your week has gone.'

'I don't get help here,' he muttered. 'This is just a threat. I do this or it's prison.'

He was breathing heavily, close to losing his temper. I started to feel uneasy.

'You people, all up in my business, not doing shit to help me.'

I turned my panic button over in my fingers.

'Please don't swear, Nathan. I'd like to find a way to work with you.'

As I said the words, I knew my hands were tied. There was much more that I would like to do for him – so little that I actually could.

Suddenly he jumped to his feet and leaned right across towards me, thrusting his face up close to mine. I felt flecks of his saliva spatter on my skin. He banged his hand down hard on the table.

'Why d'you think you can tell me what to do, you stupid bitch?'

'Nathan,' I said, 'this isn't working. I need you to stay calm. If you are abusive, I will have to terminate – '

'Terminate the meeting! That's what I mean about your lot! Nathan do this. Nathan do that. I'm stressed out! No job! No home! Trying to keep my mental health in check!'

'Nathan, I will have to report your abusive language and end this meeting.'

'Report me, then! See if I care!'

It sounded like something you might hear in a playground. *See if I care!* Underneath his crackling rage, I saw a frightened, vulnerable boy. His impulsive burst of anger and his pale, sweaty face were probably signs of substance abuse. He banged the wall with the flat of his hand, then looked around at me with loathing.

It was impossible to continue. Nathan wasn't able to engage – to talk or to listen.

'Young man, I wish you well,' I said. 'I am terminating this meeting. I will escort you from the building.'

I knew what he needed. Someone to listen, someone with the time to help him work through the causes of anger and distress in his life. Somewhere decent to live and the chance of a job that he enjoyed. What I could offer wasn't nothing – still, I knew just how limited it was. But Nathan couldn't even accept the little that that I was trying to do for him.

Until he was ready, there would only be more angry refusals to engage. That would be followed by more consequences, and then by even more anger. Until he could begin to take some responsibility for change, his life would go on spiralling down.

MARCH 1982

One ounce: twenty-eight grams. I would buy for £1,000, divide the ounce and sell each gram for £50, turning £400 profit. We worked on Pepper's kitchen table, weighing the white powder on jewellers' scales. We cut squares of white paper and folded them into little envelopes, each containing one gram of powder.

By day, we continued with our dipping. In the

evenings, we were out seeing clients, growing our new business, but only until 9 p.m. I wasn't interested in being on the road half the night and getting robbed in some crack house at three o'clock in the morning. Pepper and I were working mums. Tomorrow I would have to be up early to give Nadia her breakfast.

We used Bagga's dealer to begin with. We bought what we were sure we could sell and no more. Out on the road, I did the driving. I turned up on time, offered a fair price and gave no one any hassle. I built up some good word on the street. I made some money.

But not enough. It was going to take a while to really build my profits up. I was in business, and looking to expand.

12 August 1983, Greenwich Magistrates' Court. Shoplifting. Fined £40.00.

'So – what's in here that you want?' As usual, Pepper was straight down to business as we stepped into Crocodile, a luxury clothes and leather goods store not far from Oxford Street.

I took a look around. And then I saw it. A Louis Vuitton black leather attaché case. An absolute beauty in delicious black leather, the letters 'LV' and 'Made in France' discreetly inscribed on its heavy gold clasp.

'I like that guy's briefcase,' I said.

Pepper turned her head slightly for a look.

'Ooooh. Nice.'

'It's more than just nice.'

'Okay – it's very nice. And you're going to be a magician today, are you?'

'You think I can't get it?'

'I know you can't!'

It sounded like a dare.

'Janice,' she went on, 'it's too difficult!'

The owner had put the attaché case down. He was standing at a glass-topped counter in conversation with a sales assistant. But I could see he was still watchful – a good slice of his attention was always on his case.

I felt a stir of excitement. *There's something valuable in there.*

'I think I can see a way to do this,' I told her. 'Are you up for it?'

She pulled a face, but she trusted my judgement. She nodded. The take was on.

I stood just behind the mark, turned slightly away from him, making sure he never saw my face directly. Then I chatted energetically to Pepper. As we talked, I gently reached out with my foot. Taking my time, I nudged the briefcase towards me inch by inch. When I'd got it where I wanted it, I stopped and walked away.

I knew that this would make the mark relax. There was no one close to him, or getting in his face. He was engrossed in conversation with the assistant. Nothing around to make him uneasy or suspicious. The lift was set. And if he glanced to check, his brief-case would be plainly in view – not so close to him as it was before, but I thought he was unlikely to notice its position had changed.

Half a minute later, Pepper and I strolled back across the store together. We paused, and Pepper casually placed herself between the mark and the target. Then she started searching in her handbag. While she provided the distraction, I bent down and swiftly crotched the case.

I walked straight out of the shop, crossed the road and hailed a taxi. If Pepper couldn't make her escape, the plan was to wait for her at Victoria. But seconds later, she was safely outside too and we were both in the back of the cab. As the tension broke, we burst out laughing.

The case had a combination lock. Pepper nicked a screwdriver from Woolworth's just opposite Victoria station, then we headed to the Shakespeare. The pub was quiet in the mid afternoon and we sat there unobserved. I started to jimmy the lock apart. The metal resisted and I had to apply more pressure.

'Dammit!' I grumbled under my breath.

Pepper glanced around. The only other drinkers were a couple at a table, their backs turned to us.

'This is an awful lot of bother, Lamp-post.'

'Don't worry – it'll be worth it.'

I still had a very good feeling. Finally, I prised the lock apart. Inside, the lining was the softest golden-brown leather. I leaned forward to inhale its wonderful, luxurious smell. There was just one tiny little stain inside the lid, shaped like a heart – it looked like it might have been black ink. But even with the stain, this case was still a beauty.

But the contents were a big disappointment – only paperwork and one or two pens. A gold Cartier and a Montblanc – very nice – but still, after all the trouble . . .

'So much for your hot move!' muttered Pepper. 'We've run all the way from bloody Bond Street and there's nothing in it!'

She slammed the lid of the attaché case down. As it snapped shut, I heard a thud. Inside the case, something had shifted.

'Wait a minute . . . '

I opened the case a second time. A secret compartment inside the lid had been released. It stuck out like a little shelf. And on the shelf I saw my prize – a neat row of plastic bags, each one packed full of notes. I counted. We'd just taken £10,000 in cash.

'We got money!' Pepper whispered excitedly.

'I think you'll find that *I've* got money,' I told her with a grin. 'You done nuthin' but cuss me from mornin'!'

3 October 1983, Croydon Magistrates' Court. Handling stolen goods. Probation order – two years concurrent.

My new business was starting to make some real money. I couldn't pay it into my bank account, but I needed to keep it somewhere safe. I thought of what Ida had once told me.

'Remember – if you ever need some help, don't talk to Emmanuel. Come and talk to me.'

I went round to see her one afternoon with Nadia. My little girl was three by now, and an energetic climber. She always loved to play in Nanny's garden.

'Mums,' I said, as we sat watching Nadia running round and tripping over on the grass. 'Could I ask you the biggest favour ever?'

'Well, I wonder what is this now?'

'I have some money. And I was wondering if you could maybe help me. If you'd keep it in your house, like the pardners do, I'd know it would be safe.'

'Money? What kind of money?'

'Ah – some cash I made. From selling things. Most people pay in cash, you see, and . . . '

'How much money, Janice?'

'It's packaged already. It won't take up much space.'

'I didn't ask you how much space. I asked you how much money.'

I knew exactly how much. By now it was nearly twenty grand.

'Maybe I should fetch it,' I said hastily. 'I've got it in the car.'

I'd packed the money in a handbag. When I passed it to Ida, she slipped the catch apart and looked inside. For a moment, she didn't say a word.

'Janice – where did you get this?'

'Mums – if it's a problem then just tell me.'

'I didn't say it was a problem. But I want to know where you got this money from.'

'Mums – I can't tell you all of that.'

'Then I can't store this money in my house.'

Whatever secrets were hidden in Emmanuel's past, Ida was aware of them all. This woman was no fool.

'I'm selling furs,' I told her.

'Selling furs?'

'Yes. For a business in Knightsbridge.'

'In Knightsbridge?'

'End of season stock. Stuff that won't fit on the rails. So sometimes – it falls off the rails. You know.'

'I do know, Janice. And I want you to be careful.'

'I'm always careful, Mums.'

'Alright then. I will help you. It's money from your business. That's what you told me. I believe you. You will never tell me any more than that.'

'Okay. So . . . . Mums? There's something else as well.'

Ida sighed.

'It's nothing bad. It's the case I keep my jewellery in. An attaché case. Would you please store that too?'

'Yes, I'll store that too. I'll always help you. Remember – you're family, no matter what.'

'No matter what?' I asked her. I could see that she looked sad as she said it. 'What do you mean?'

'I'm not blind,' said Ida gently. 'I can see that there are problems between you and my son.'

We sat together for a moment in silence.

'I'm sorry, Mums. I didn't want to tell you. I thought you'd be upset.'

'And I am upset, Janice. But we need to think of Nadia. All of us do. I love her very much. I hope I'll always be a part of her life. And of yours.'

'Of course you will!' I found that I had tears in my eyes. 'Don't even say that!'

'Good. We're family and we'll act like family,' said Ida. 'We'll help each other out and we'll be there when we're needed. Always.'

But Emmanuel and I were almost strangers by now. I knew that our relationship must end. I would have to leave his house and find a new home for me and for Nadia. But still, I dreaded telling him. And far worse than that, I dreaded telling her.

'When will you talk to him, JanJan?' asked Sabrina. She looked across at me as we sat watching the kids on the swings in Brockwell Park.

'Soon.'

'When?'

'Very soon. I definitely will. I promise.'

Sabrina sighed. 'You keep saying that. Babe, you need to deal with this.'

'I will, Sab. I have to get my own place sorted first.'

'So do that. Get on with it. Leaving things like this – it's no good for anyone.'

That was why I loved her. She'd tell me the truth, even if I didn't want to hear it.

'Ah, Sab – but it's difficult.'

She laid her hand on mine.

'I know it is, Jan.'

By now I longed to be free to live my own life. But a part of me still clung to Emmanuel. He'd made me feel safe for the first time in my life. It hurt so much to let that feeling go. I summoned up my courage and asked him to help me get a flat from the council. It was as close as I could come to saying the words: *It's over.*

When he'd listened, he was silent for a very long time. Finally, he said: 'When you've got a job, Janice. A proper, straight job. Then I'll help you. Not until.'

But I wasn't taking no for an answer. I applied for a flat, and was offered one not too far away. I kept the new place secret for months. In the daytime, I'd stop round there – take some small things along to make it homely, start to decorate. But then a wave of sadness would engulf me. This was going to cause Nadia such pain. She loved her father so much – and deep down, so did I. Lying to him was killing me. Every evening, I still wanted to go home where I was safe – just for one more night.

AUGUST 2015

Izzie's hands were red raw. I noticed it as soon as she walked into the meeting room. She had started to feel terrified of germs and was compulsively washing them again and again. It had been going on for two or three weeks.

The desperate need to wash had come just after she'd got rid of her terror of spiders. Suddenly she'd thought that they were everywhere, down the sink and in the corners, hiding down the cracks in the floorboards. At night she paced her bedsit, too terrified to sleep in case they scuttled out and ran across her face. And just before the terror of spiders, she'd thought her place was bugged. She was convinced that everything she did was being filmed and would be broadcast on the internet. As soon as one dread faded, it was instantly replaced by another. She was caught in an unending spiral of anxiety.

'I think I know what's worrying you, baby,' I said to her.

A talk like this between us could go two ways – she'd be terribly angry and storm off, or she'd listen.

'You keep on telling yourself that you're okay,' I continued. 'But really – you know that isn't true. Your inner self, your real self – it knows better.'

'What do you mean?'

'You need to face reality. You're trying to believe your own lies. And other people's lies as well. The longer you go on like this – hanging out with these guys, taking heroin, doing what you do – the louder your inner voice will shout. You can't suppress your feelings like that. The longer you try to, the more afraid you'll feel.'

She hadn't argued yet.

'The truth is – you're killing your future. Your ambitions, your dreams. All the things you wanted to be when you were a little girl. All those things are dying, and it's drugs that are killing them.'

She was listening. The process was slow, but I could see her getting stronger. And she was helping me grow stronger too. She took me to a different level in the way I interacted, not only with her but with everyone.

I saw what she was capable of, and through this, I saw what I could also do.

'Izzie,' I said to her, 'I've been there, and I know. The closer you come to reality, the less afraid you'll be.'

MARCH 1984

'I heard you're doing business,' said Gill's voice down the phone.

We'd lost touch for a while after Lucy and I had fallen out. It was good to hear her rapid, throaty growl.

'Where did you hear that?'

'Aw, c'mon, Jan. I'm on the road, for God's sake. I hear things. Got any time to meet up and chat?'

'About what?'

'About your business, of course.'

It was great seeing Gill again. She still smoked her fat spliffs and we chatted non-stop until late into the evening. She'd been making money doing mule work – drug runs through Heathrow, travelling to the Caribbean and smuggling back parcels. I told her she was out of her mind to be taking risks like that. People do all sorts of craziness – they swallow packages of drugs to get them through customs, then the package bursts in flight. They wrap coke in condoms and clingfilm and push it into the cavities of their body. It's messy and it's dangerous – you're dicing with death.

'You have got to be mad,' I said. 'That's playing with your life, girl. You can't be that desperate.'

'I hear you, Jan. Anyway, something better just came up. One of the young dons from north has an operation. The money sounds good so I'm taking the chance. Would you like to meet the link? He's a serious guy.'

I laughed.

'Yeah. I suppose so. Gill – you're sure he's alright?'

'Jan – he's safe. How 'bout Tuesday night? I'll introduce you. His name is Scully.'

'Hello, Janice.'

He sat behind a desk piled with paperwork – a chill-looking Jamaican guy, mid-forties, softly spoken, dressed in ordinary working clothes. He ran a busy and successful scaffolding company – a front for his drugs operation – in Stockwell, south London.

He don't look like no big man. He don't move like no big man. But there's something about him. Why did I feel that stir in my belly?

I looked at Scully and I knew. *This man is powerful. I can smell it. This man is used to bein' in control.*

My life was going to change. My future would be different now that we had met.

'So – young lady. I heard you're looking for work?' he asked me.

'Yes. But nothing major for now. Just an ounce. What price are you offering?'

'Fourteen hundred.'

'Okay. I'm good with that. But I don't have all the cash at the moment. I can leave you my Omega watch.'

He sat back in his chair. His gaze never left my face.

'I see.' He looked thoughtful. 'Okay. I'd be cool with your watch.'

From the corner of my eye, I saw Gill. She was half-smiling.

'Give me a couple of days,' I said, 'and I'll call you.'

'No problem, young lady. When you're ready.'

I took off my watch. He held out his hand. I dropped its heavy gold links into his palm. The metal was still warm from its contact with my skin. Scully smiled.

'It's good to do business with you, Mama J,' he said.

My new flat was looking more like home. I'd paid a few working visits to Oxford Street. Each time, I picked up something new, then on my way home to Thornton Heath, I'd drop off the latest addition. I stayed the night a few times, just to settle in. I told Emmanuel I'd been out with friends and slept over.

'That's okay, babe,' was all he replied. I'd no idea at all if he believed me. Next morning, he'd always get Nadia ready for school.

One afternoon, as I was walking to my flat, a familiar black Mercedes came round the corner up ahead – the High Commission car. The pavement was empty – there was no place to duck down and hide. Emmanuel pulled over and wound his window down. If he was surprised to see me there, he didn't show it.

'Hey babe.'

'Hey honey.'

Then there was a pause.

'What you up to round these parts?' I asked him.

'Just had to drop some top fellow off in Clapham.'

'I've been round Gill's new place,' I offered.

'That's cool, babe.' There was no way to tell what he was thinking. 'Take care. I'll see you later.'

When he got home that evening, all he said was, 'Janice, let's talk.'

'Okay.'

As I told him about the flat, I felt a sense of relief. He didn't ask me many questions. It was over between us. What would be the point?

'I'd like to see your new place, babe. 'Specially Nadia's room. I'm sure you've done a good job.'

'I'll be staying over sometimes, just to get used to it. You okay with that?'

Ordinary words, but such terrible finality. At least he didn't argue, or make our parting any harder than it already was.

'That's fine, babe,' he said. 'Take your time. Let me know if you want some help moving.'

'So Daddy won't live here?' said Nadia when I took her along to show her our new home.

I'd explained very gently how both of us still loved her, and that even though we wouldn't be together any more, she could see Emmanuel as often as she wanted. But I knew that it hadn't seemed quite real to her. Now that she was looking round the flat, she began to take it in.

'No, baby. Mummy and Daddy don't live together

anymore. But he will often come to see you, and you can go and stay with him.'

'But I want Daddy! I want him to live here too!'

I felt my eyes begin to sting. More than anything, I wanted what was happening to her not to be painful. But it was.

'Nadia – honey – I told you – '

She was only four years old. She loved her daddy, and she didn't understand. Knowing I had hurt her was a horrible feeling, like rocks in my throat. I kept swallowing and swallowing, trying to make the lump go away. Nadia started to cry, and now tears filled my eyes too.

'I want Daddy! I want Daddy!' Suddenly she turned on me, furious. 'Why did you make my daddy go away?'

A couple of weeks later, I drove Nadia round to her daddy's for an overnight visit. As I drew up outside the house, Emmanuel was standing by the door waiting for her. He walked down the path as I drew up at the kerb, and reached across to open the back door.

'Hello, sweetie!' Emmanuel called to her.

As Nadia scrambled out of the car, something on the floor caught her eye. She leaned forward. I thought she must have dropped one of her toys.

'Look, Mummy,' she said. 'Auntie Gill dropped her weed!'

Emmanuel froze.

Nadia picked up a little plastic bag from the floor. In the bag was a big bud of weed. How did she know what it was? I'd never told her anything about it. I hastily held out my hand.

'Pass it to me, baby.'

Nadia jumped happily into Emmanuel's arms. As he scooped her up and hugged her, he looked down at me over her shoulder. Disgust was written all over his face. I had to wait two days before he knocked on my front door.

'How did she know, Janice? How did she know what it was?'

'I don't know, Em.'

'What do you mean, you don't know? What has she seen? What has she heard?'

Nadia was often in the back of the car. She heard me chatting with my visitors and friends. I'd thought she wasn't listening because she was playing or reading or singing to herself, but Nadia was listening, alright. She was a smart, observant little girl. She understood everything that people said around her. I should have known. I realised I had been very careless.

'Em, look, I'm sorry. I've not dealt with this too well.'

'Not dealt with this too well! Is that how you put it?'

'I'm sorry.'

'You keep on saying that! But it's too late to be sorry.'

I knew how much he loved our daughter. Arguing with him would only make things worse.

'I told you I didn't want to lose another woman!' Emmanuel cried.

'I remember.'

'Well, I have.' He shook his head slowly, disbelievingly. 'I've lost you – the very same way. And lost my baby too!'

'You haven't lost Nadia. She loves you very much.'

In a voice full of bitterness, he answered: 'But you've got her behaving just like you.'

His words slapped me in the face. Our love had once been strong. Now he meant to kill what was left of it.

'I thought I could keep you away from the wolves,' he whispered. 'I really tried to do it. But you can't be kept away. And do you know why? It's because you are one of them.'

The break-up took its toll. Although she loved to visit him, Nadia was constantly asking for her father. I decided that we should have a holiday. I bought an all-expenses-paid trip to Jamaica for us both.

I wanted Pepper to come with us. She was stressed out, and desperately needed a break. Scorcher had only just come out of prison, but already he was back to his game of cheating. His latest woman was hanging around. Yet again, I wished that Pepper could find the courage to end all this. But I knew how hard it was. She loved this bastard. He didn't deserve her.

'Pep – come with me,' I urged her. 'I'm sure your mum will have the kids – she knows you need a break. You seriously should take time out.'

'Nah. I can't. There's too much going on.'

The night before we left for our trip, with our suitcases packed and standing by the door, I phoned her again. I felt uneasy and I didn't know why.

'Pep – I think you should come with us.'

I heard a sad little smile in her voice as she answered.

'I love you, JanJan. I can't come this time. See you when you get back.'

I sat on my balcony at the Pegasus Hotel in Kingston. Inside our room, Nadia was sleeping. It had been a good day – and the Caribbean sun always lifted my spirits. Now it had set, and the outline of the mountains could barely be seen against the darkening sky.

I heard Nadia wake up with a cry. I went inside to comfort her.

'Mummy! Mummy!' She was sitting up in bed sobbing.

'It's okay, baby, it's okay.'

'I dreamt about Auntie Pepper!'

'Did you, baby?'

'I dreamt that she was lying in a bed with loads of wires. She said to the doctor, "I'm not dead" but then I looked at her again and her eyes were closed.'

The room was in half-darkness. I was glad that Nadia couldn't see the expression on my face.

'Nadia, baby.' I tried to soothe myself as much as her. 'Sweetie, it's okay. It was only a dream.'

I kissed her and stroked her hair until she fell back to sleep. But I couldn't settle down. I didn't understand how a little girl's nightmare could frighten me so much. I decided to ring London. But in Pepper's house, the phone rang and rang. Unusual for her not to be at home. I began to pace the room, telling myself that I was overreacting, imagining things. Nothing helped. In the end, I phoned Bagga.

He picked up in one ring.

'Janice? You need to come home,' was all he said. My heart began to pound.

'Why? Bagga – what happened?'

'There's been an accident. Pepper's in hospital.'

As early as I could the next morning, I went to change our flights. It seemed forever before we landed back in London. There was the hassle of getting through customs with a tired little girl. Bagga was waiting to meet us outside. As he drove us away, I asked him which hospital Pepper was in.

His face was rigid in the rear-view mirror.

'Bags? Can we just go straight there?'

'Jan.' His voice was flat and strange. 'Jan – I couldn't tell you while you were still out there. I knew it would be bad when you heard. Pepper's dead.'

Nadia burst out crying. I tried my best to comfort her. I couldn't ask what happened. I was numb.

We made our way to Pepper's parents' house, and her dad came to the door. He almost collapsed into my arms. From inside I heard her mother's voice: 'Who's there? Who is it?' She stumbled towards me down the hall, then started sobbing loudly and pounding at my body with her fists.

'Why did you leave her? If you'd not left her – '

'What happened?' I asked.

Pepper's dad answered in a dull, flat voice.

'My daughter was murdered.'

I could barely take it in. The story was that Scorcher was out of jail, and up to his old cheating tricks. But this time, the woman was hot-headed, and furiously jealous of his wife. She'd tracked Pepper down while she was working up West. She'd made an awful scene, screaming and shouting hysterical abuse, telling Pepper that her husband didn't want her and was going to leave for good.

I knew at once how horrified Pepper would have been. She wouldn't want to deal with her husband's raging girlfriend. And raised voices and attention were disastrous for business. She'd tried to walk away up a side street. The woman followed her, and stabbed her with a pair of scissors. Pepper died in a pool of her own blood on a West End pavement.

For months, that scene filled my mind. I saw its horror and violence again and again. Each time I longed to be there – to be with her, to be able to protect her. But it had happened. It could never be undone. As time went by, I could sometimes feel my energy and cheerfulness returning. But next day I'd be paralysed with despair all over again, barely able to get out of bed.

I couldn't bear to set foot in the West End. But a little while later, I agreed to go up to Knightsbridge with Suzi Q. I hadn't seen her for months, and I hoped that it might be like old times, working as friends. Still, as we set out, unease hung over me. I thought it would be good to distract myself with work. I decided to push on.

We went to Harvey Nichols for a browse, checking out the marks. I tried to feel it like I used to in the old days. But it didn't take me long before I realised I was done. I had no concentration. Nothing would be happening today. Then I noticed a store detective watching. She was dressed all in black – a leather jacket, expensively cut trousers, a couple of carrier bags in her hands, and eyes locked on me. Damn it. I must have been recognised.

I paused at one of the confectionery counters and bought a few loose chocolates, trying to decide what I should do. The detective stopped too. She was tracking me for sure. But since I'd taken nothing and made no attempt to do so, I was still in the clear. I could leave. I headed for the street.

Outside on the pavement, I quickly picked up speed and strode away. On the island in the middle of the road, I looked back. The detective was already at the kerb, giving chase. Tense and disorientated, I broke into a run. As I reached the Hyde Park Hotel, she came racing up behind me. I felt her hand grip onto my arm.

I panicked and resisted, forgetting that I had nothing on me. She must have radioed before she came out after me, because now two other detectives were approaching. She was trying to keep hold while I pulled away, kicking out at her to make her step back.

Then suddenly, I stopped. I'd no more energy to fight. The surge of panic ebbed from my body. I gave up. In a haze I remember the police van pulling up and being taken to Bow Street. I was charged with resisting arrest. The woman only followed me because she knew my face, not because I had committed any crime. Nothing would have happened if I'd managed to stay calm. Where had my judgement gone?

Because I had no history of absconding, I was quickly given bail. Later that night, I got a phone call. Q had been arrested too, at her home. We were both due in court in two days.

On the day of my appearance, I still felt completely overwhelmed. I knew a warrant could be issued if I didn't show up. But I couldn't leave the house. I just wanted to hide. Then my solicitor phoned.

'Janice? Listen, there's been a change of plan. I'm sorry to have to tell you this – Suzi's gone QE on you.'

'What?'

'Yes. I'm afraid she's turned Queen's Evidence. She's giving information about your involvement in the dipping squad in exchange for a lighter sentence.'

I remembered all the evenings Q and I hung out, the laughs we'd had, the times I'd babysat her kids. The crazy day she'd helped me lift the leather pouch in Soho – how I'd legged it like mad with a gang of angry Christmas shoppers in pursuit. How could she turn QE?

'What do I do now?' I asked the solicitor.

'Present yourself to court next Monday morning. We'll try to get probation for you – so you'll need to make sure that you meet your conditions. No excuses at all. If they give you a work order – you'll have to find a way to attend. No childcare problems – nothing. Otherwise – '

'I know,' I said. 'I know. I'll make sure I'm there.'

My solicitor's plan worked. I escaped with probation. But I couldn't feel relief. I had acted like a fool. And in the dock, my former friend blamed everything on me. I would have given my last penny to that girl, yet she had tried to bring me down to save herself.

Pepper's funeral was held on a cold, bright day in Thornton Heath. Scorcher came to the church with a couple of his heavies. There he was – the grieving widower, dressed all in black, in his crocodile skin shoes. I felt sick at the sight of him. He was wearing his screw face – his bad man face, the one he wore when he was trying to look powerful and scary.

Pah – him tink him such a gangster. I felt nothing but contempt. As Pepper's body was lowered into the ground, I was consumed by hate.

After the service, he tried to approach me. I don't know what he wanted to say. I wouldn't look at him. I couldn't speak a word. *If it wasn't for this lying, cheating bastard, my girl would still be here.*

This is all your doing, Scorcher. She died because of you. I will never forgive you. I will never forget what you have done.

8

YOU'RE A DIFFERENT CAT, MAMA J

WHEN I LOOKED AT my work diary for the day, my heart sank. My first client appointment was with John, a young chef. I very much doubted he would make an appearance. He'd missed our previous two meetings, and was very close to breaching the terms of his probation. If he didn't show up today, I would have to take action.

John worked shifts in a west London restaurant – long, tense hours under pressure. That was the reason, he told me, that he started to use cocaine. It was a way to unwind and decompress after his hot, demanding kitchen shifts. But then he did some dealing, and that got him arrested. His community service order was 120 hours.

I asked him to give me his restaurant rota, so that I could structure his hours for the days that he was free. Probation would never disrupt a steady job. It's a service user's best chance of making progress and avoiding offending in the future. But John was evasive and unhelpful.

'My shifts keep changing at short notice! We're busy – I can't keep bothering my boss to let me know about next week!' Weeks went by and still I didn't have the rota.

When I finally managed to set up a schedule for John, he didn't attend the first two sessions. He'd had to do overtime, he said – it was Christmas. He came to the next one and I thought things were improving, but by the start of March, he'd done less than thirty hours' work.

I tried ringing him, but John dodged my calls. When I managed to get through, he brushed me impatiently away: 'Yes, yes, I know, I know, next week, next week.' To him, his probation wasn't a serious matter. And I was clearly not a person whom he needed to take seriously.

He was due for his appointment at 10.00 a.m. By 10.15, I knew I had a problem. I was going to have to breach him.

Regretfully, I filled in the form, detailing everything I'd tried to encourage him to do, the dates and times of our contacts and the endless excuses he had offered. One of his comments – a text he had sent me – summed up our whole relationship. 'Leave me alone,' the text read, 'you miserable old lady.'

Two weeks later, John's case was heard at breach court. We adjourned, waiting for the judge's consideration, and I went to take a seat in the waiting room.

As I stepped outside, I overheard a comment by the clerk. 'They're sending for the jailer,' she said. That was when I knew – although I'd guessed it already – that John was going down.

I felt sick. He wasn't an unlikeable young man – just rather cocky, determined he knew best, but not quite as smart as he imagined. And this was where it started unravelling for him. Up until then, he'd kept his job – a good one with a future that might even be exciting, with his talent for cooking. But his sentence would soon put paid to that. A few weeks from now, he'd be facing unemployment, with a prison record as a blight on his prospects. While he was inside, he wouldn't make his rent. Then he would be homeless. It would bring about the total collapse of the purposeful life that he'd built. All because he wouldn't listen, wouldn't think, wouldn't face up to reality.

I was once like that. I identified with him, in that place of wrongful certainty that comes before a dreadful crash to earth. My job was to use what I knew to persuade him to listen. To cut through all the attitude and stop this situation from spiralling far further – before it was too late. And this time, I had failed.

I wondered what it was I hadn't done – what words I hadn't spoken, what understanding I hadn't managed to show. If I'd reached him, perhaps he could have conformed to the system – for all the flaws I knew that system contained. He might have fixed things before it was too late. There must have been a way. I believe very strongly that there is, in almost every case. But right here, the fact was stark – I hadn't found it.

I didn't want to hear his sentence handed down. I couldn't bear to see the misery and shock dawn on his face. I did something that day that I very rarely do – I slipped away from court. I couldn't sit there and listen as a young life fell apart because I hadn't found a way to prevent it.

My eleven o'clock appointment looked more positive.

Brenda was an unusual client – a middle-class lady not far from the age of retirement who worked in an office in Canary Wharf. She'd been convicted of benefit fraud. Following the death of her husband, she took sick leave from her job and signed on to receive her benefits. But when she went back to work, she forgot, or so she claimed in court, to sign off again.

It was hard to be sure what had happened – and easy to demonstrate that Brenda must have known she was receiving her sickness benefit payment. But grief does awful things to the mind, distorting reality, leaving people struggling and bewildered. Brenda also, perhaps, was not accustomed to tracking her income and bank account in detail. She'd been married a long time and for a woman of her generation, it was common for her husband to take charge of all financial matters. I felt the explanations she gave were quite likely to be true. Her employer thought the same, and happily, Brenda kept her job.

Most of all, I didn't think she would ever have risked

the shame of standing in the dock. She pleaded guilty in a trembling voice that could barely be heard. Her whole body shook. The entire experience was a horror. For her, the fairly small amount of money would never have been worth it. I was very, very sorry for Brenda.

But she did make my life easy. She was the most co-operative probation client you could ever wish to meet. She turned up promptly for our meetings, smiled and chatted about what she'd been up to that week. But I knew she couldn't wait until probation was over. As soon as it was, she would never want to see my face again.

In the end, it didn't take her very long. Brenda booked annual leave and completed her community service – eighty hours – in a month. Afterwards, she even kept on working Sunday shifts at the charity shop where I had placed her. As a widow, she felt lonely and lost every time Sunday came around. Working at the shop meant someone to talk to and somewhere to go where she felt valued.

For Brenda, one mistake wouldn't ruin her whole life. And that's how it should be. Everyone deserves a second chance. When people see the best in you – the fullest potential that you have – it's more likely you'll become that best self. For at least one client this morning, the story would end happily, with hope for a better day tomorrow.

Then there was my twelve o'clock, Christina.

As I waited for her to arrive in the waiting room

downstairs, I leafed through her file, reading back my notes and trying – again – to work out the best way to help her deal with her problems. I hadn't found anything that worked yet, and I knew that time was running out.

She came from a well-to-do family. She owned a large house in Wimbledon Village where she lived a very comfortable lifestyle without the need for work. She was privileged in background and education too – it showed in her clothes and voice and manner. With all those advantages behind her, I'd wondered at first what on earth she was doing on probation.

But she had eighty hours of community service to complete, following a conviction for drunk and disorderly behaviour. When I asked her about it, she said she'd been having a bad time when she'd committed the offence. She wouldn't tell me anything more. I noticed her attention span was very short indeed – within seconds of being asked a question, she was chattering away about some completely different matter. She talked at length about caring for Pepe, who I thought at first must be her son. His multiple food allergies and health problems seemed to dominate her life. But looking after Pepe also gave her days some structure – a positive sign. I expected a good outcome to her probation, and arranged for her to work in a shop run by the charity Oxfam.

But she didn't turn up. It happened three times. I tried to talk to her about it, but heard endless excuses – Pepe's health again – that never identified the reason.

I sent a formal letter, explaining that if this went on, she'd have to be breached and sent back before the court. In response, I got a long and frantic text. Pepe was seriously ill. She couldn't leave him for a moment. She attached a photo. Pepe was a Yorkshire terrier – and one that looked quite healthy and well.

Christina was in trouble, I realised. She just couldn't find a way to tell me. I decided not to breach her – not yet. I wondered if the long working day at the Oxfam shop might be her problem. After all, it was a struggle for her to concentrate on anything for more than five minutes. The shop agreed to split her weekly hours into several shorter sessions. Surely now she would find the work more manageable. I also noticed that she talked to me more easily by phone. Face-to-face contact overwhelmed her. So I started ringing regularly, just to check in. I asked her what was happening, and listened to the details of her day.

That was how I learned about her problems. Christina believed that she had friends, but in reality, these friends were abusing and exploiting her. They treated her lovely house in Wimbledon Village as a place to hang out, but gave her nothing in return. To them, she was just a source of free booze. They held parties in her living room. The atmosphere she lived in was highly alcoholic, with lots of people drinking day and night. They stole her money. Her possessions kept on disappearing. Caught up in all of this, Christina's problems with addiction were growing worse and worse. But it was difficult to get her to see that there was anything wrong with these 'friends', or that their behaviour wasn't really very friendly.

'Does anyone bring anything for you?' I'd ask her gently. 'When they come round to see you? Perhaps some food to share? Or maybe some flowers, to say thank you for all your hospitality?'

Christina sounded puzzled. She was needy and confused, terrified of being left alone. She also seemed depressed, in need of treatment and support. She couldn't fulfil her community service order, I realised – the whole thing was unworkable.

So I'd applied to the court to revoke the order. I completed a form that stated why I believed it was impossible for her to do it. But sometimes applications were pushed back and the reasons we gave were not accepted – a terribly frustrating situation. Unless I was certain that my client was in crisis, I wouldn't have applied for revocation in the first place.

In Christina's case, I'd been met with a 'no' from the court. I felt strongly that this ruling wasn't right. But still, at this meeting, I was going to have to tell her that she must complete her order as directed. I knew how she'd respond – puzzlement at first, and then distraction. But if she failed to complete, she would be breached and sent to prison. And if she ended up there, I didn't think she'd cope at all.

And – as if all this was not enough – an even bigger shadow hung over our meeting. Change was coming to the way probation worked. It wasn't change that I welcomed. As our working practices were altered, I would soon be moving away from day-to-day involvement with my clients. In future, I'd be speaking to more people, but less often to each one. What that would mean in practice was an end to the very careful listening which identified a problem like Christina's in the first place. It took up too much time.

She needed positive engagement. Someone to go round to her house, take an interest in what she was eating and drinking and doing and the lifestyle she was living. It helped her feel supported, and also said to anyone who might be hanging round her that somebody responsible was watching. If the so-called friends could see this, they might leave her alone.

Christina did manage to stay out of prison. But just as I'd feared, I lost touch with her. When Christmas came around, a card arrived for me, signed from her and Pepe. His picture was stuck onto the front. He looked bright-eyed and healthy as ever. The two of them were out there, still surviving. I only hope they go on doing so, until maybe one day, the real help they need can be provided.

SEPTEMBER 1985

10 September 1985, Knightsbridge Crown Court.
Shoplifting charges. Resisting arrest. Failing to attend probation appointments.

*

This court appearance was different. I'd been breached. I knew that I was facing time.

The night before the sentencing, I had a talk with Nadia, trying to explain what would happen tomorrow in a way she could understand.

'You're going to a school for naughty girls, Mummy?'

'Yes, baby. It's because I was naughty at work.'

'Were you a lot naughty?'

'Yes,' I told her. 'I was very, very naughty.'

She was nearly six by now, and logical.

'But Mummy – if you knew you would be sent there, then *why* were you naughty?'

I tried to keep on chatting, struggling to make this seem okay. But it wasn't okay. When I thought of tomorrow, dread rolled over me. When Sabrina phoned me to offer words of comfort – 'Babe, if they do send you down, it won't be long. We'll all look after Nadia, don't worry.' – I choked as I tried to speak to her.

Now I blessed Emmanuel for taking me to see my mother in Leicester. Thanks to him, we'd partly mended our relationship. Mummy had agreed that she would live in my flat and care for Nadia during my sentence. But when she arrived, though she hugged and kissed her granddaughter as always, she barely spoke to me. She was bitterly angry.

Next day, I got nine months.

From court, I was driven to Holloway in a prison van – the squeeze box. Night had fallen, and secret tears streamed down my face in the darkness. Through the blur I saw the two stern stone griffins on the gateway as it opened with a harsh metallic scrape. I missed Nadia so much. A great jolt of loneliness took my breath away. Waves of nausea and fear spread through my body. I was all alone, and near to panic.

I clenched my fists. *No room for crying now. Mi need to lock down tight. Always remember: if you control your mind, then your mind controls your face.*

I told myself that I would get through this. It was time to close down my weakness and my fear, to find a will of iron, to survive.

During that first sentence, I met Zeta.

I'd hadn't been inside for a day when I heard whispers about her. She was mafia, serving eighteen years. Her husband was involved in the same crimes, doing his time in Wandsworth. The two of them were heavy – met with fear and respect from everyone around them.

Eighteen years inside. It was hard to get my head around that amount of time. But when I saw her, she amazed me. She was graceful and stylish, absolutely calm, dressing each morning and emerging from her cell as though she was heading for a smart city office. Nothing seemed to bother or upset her. She had total self-command. This woman was a boss. The sight of her inspired me. If she could be this way, I saw that maybe I could be a boss too.

Shoplifting? Dipping? What kind of pettiness was that? I was ashamed of the smallness of my crimes. I'd certainly learned from my mistakes, but what I'd learned was that I wanted to go harder – much harder. I made a big decision: as soon as I had done my time inside, I was stepping it right up. I was ready to rise to the next level.

And di way forward is wit' the big man – Scully. I was certain of it. I grew more and more impatient to meet him again.

The two of us had done some deals already. It was just small business at first – after I had accepted that one ounce of white in exchange for my watch, I'd wrapped it out in grams for sale. My customers seemed happy – *'Jan – this work's propa,'* they told me. Scully only sold the best. I went back to him and bought a second ounce, and then a third. He never put pressure on me to take more than I could manage. He let me take my time.

Days after my release from prison, I knocked on his door. The Stockwell yard was quiet. As usual he sat behind his desk in his office. His piles of business paperwork covered its whole surface – bills, receipts, booking forms for jobs. His calm brown eyes were watching me steadily.

'Time for reload?' he asked me.

'Yes. But I've been thinking. This time I'll take more. I'd like four ounces. It's selling well.'

Scully smiled.

He opened a drawer and took out six plastic packets.

'Uh – I only said four ounces. I can't pay you for six.'

'Take them. You can owe me. I know you'll make good.'

147

I looked at the packets. Could I do it?

'Okay,' I said. 'Okay – yes, I can.'

'I thought you'd say that,' said Scully with a smile. 'Word on the street is that you're tough.'

'Word on the street?'

'I been listenin'. What I hear is you're doing your thing. People understand you take your freedom seriously. If they're not on spot when you get there, you're gone.'

'That's right, yes. That's how I've been doing it. I'm not playing around out there.'

'I like that,' he told me.

'Well, thank you. Here's money for the four ounces, and I'll bring the payment for – '

'I thought about offering you more,' said Scully, interrupting me. 'But then I thought – Janice is a woman.'

His words sent anger speeding through my body, but I wouldn't let him see it.

'That's right – I always have been!' I answered with a grin.

He grinned back, but then he looked thoughtful.

'A woman in this business would be vulnerable,' he said.

'A woman's vulnerable if she makes herself vulnerable.'

'Is that so?'

'Yes,' I said. 'That's so. Don't put me in a glass house. I can look after myself. If you're putting a proposition to me – let's hear it.'

'You want to be out on the road selling work all hours of night? This is bigger stakes, now, Janice. Are you sure?'

'Yes,' I said. 'I am.'

'Then you're a different cat, Mama J.'

'I guess I must be.'

Scully sat back in his chair. He placed the tips of his fingers together.

'Well then. That should mean you'll have no trouble selling your six ounces. Let's see how you get on.'

Scully was right. I had no trouble selling those six ounces. I made enough profit to buy an extra ounce. Next time, it was going to be seven.

'Seven ounces?' he said thoughtfully. 'Well now, that's a shame. I was thinking of starting you with one.'

'One?' I questioned, keeping my voice even.

'Yes. One ki.'

'And how much will I owe you for that?'

'Thirty grand.'

What the fuck? yelled a voice in my head. *Thirty grand! Selling wraps to my contacts and friends won't move all this! I can't sell a kilo in one go!*

'Er . . . how would I sell it?'

'Don't worry 'bout that.'

'But – um – I'm going to have a kilo of cocaine in my house. My customers buy small. It's going to take me ages.'

'You'll need new customers, babe. And don't keep

it in your house. Never in your house. Always go home clean.'

This was the moment of decision. If I wanted to rise to the next level – he was offering me my chance.

'Okay,' I said. 'I'll do it.'

'Right, Mama J. You need to buy a new phone. When you've got one, you come back and collect.'

My Motorola brick cost eleven hundred pounds. With that phone, I felt like a boss.

Three days later, Scully placed another package on his desk. This time it was the size of a paperback book: a block of tightly pressed powder wrapped in plastic. Then he showed me how to divide up my first ki into packages of twenty-eight, fourteen and seven grams.

He told me he'd direct people to me. But this time, they wouldn't be customers who wanted to party. I was working on a different level now. These would be dealers, buying wholesale.

'I'll phone you later,' he said when our business was done. Always the gentleman, he rose to show me out of his office. Suddenly I saw – in a vivid mental flash – just how enormous and how dangerous this game was becoming. I stopped dead still. I could feel my heart drumming. This was the place where the roads divided. Whichever way I went, there would be no turning back.

'Scully?'

'Yes?'

'Thirty thousand? I can't believe I owe you that much money.'

He gave me his warm, wide smile.

'Yeah, babe. But I trust you. You have a pleasant evening now.'

Two minutes later, I was standing alone on a quiet suburban street. I had thirty thousand pounds' worth of class A drugs in my handbag.

How the fuck am I going to sell all this?

I sat in my living room. I was excited. I was also very nervous. Then my new Motorola started ringing.

'Hello?'

'Hello. Scully gave me this number.'

It was a voice I didn't know.

'What d'you want?'

'Scully told me I can get something from you.'

'Okay, you can.'

'Where are you?'

'Near Brixton.'

'Meet me in Somerleyton Road. I want twenty-eight – an ounce.'

I drove down there. My new customer was standing by the bus stop. My only problem was his payment – the bundle of cash he handed over was too large for me to count.

'Is your money right?' I asked him.

'Yeah, man.'

I took his word – there didn't seem much else that I could do. I shoved the cash quickly into my bag and drove off. When I got home, I counted. To the very last penny, it was right.

I'd just sold my first ounce.

I sat on the sofa feeling breathless but elated – and stunned at how easily it all happened. The Motorola rang again. A different voice was speaking.

'Hello? Scully gave me your number.'

Very late that night, the phone rang one last time.

'How was your evening?' said Scully in my ear.

'Oh – it went well.'

'Any issues?'

'I don't believe so.'

'Well, that's good news. We should celebrate.'

'How should we do that?'

'Well, Mama J, I was thinking I would take you out to dinner.'

'Oh wow – I love your car!' said Sabrina.

'Thanks, babe.'

She climbed into the passenger seat of my new Vitara jeep, looking admiringly at its white leather seats with their smart black piping. I'd customised the car, and now the words 'Nasty Girl' were written in red and silver across the door on my side.

'Jan – this is so cool.'

'Yeah, it's alright.'

I loved Nasty Girl. She drew envious stares from the street. She was larger than life. That was how I wanted to be.

'Lucky you,' said Sabrina. 'Mine's in the garage – again.'

'Still making that noise?'

'Of course it is. Blasted old banger. I really need a new one.'

'I just got this,' I told her, patting the steering wheel. 'But if you can wait a couple of months, I can get you something nicer. And definitely more reliable.'

'Jan, I didn't mean – it's just – you know – the kids always need things, it's difficu–'

'Honey. It's okay. I'd be happy to.'

Sabrina gave me a quick little smile.

'If you're sure you don't mind . . . '

'Of course not.'

She'd been there for me in my darkest moments: when I lost Pepper, when I went inside. Of course I was happy to get her a car. She was my same-birthday-sister.

'Are you okay now, JanJan?' she asked me. 'After – you know. Nadia alright? You both back on your feet?'

'Yeah, honey. We're good. And getting you the car won't be a problem.'

It wasn't a problem at all. In my new partnership with Scully, I was making serious money.

The Motorola never stopped ringing. A few months later, I bought another. My two huge money phones went everywhere with me – and the cash was coming in fast. Scully introduced me to his partners, Chubby and Glen. At first they were surprised that he was working with a woman, but Scully was the boss. If he vouched for me, the others would be cool with it. I had a chance to prove my worth.

I still sold the odd gram to friends, but now there was no need to sit around the kitchen table wrapping with Gill. No more visits to the smokers down in Streatham. The game was selling wholesale, working with dealers only.

I did some business with Bagga, for old times' sake – until he suggested that we cut our product with bicarb to raise profits even further. The syndicate's unbreakable rule was that we never cut the product. We sold quality – that way, we didn't get complaints, or have to waste our time with customers who thought they could haggle over price. The cost was what it was – and it was worth it. When I received a rare call from a buyer unhappy with our goods, I'd give a refund straight away – even though I knew that the problem must be further down the line. If someone cut what we'd sold them, that was certainly a nuisance, and I noted for the future not to use that contact again. But what mattered was to keep our reputation for straight-dealing.

We ran things tight, reducing the danger as far as we could. But still we faced the constant risk of being monitored by the police. Nobody ever phoned a land-line. We were careful on our mobiles and used coded language, aware that the connection might not be secure. *'I was looking for a half pint of milk.' 'Got any sugar?'*

But Scully still transported his work around in carrier

bags. He'd stroll along with his shopping, but alongside the carrots and tins in his bag was a kilo of white. Other times, he used pretty gift bags with ribbon handles from WHSmith's. *Birthday boy!* the bag would read, or *21 today!* I saw that this amused him.

'You carried that here in that bag?' I said to him one day in amazement.

He gave me his most mischievous smile.

'Do you think the police got X-ray eyes? You think they can see through the bag? Just play it cool.'

The big man had the confidence to hide in plain sight. He dressed in balding old fleeces and polo shirts carrying his company logo. His work boots were battered and flecked with paint.

'If I start dressing up,' he said to me, 'people gonna say that I have money.'

'But they already know you have money!' I told him.

'Ahh, Janice – not everybody knows.'

What everyone knew was that Scully always had quality work. He had contacts everywhere, and all of them respected the way he did his business. I was playing a very big game – and now it was going to get bigger.

'Mama J? It's Andrew. I've got good news – the prince is in town!'

Andrew was another one of Scully's connections. He was a concierge at a luxury hotel in Knightsbridge, SW1 – and whenever the prince came to town, Andrew would pick up the phone. The prince got through an ounce of white a night.

My selling price to Andrew was £1,400 an ounce. When he sold to the hotel's guests for £1,800, he was nicely in profit. I drove over to see him in my new BMW 328i. That way, I wouldn't stand out among the Porsches and Lamborghinis. I'd drive into the courtyard and Andrew would come outside. We'd air-kiss – *'Hello darling!'* – and I'd hand the gift bag over. On other days, I'd nip inside and linger for a while with a glass of champagne.

The prince was always grateful and his payment was prompt. He liked to show his gratitude with a Christmas bonus too – a case of Dom Perignon.

There were still some things I couldn't quite resist. Although my shopping trips up West got me in trouble, that buzz of danger had always excited me. So many beautiful things all around – they pulled me back again and again. Court appearances and sentences were tiresome, but I could work around them. Every job has a part that you don't like.

30 January 1987, Southwark Crown Court.
Theft. Shoplifting. Imprisonment – 6 months.

18 February 1987, Southwark Crown Court.
Attempted theft from person. Imprisonment – 6
months concurrent.

18 February 1988, Southwark Crown Court.
Shoplifting. Imprisonment – 6 months.

Out on the road, I learned from Scully's watchfulness. A second eye became a part of me. When I entered a building for a meeting – who else is waiting inside? Where are the doors? How could I leave quickly if I needed to? I turned up early and checked the place out, just so I knew my information about who I was meeting was good. I trusted my instincts, just like going out dipping. If I wasn't comfortable in any location, I'd leave, or immediately take the discussion outside.

I loved handling the money. It felt natural to me. Scully observed me doing business for a while, then made me his banker. Once our cash was counted, we bound it in wraps of a thousand, packed them ten at a time in handbags, and passed them to a safe house – a low profile address owned by someone we knew we could rely on. We paid our safe-house keepers well.

Of course I still trusted Ida, and kept some of my money and my valuables with her. But the amounts had grown so large, I knew I needed to spread the risk around.

The syndicate kept most of its profits offshore. When I was ready to go banking, I flew out to Antigua. There I was regarded as a wealthy ex-pat come home on business. There weren't a lot of checks and I could bank some cash myself, then pass the rest to local contacts who would bank it for a cut.

'Blimey, Jan – a BM now! What happened to the jeep?' asked Sabrina.

'Oh – I've still got it. This one's my runaround.'

'Wow.' She glanced in through the BMW's windows, admiring its gleaming interior. Something was wrong – I could tell. She didn't seem herself.

'Are you okay?'

'Yeah, yeah. I'm good.'

'Could you use some extra cash, Sab?'

She didn't answer for a moment. Being short of money wasn't something that she'd like to admit.

At last she said, 'I'd like to earn some.'

'Okay.' I'd had an idea for quite a while. 'I need a safe house. How about how I use your place?'

I'd set up two safe houses already, but I wanted another. If Sabrina needed money, this could work for both of us.

'You mean – somewhere to leave your stash?' she asked.

'Usually just money. Sometimes work. I need a place to put it where there'll be no attention. You've got no criminal record. You're off radar.'

'And I want to stay that way, Jan.'

'Don't worry, babe. You'll be safe.'

I'd chosen my first two safe houses carefully – people I could trust who weren't known to police, with little risk of attracting attention. They also didn't know about each other, so if anything went wrong, they couldn't give the police information. Like them, I wanted Sabrina to believe that she was working on her own.

'How much would I get for doing this?' she asked.

'A hundred pounds a week. Plus your shopping.'

'My shopping?'

'Yeah. I'll do a shop for you. You meet me at Sainsbury's and collect it.'

'You being serious?'

'Of course, Sabrina. You're my sister. I'll get you something nice at Christmas as well. Toys for the kids. I'm making money. Family comes first.'

Sabrina shook her head.

'Janice – you are really something else.'

I gave her a smile. But she was still looking worried.

'What exactly do I do for this money?'

'I'll give you a lock box. Keep the box safe, some-where the kids won't see it. Whatever I give you, put it straight in the box. When I want it back, I'll tell you where to bring it.'

'How often would I have to do that?'

'Couple of times a week. I won't ever come to your house unless I have to. I'll hold a house key for emer-gencies, but apart from that, I'll stay away. The police might be watching.'

Those words scared her. 'Um,' she said, 'um, look – I'm not sure.'

'Sab, I'm always careful – really careful. I'm working with experienced guys now.'

'Who are they?'

'The top boss in London. He's got contacts all over.'

'My God, Jan. Are you sure you know what you're doing?'

'Babe, it's okay. The people at the top of the game – they're always in control. No taking chances. No using the product. No getting all mashed up and losing judgement. We manage risk very carefully.'

'Risk?'

'Yes, some. But it's on me. I won't let it fall on you.'

She was still frowning.

'But these are people I don't even know,' she said worriedly.

'No one else knows who you are. Information like that is controlled. It's my safe house. You'll just be working with me.'

This seemed to reassure her.

'Okay, JanJan. Okay. And the money would be nice.'

'So let's do this.' I smiled at her to break the serious mood. Then I noticed a graze on her cheek.

'Did you walk into a tree, Sab?'

'What?'

'You've scratched your cheek. It looks sore.'

'Oh.' She raised her fingers to the mark on the side of her face. 'Yeah – actually, I did. It was ridiculous.'

'You got some antiseptic?'

'Yeah, I'll use it. It's fine, Jan. It's nothing.'

To Sabrina, all this had been just words, and I knew it. She didn't truly understand how far down this road I'd gone. That was fine – she didn't have to understand. Although I trusted her, the less she knew the better, for her own peace of mind.

The voice on the phone was hoarse and strained.

'Hey, Mama J. I'm in trouble. Can you help me out?'

'Ivan?' I said. 'What's happened?'

'I – I got robbed.'

'You got *what?*' I thought quickly. 'Let's not discuss this on the phone. Why don't we meet?'

I'd got to know Ivan pretty well. He was a runner, helping to make drug deals that reached across the world to Venezuela, Guyana, Africa, Brazil. Scully always gave me a heads-up when an international customer was bringing in their work. Agents in London took delivery – guys known as contacts. A good contact was the key to keeping the business running smoothly. Once the work had landed safely, the phone would ring and the sale would be arranged.

I checked the quality myself before I bought. The men I dealt with were amazed that I could be the chemist, taking my sample from the middle of the parcel of white, then heating it to see how well the stone would form. If it was peng – the kind of quality I wanted – I'd pay the agreed price right away. If it wasn't, I would walk away. There had never been a problem with Ivan. Up to now, I'd had him down as a pretty chill guy. It was hard to imagine how he'd made such a serious mistake.

We met at the Hot Pot in Landor Road, Brixton. He was sweating. He told me he'd been played – swindled into handing over two ki with payment for just one. Then he never saw the guy again. He was angry with the dealer who had tricked him, and angry with himself – but mostly he was frightened.

Now he was down a ki – and that could mean big trouble. The missing merchandise belonged to a major player called the Captain, based in Guyana, South America. When the Captain found out that he was thirty grand short, he was going to be very unhappy. The problem would be proving that the robbery had taken place at all. How did the Captain know that Ivan hadn't sold the missing ki and pocketed the proceeds? He would have to explain it – and he wasn't sure how. No wonder he was sweating.

I saw a way to help him. It meant taking a risk – but to my mind, a good runner was worth keeping.

'Here's what we do,' I told Ivan. 'I'll buy another ki from you and smash it out for sale. If we sell in smaller amounts, we make more on it. That way, the Captain gets some money back at least.'

'Yeah,' he said thoughtfully. 'Yeah – that might help. And at least he'll know I tried.'

'Exactly. If you'd been trying to cheat him, you wouldn't bother trying to make up for it.'

'But – '

'But what?'

'Janice – this is serious shit. What if he doesn't believe me?'

'It's the truth,' I said. 'If the Captain's got good judgement, he'll know it when he hears it.'

'Can I tell him about you?' asked Ivan nervously.

'Yeah,' I said. 'For sure.' He looked relieved.

The deal went smoothly. Ivan got his money. A day or so later, he rang me again. He sounded much happier.

'Janice,' he said, 'you did good for me, you know. The boss says he'd like to meet you.'

BREAKING OUT

The Captain was the top of the tree – a big international operator. I knew he must be ruthless. There was no way to run a set-up like his without taking some very tough decisions. And he wanted to meet me and talk business. This was serious now. I was up there at last, with the real players. Just where I'd wanted to be.

I flew out to Guyana and booked into a hotel in Georgetown. Next morning, a chauffeur-driven car arrived to take me to the Captain's villa. It was a beautiful journey, close to the banks of the deep brown Demerara River. We passed the old towns of Diamond and Grove, winding our way through open fields where sugar cane was growing. As we crossed the pontoon bridge, the road gently rose and fell beneath the car. The wealthier suburbs were approaching. I saw pavements lining the road in the place of muddy tracks.

The car slowed. I felt a prickling of nerves as the moment approached. Electric gates swung open and we climbed a gently winding slope, surrounded by trees. We came out into a wide, sweeping driveway in front of a colonnaded house. Three expensive-looking cars were parked, one of them an old Morris Oxford. As I glanced through white arches to the side of the building, I caught the bright sparkle of a pool. There was no one to be seen – but everywhere around me I could feel the Captain's enormous wealth and power.

Two men led me through the cool of the house then out at the rear of the building. There was the swimming pool with plush-cushioned loungers and a bar. A dark-haired man in shorts and a vest was sitting at a table underneath an umbrella, smoking a hand-rolled cigarette. The Captain rose to his feet as I approached.

He held out his hand in welcome. I had resolved not to give this man the slightest sign that I was intimidated. *Control your mind*, I remembered, *and your mind controls your face.*

As I greeted him, I heard screeches. Behind the pool was an enormous aviary. Inside I saw flashes of colour – the brilliant wings of half a dozen parrots.

'Mama J!' the Captain said. 'What a pleasure to meet you.'

He spoke with an American accent.

He took my hand in his, and looked into my eyes.

'Take a seat, please,' he said. 'Can I offer you a drink?'

'Thanks – that would be great.' I was glad to be under the shade of the umbrella, shielded from the strong morning sun.

He raised his hand – hardly more than a movement of his fingers, but a young man in a smart white shirt immediately came hurrying out from the house.

'Bring some rum for my visitor!' the Captain instructed. The young man turned at once and went to fetch it. As he disappeared into the shadows of the colonnade, I noticed that the two men who had welcomed me were still standing there, half-visible, watching.

'Ivan has told me about you,' the Captain went on. 'And about your work in London. You know Scully?'

'Yes, I know him very well.'

'I respect him,' the Captain told me.

'So do I,' I replied.

'But,' he went on, 'I have a question for you. The business you are in – why would a woman do this?'

'Strong women know how to work with men. We can do business.'

He sat back in his chair and watched as his young attendant returned with a tray, two glasses with ice and a bottle of High Wine rum. When the drinks were poured, he raised his glass and I raised mine. The ice cubes clinked.

'Cheers!' the Captain said.

'Cheers.'

'So – you helped Ivan when he made his unfortunate mistake.'

'I did.'

'Because you were sorry for him. Tell me – would a man have done that?'

'Maybe not,' I answered. 'I don't think a man would have such good judgement.'

'It was good judgement?'

'Ivan is a man I know and trust. When he had a problem, I decided I should help him. Now, if I ever have a problem, Ivan will do the same for me. That makes it good business.'

There was a silence. I sipped my rum. Then the Captain smiled.

'Mama J, they call you. People like you are very rare. I have a proposition for you.'

'A proposition?'

'You are good at what you do. If I could get merchandise to you – would you be able to dispense it?'

'What kind of merchandise?'

'Come and see,' the Captain said.

He rose and walked indoors. He led me down a short flight of steps at the side of the house. There was a door, fitted with three heavy locks. One of his men had followed close behind, and stepped forward with the keys. Unfastening the door took several minutes. To step inside, I had to slightly bow my head because the archway was so low.

The Captain's strongroom was lined with shelves. Tightly wrapped packages were stacked on every shelf. There must have been a hundred ki right there. The Captain pointed to each shelf in turn.

'Peruvian,' he said. 'And here, Bolivian Flake. This one – Pink Champagne. The very finest quality.'

'You can send this product to me in London?' I asked.

'Most certainly.'

'How much? And how often?'

'To begin with, five ki a time. Let's say – a shipment arriving every twelve weeks.'

'Every twelve weeks? That's very precise. How can you bring it in so regularly?' I questioned.

'We have a reliable green channel, from Georgetown to Dover. A route where our shipment will not be examined. We have our own people in place.'

'I see. Well then – yes, I guess we can handle that.'

'Good. Now – would you like to see the rest of the property?'

We strolled in the sunlight. The young man who waited on the Captain came too, in case there was anything his boss might require. His bodyguards watched us from the edge of the trees. Behind the manicured grounds of his home, the Captain had a farm. He showed me round it enthusiastically, talking at length about his animals. He was just as proud of them as he was of his opulent poolside luxuries.

'Mama J,' he said suddenly, as we leaned on the low wall alongside the enclosure where his goats were grazing. 'There's something I would like to know. How did you come into this game?'

I looked at him. I thought for a moment.

'I could tell you,' I said, 'but then I'd have to kill you.'

There was a breath-holding silence. Then the Captain roared with laughter. As soon as he laughed, his attendants all laughed too.

When I checked out of my hotel in Georgetown two days later, I found that my bill had already been paid – by the Captain. A few days after that, my mobile rang in London.

'Mama J?'

'Who is this?'

'I'm calling from the farm. Boss says I have to send something for you. Just making sure that you have room for it when it arrives?'

*

Ivan had been robbed because he was impatient. He didn't check out who he was dealing with. I thought hard about that.

My contacts were always in a hurry. It goes with the job. Holding on to merchandise is dangerous. When a mule comes into London with product, he passes it on to the contact as quickly as he can. The contact also wants the shipment gone – and fast. And I could use this haste to my advantage. This was the moment to have the notes ready – and negotiate for discount.

'I can't pay thirty grand a ki,' I would tell them, 'but I'll take five ki off your hands right now for a hundred grand.'

They'd always go for it. Then I'd get in touch with my buyers. I didn't want to sit on product either. Holding on to work was the biggest risk anyone could run.

Go home clean. That's what Scully taught me – every time, no exceptions. Get rid of product as quickly as you can. Above all, don't ever, ever store it where you live.

9

MONEY TALK, BULLSHIT WALK

GODFREY HAD BEEN AGITATED when he arrived at the probation office. Now he was becoming even more so. A heavily built young black guy, he marched up and down the waiting room, breathing hard. He looked distressed and disorganised. His clothes were dirty. Every minute or so, he kept raising his arms to his head and frantically mussing up his hair.

'I'm not leaving!' he cried. 'I'm not leaving!'

I was watching through the window from the safety of the office. I could see that he had a white mark on the side of his mouth – like a skin tag, as though his lips were chapped. I'd noticed this before. People on anti-depressants quite often have this symptom. He must have a prescription to help him with his changes of mood. But judging by the look of him, whatever medicine he needed, he hadn't been taking it.

'He was like this when he came in last week, Janice,'

the receptionist told me. 'And he said he was going to kill Emma. Are you okay to see him?'

Probation work sometimes required us to put ourselves at risk. That was a fact. But still, there was a difference between talking to a vulnerable, agitated boy and facing someone violent and dangerous. How could we judge that risk? None of us were doctors. All we had to rely on was experience and instinct to try to make the call.

Godfrey's threat to harm Emma had been recorded. Any threat should be taken very seriously – but this didn't always happen. There was pressure on all of us to carry on working, marking matters up as having been attended to. That was what the system required us to do. See the client. Tick the box. Submit the form. Next case. And do all this whether or not the situation had actually been resolved. But not everyone we saw could be dealt with in a standard way, within a tightly set amount of time.

Under that kind of pressure, a conscientious officer might feel that she had to put herself in danger, just to meet her target. Or a fatal misjudgement might be made. I thought carefully before I replied.

'Yes,' I decided. 'I don't think Godfrey is a dangerous person. I think he's making threats because he's feeling upset. He's not been taking his medicine.'

'I'm not leaving!' Godfrey yelled from the waiting room.

'He's feeling vulnerable here. He's more worked up than when he arrived. I'd like to talk to him outside.'

I opened the waiting room door, moving slowly, not wanting to startle the nervous man inside.

'Godfrey?' I said. 'Hi there. I'm Janice. I'm an engagement worker here.'

He stopped his pacing for a moment.

'I don't think we should stay indoors,' I went on. 'It's too stuffy. Would you like to get some fresh air?'

It was the middle of the morning. The sun was shining. The air was warm. As we walked side by side, his agitation lessened.

'So, Godfrey,' I said, 'there's something that's upsetting you. Can we try to find out what that is?'

'It's – it's – ' He raised both hands to his head, just as he had inside.

'Take your time,' I said. I didn't want him to feel rushed. Important things get missed when everyone is always short of time.

'It's – oh, I don't know, miss. I – I – '

I touched his arm to calm him. 'Godfrey. It's okay.'

'Miss!' he burst out suddenly. His voice was filled with total desperation. 'Miss, I'm homeless. I'm sick. I don't get no attention. Bet if I got a gun and shot you, I'd get the attention then!'

I knew I had to take what Godfrey had just said very seriously. But I didn't want to frighten him, or harm his trust in me.

'Godfrey,' I said, keeping my voice light. 'What did you really just say there?'

He didn't reply.

'Because I don't think you really want to shoot anybody. Do you?'

'It's the only way it seems like you get help,' he muttered. 'Do something bad to one of you lot.'

'I don't think there's any need for that. I'd like to help you anyway.'

'But miss – you don't understand!' He lifted his arms in distress.

'What don't I understand?'

'Someone's fucking with my head!'

'Who's doing that?'

'People!'

'Which people?'

'They've called the police! They're going to take me!' Suddenly, Godfrey started to cry.

'Please listen. I think the problem here is your prescription. You've not been taking it. That's why you're so upset and angry. If we can see a doctor and get that sorted out, things won't seem so hard.'

I thought he'd had enough for today. The probation office waiting room upset him, so taking him back there now wasn't going to do much good.

'Why don't I book you a doctor's appointment?' I said. 'I'll phone you tomorrow and tell you when it is.'

He seemed to agree, and drifted away up the street. I didn't have much time to put a rescue plan in place. The moment I got back to my desk, I hit the phones. I had to make him a doctor's appointment. But I quickly discovered that he wasn't just excluded from the hostel. His surgery had banned him as well, for abusive and threatening behaviour.

The more I learned, the more desperate his situation seemed. Godfrey had been released from prison with nowhere to go. For seven days he'd stayed at the local homeless hub – but that was the longest that anyone could stay. There was heavy pressure on the service. He was sent to a hostel. But by himself in a room, and off his medication, his mood crashed. He became so disruptive that the hostel had no option but to ask him to leave. Now he was sleeping on the street. Meetings at probation were the only anchor he had left.

From the surgery's point of view, of course I understood the ban. They had the other patients to think of. But he urgently needed to find another doctor. Everywhere I tried, the list was full. After several fruitless phone calls, I felt as though I was going round in circles.

I also had a difficult decision to make.

I bet if I got a gun and shot you . . . Those were the words that Godfrey used. This was a threat. I must inform the manager and record this event on the system. If another, future officer were to be exposed to danger from this client and I had not done so, it would bring my job into question. My instincts said that Godfrey had spoken from illness and desperation, not because he really presented any risk. But the process was vital for everyone's safety.

Godfrey needed someone to guide him as he peeled back all the layers of problems that were causing him to behave in the way he did. But how could he get it? His circumstances were a hopeless tangle. The system wasn't responding to his needs.

I talked to a senior manager about Godfrey's threat. She called the police. The incident was formally recorded to alert other members of the team who might deal with him in future. The matter went no further. For action to be taken, things needed to get worse. That's quite often the case. Nothing happens until there's a crisis. With limited resources, there isn't the capacity to see trouble coming, or help a person who is struggling before they just can't cope any more. If there was, so much misery and suffering could be prevented – and so much money could be saved.

If Godfrey ever does hurt anyone, further down the line, when his situation has deteriorated – there had been a warning. I heard it clearly on that warm sunny day on the pavement in Stockwell. Then I made sure that others heard it too. The problem was that no one was listening. Or even if they were, they were unable to respond.

MAY 1988

I decided to grow the syndicate's UK network. That meant getting out of London. It was safer to deal volume away from the city.

I based the new operation up country, in Northampton, Birmingham and Leicester. I worked with Diego, a contact who'd proved to be reliable. To get him sweet, I sold him two ounces of the Captain's finest flake for £900 each. I knew how much profit he would make. He was on the phone again before the end of the day.

'Janice? That stuff's proper. I want anything you've got.'

'I got a ki right now.'

'Okay. How much?'

'Thirty-six. I'll bring it up there.'

The extra six thousand was danger money – covering the chance I would be taking in transporting the goods. Moving merch is the riskiest part of any operation. Every few weeks, I headed up the M1 to meet Diego at Toddington Services. He introduced me to his mate Mank, and I tapped into their network of contacts in the Midlands, West Country and Wales. I travelled down to Bristol to meet up with Mank's bikers in the Black and White cafe. They were surprised to be dealing with a woman. They struggled to accept that I was capable of handling business on this level.

'Hey babe. You look sexy. We could have good times,' they'd always sigh.

'My name's Janice, not sexy. You're here to buy a product. I only want to talk about money and drugs.'

Everyone went quiet.

'Right then. Let's do business. Money talk, bullshit walk.'

'Ah, Mama J, you're the lady,' they'd say.

'I'm not the white lady. I just *got* the white lady.' They'd smile, but by now we'd both know who was in charge.

Long ago in Holloway, I'd found my iron will – the will of a boss. I wanted total control – so everything about me sent that message loud and clear. I showed those men no fear, no hesitation, no self-doubt. *Control your mind, and your mind controls your face.*

I parked outside the house in Northampton at half past nine in the evening. It was the middle of summer and still almost light. I wasn't expected until ten o'clock, but I was early. I needed to know who was going to show up – and I wanted a look at who they might bring with them.

As the sky slowly turned from deep pink to dark blue and car headlights came on, I sat tight and watched the house. At five to ten, I picked up my phone.

'Mank? It's Janice.'

'Hey Janice – where are you?'

'Five minutes away. He there yet?'

'Er, no, actually, he's not. Any minute, though.'

'So – the customer's not arrived?' I said.

'Any second now. He'll be here. Simon is straight with me. He's a good guy.'

Already I had serious doubts about that.

At two minutes to ten, I got out of the Cosworth. I checked myself over, smoothing down my black Apple Bottom top over my tight leggings. When I was ready, I walked up the garden path and rang the doorbell. Mank answered. I noticed he was acting super-friendly, seeming even more delighted than usual to see me.

'Wha' ah gwaan, Jan?'

He was a good guy and I liked him. But I wasn't going to chat patwa right now. In my big blue and white Chanel handbag was a ki, packed inside a sparkly yellow giftbag. £36,000 was the street price, including danger money for the journey.

I followed Mank into the house. In the living room stood Diego. He was peering round the curtain. Both of them were smiling, but I noticed at once that they were tense and on edge.

'Well?' I said. 'Is he here yet?' They exchanged glances.

'Janice – he's coming. He's driving down from Birmingham.'

I looked at my Cartier watch.

'It doesn't matter where he's driving from. I drove here from London,' I replied. 'This guy's late.'

'Yeah. Yeah, sure. Absolutely.' Diego picked up his phone and pressed the buttons. He paced through the house with his finger in his ear, talking softly. I heard him say, 'She said ten o'clock.'

I turned to Mank. I kept my voice level.

'Mank,' I said, 'you think I'm travelling with sweeties? You're taking my freedom for joke. Why ain't he here?'

Diego put down his phone.

'Jan, I'm really sorry. The guy's on the motorway. He's coming, but he's going to be late.'

'Well, I hope he didn't spend too much on petrol.'

Three minutes after ten, I left the house. I got into the Cosworth, flicked on my headlights and drove away.

By 11.30 I was back in the city. My phone had rung

three times on the journey. I didn't pick it up. I drove to Herne Hill in south London, and let myself into a house in a quiet leafy street. My friend Krystal heard me arrive and came downstairs. She looked surprised to see me. Krystal's place was one of my safe houses. I usually stayed away – but in tonight's circumstances, I had to make an exception.

'Hey JanJan – what you doing here? I'm just getting ready for bed.'

'Sorry about the late visit. I got a last-minute problem. I need to leave a present.'

I put the yellow giftbag in her hands.

'Sure.' She took the bag from me. I didn't know where in the house she stored my goods. I didn't need to know. What mattered was that I could go home clean.

Just after midnight, I let myself back into my flat. Nadia was in bed and the place was dark and silent. Ida had been minding her and now they were both sleeping. In the kitchen was a note.

We had fish fingers and chips for dinner. Bed by nine. Love, Nanny.

Frustrated by the evening's wasted journey, I sat down and lit a cigarette. The phone rang again. This time I answered.

'Hey, Janice.'

'Hey, Mank.'

'I'm with the guy now – Simon. We're in his car. We're coming down to London.'

'I see.'

'We'll come round and pick up the work then head straight back.'

'You won't. Not tonight. That parcel's gone.'

'Gone?'

I heard him relaying this information to whoever else was in his car. 'Gone? Already?'

'But Janice – you knew he'd be coming!'

'Mank, let him understand. I drove from London to Northampton. Our agreed time was ten o'clock. Now it's midnight and I'm in my bed. The parcel's gone.'

'But can you fix him up?'

'Not tonight. You lot jam at a hotel.'

'Aw, Jan, c'mon! You can get it. Please! Do this now – I'm begging you.'

'No. We had a deal. I'm not risking my freedom driving all the way up there so you can fuck me about and tell me he's not here yet. That's not my responsibility.'

I pressed the cut-off button.

When I woke next morning, I could hear the cartoons on the telly. Nadia was listening to *Thunder Cats*. I got up and fixed her and Ida their breakfasts. Nadia sat at the bar in the kitchen, eating her cereal and chatting to Nanny. We searched for her school things, which were strewn around as always. This morning, she couldn't find her reading book.

'Nad – look in your bedroom, quick! Auntie Monica's here any second!'

'Can Nanny come with us to school?'

I took a quick glance at Ida. Ida smiled.

'Of course she can. Now find your book!'

Nadia shot into her room. I could hear her searching. By the sound of it, everything she owned would soon be lying on the carpet.

'If you kept your things tidy, Nadia, you wouldn't lose your book!' I called to her.

'Uhhhhh!' she went – the noise she always made when something annoyed her. *It's going to be no time at all,* I thought suddenly, *before I've got a teenager on my hands.*

'Look under your bed!' I told her.

My mobile phone rang.

'Janice?' said Mank's voice. 'I'm in Clapham with Simon. Where d'you want to meet?'

BZZZZZ. The front door intercom sounded.

'Mummy! Auntie Monica's here!'

'Have you found your reading book?' I asked.

'Have I found my what?' said Mank on the phone, sounding surprised.

'Yes, Mummy!'

I gave Mank an address. 'Forty minutes,' I told him. I kissed Nadia and off she went with Ida and Emmanuel's cousin Monica, who regularly walked her to school. I heard the door of our building closed behind them. In the sudden quiet, I picked up the mobile and rang Krystal.

'Bring the gift bag, darling. I'll be at the Monkeys. Twenty minutes okay?'

I got dressed. My shell suit was Gucci – white

trousers that matched my white ballet pumps and a grey, white and plum patterned jacket. I drove to Herne Hill to meet Krystal outside the Three Monkeys restaurant.

'Thanks, babe. Don't forget – Wednesday for your shopping, yeah?'

I headed for the address I'd given Mank – another safe house nearby. This one was run by Scully's partner, Glen. As I parked, I saw Mank and Simon waiting in what must be Simon's car. Mank jumped out as soon as he saw me and started to apologise.

'Janice – look – I – '

'Inside,' I told him briskly. I let myself into the house and both men followed. Simon was tall and dark-haired, in his thirties, dressed in a black leather biking jacket.

In the kitchen, I turned to face them.

'Well?' I demanded.

Mank tried again. 'Janice,' he said, 'look, I'm really – '

Then Simon held out his hand. He was well-spoken and confident.

'Mate – I'm the one who should have an explanation. Except that there isn't one. I really do apologise.'

He sounded like he meant it. I accepted the handshake.

'That's okay, Simon. But when I say ten o'clock, I mean ten and no fuck'ry.'

'Of course.'

'Now – thirty-seven and we're good. I charge for transportation.'

'I got ya.'

With a nod, he took the money out of his knapsack: bundles of fives, tens and twenties, each one totalling a thousand, held together with elastic bands. I quickly scanned the pile to make a practised estimation. All good.

'That's cool,' said Simon. 'And from now on, I'll make sure I'm always on time.'

31 October 1988, Southwark Crown Court.
Theft from person. Shoplifting. Probation order – 2 years.

23 February 1990, Middlesex Guildhall Crown Court.
Attempted theft. Imprisonment – 1 year.
Breach of probation. Imprisonment – 6 months consecutive.

I was driving through the Oval in Nasty Girl. At the junction by St Mark's church, I saw blue lights behind. The police made me pull me over.

'Hello, Janice.'

I was always half-waiting for trouble. I was an ex-con, known to the feds. And I recognised this guy – he caused regular hassle. We called him Steven Seagal.

'Good morning.'

'I see we're in a different car today!' Seagal said.

I answered with a smile and shrug.

'Can you tell me who this car is registered to?'

I was in a sparky mood today. I felt dangerous. Suddenly I decided to give it some swag.

'What's the problem, officer? You want to search my car?'

The instant I said it, my stomach did a cartwheel. *Why did I just say that? Because if Steven Seagal takes me up on my kind invitation, he gonna find the white that I got stashed in the boot.*

He gave me a considering look.

'Just wanting to make sure that everything's in order.'

'Well, thank you very much, and it is.' I leaned my arm casually out of the open window, trying to play it cool.

But if he does this search, my arse is grass.

Steven Seagal walked slowly round the jeep, inspecting it. I could feel the adrenaline surging through my body. Every second, the tension increased. I'd taken this one right to the edge. I kept right on smiling, willing him to get back in his vehicle.

'That's alright for now,' he said to me. 'You enjoy your day.'

'Why thank you – I will!' As I drove away, I burst out laughing at the close shave I'd had. I was up to the sky on danger. When I described the scene to Scully, he laughed too, but then quickly looked serious.

'You did it for the hell of it. You were out of your head, babe. Don't do that again.'

That was the last time I trafficked any drugs in my jeep. Nasty Girl was just too outstanding. She was a risk I couldn't afford to take. Scully drove an ancient scruffy Volvo – and he did it for good reason. Once again I learned from him. I started buying bangers from dealers down in Thornton Heath. They cost a couple of hundred pounds a time. As soon as each banger packed up, I'd buy another. I used them – and only them – to move work, and kept my fun cars for fun.

Scully was my lover, my teacher and my friend. He didn't offer me a safe suburban life. He knew I didn't want it. We didn't do domestic. But what I had with him was solid.

He gave me a Kutchinsky lapis and diamond ring as a gift – the most beautiful thing I've ever seen. I took it to Ida's house and put it away for safekeeping in the Louis Vuitton attaché case that was my last link to Pepper. Whenever I touched its soft leather, I remembered her. The day I stole the case in Crocodile, our laughter in the cab, the astonishment of finding the money in the secret compartment. A friendship like Pepper's is precious and so rare. Now that Vuitton case held both the loves of my life.

But Scully gave me something even more precious than that ring. He gave me trust and respect. He showed me that I was an equal in his world.

With all his years of experience, he never once forced me to do what he wanted. If I disagreed with him, he'd only say: '*I'll let you think on that.*' He'd let me work it out for myself. He gave me his trust without question, to run my business as I thought it should be run.

The first sign of trouble was the robbery.

I'd been at home all day. When I left just after three to pick up Nadia from school, I carefully locked the barred security gate on the outside of my front door. I met her and we strolled happily home together while she told me all about her adventures. Everything seemed normal – the outer gate still locked, the door still tightly closed. Except that now, the door refused to open. For a minute or two, I shook the handle in annoyance. Then I realised it was bolted on the inside.

It felt a little strange to do it, but I thought I should call the police. The London Fire Brigade also arrived, to help break in. What we found was a great jagged hole in my living-room ceiling. Plaster fragments and broken bits of timber were scattered everywhere.

'It was a break-in through the loft. He must have planned to leave by your front door,' said the policeman who attended, 'but apparently your deadlock changed his plans. So he climbed back out the way he came. At least that way he couldn't take much with him.'

My burglar had got access to the loft via the stairwell, then smashed through my ceiling with an axe. As the policeman said, he'd not taken very much – just two watches, a Cartier and an Omega, along with my cheque book and card. But something told me those weren't what he'd come for.

The incident was troubling and strange. I'd been

targeted – my flat was the only one he robbed. My burglar had also been watching me – he struck in the only half hour when I wasn't at home. What was going on?

'Janice,' said Mikey Shoes, 'you're handling big now. There's issues happening. You need to be strapped.'

I knew what he meant. It was time for me to carry.

'You're Scully's right hand,' Shoes continued. 'That means people will test you. Be ready.'

Sharp Man, Leggy and Mikey were some of the first customers Scully had given me. They'd been together from way back in Spanish Town, Jamaica. Sharp Man was a dealer, very well-connected, and Leggy was his muscle for hire. But Mikey was the danger man. And I knew just how dangerous he was.

When I rang him, he'd come straight down to London from up country. We talked. He was a gentle-seeming, tall and gangling black guy in his late twenties – so cute-faced he looked far younger than his age. He towered over me, and got his name because he had enormous feet. But his lop-sided smile and lanky walk were misleading – no one fucked with Mikey Shoes. They didn't dare. They knew he carried a gun.

I didn't need him all the time, I told him. I just wanted to be seen with him now and again. It would send out a message: mess with me, you'll talk to Mikey. Shoes nodded. He was cool.

He brought me my blue steel Beretta Bobcat, a semi-automatic pistol, and taught me how to use it.

Coiled in my hand, small and silent, it gave me a feeling of power like nothing I had ever had before. I gently eased my finger into place on the trigger. Just one tiny movement, and that Bobcat would snarl.

'You're a woman,' said Shoes. 'And a very tough woman – but this game is run by men. Now if anyone wants to try it on you, Mama J – you're prepared.'

The moment I heard Glen's voice on the phone, I knew there was more trouble. It wasn't often that the syndicate's partners rang each other.

'I'm in the gambling house,' he told me, 'and I heard your name mentioned. Word is – someone's planning to rob you.'

The gambling house was in the basement of a shop in Landor Road, Brixton. Men hung out there all hours, listening to music, eating, smoking weed. Poker and dice went on all night, and there was always some excitement – a dangerous stake on the table, a woman come in looking for her man when she's not seen him for three days and there's only one place left that he could be. It was a good place – the best place – for rumours and street news.

'Again?'

'That's the rumour,' Glen answered grimly.

'Who's planning it?'

'The north London boys. I've got no names yet. Janice – where are you?'

It was past ten at night. I was on the South Circular.

'Still on the road. Nearly home.'

'If I were you,' Glen warned me, 'I'd be careful when you get there.'

The streets around my building were in darkness. I drove slowly past the rear. A car with two men in it was parked by the kerb. As I cruised by, one turned his head. So I was under surveillance. Someone was checking the place out.

I went round to the driveway at the front of the flats. The dustbins were kept in a small bricked enclosure near the gate. Now one bin had been moved. It was sitting dead centre in the entry. If I wanted to drive in, I would have to get out of my car and move it. I looked around. A few yards down the road I saw a second parked vehicle. Two dark figures sat there motionless, waiting. Another two-hander. I definitely wasn't getting out of the car – or going home tonight.

I drove to Chelsea and checked into the Harbour hotel. Once I was in my room, I rang Ida, who was babysitting Nadia at home. I didn't want to scare her in the middle of the night, but I told her that I needed to stay out on unexpected business. She agreed to stay till morning.

At 8 a.m., I rang her again, sounding as casual as I could.

'Good morning, Mums. Is everything okay?'

'I think so.'

'Has anybody come to the door?'

'No, Jan. Why – what's wrong?' Unease was creeping into her voice.

'You didn't hear anything last night?'

'Nothing at all. Jan – '

'Look – don't worry,' I said to her, 'but when Nadia gets home from school later, can you pack some clothes for her and both of you come round to Chelsea Harbour? We three need to hole up here for a while.'

Two weeks later, Scully was robbed in the street, outside Peggy's Cafe in Brixton. Some guy grabbed hold of him, pushed him to the ground and took all the money he had on him. I could scarcely believe what had happened. But when I went to see him, I found that he was calm.

'I'm leaving it alone. I won't be taking action,' he told me. He lowered himself gingerly into a kitchen chair, rubbing his back.

I could scarcely keep my anger from bursting out.

'You're mad! You're going to let this go? Do you know the message you'll be sending? And you're hurt!'

Scully gave me a rueful smile.

'I landed heavy. Not as young as I used to be, Janice.'

'I don't understand how you can joke about this!'

'I'm not joking. I'm serious. It's finished. I'm leaving it alone.'

'But if somebody can get away with it, then – '

'He won't get away with it,' said Scully.

'What d'you mean?'

'I know who it was. And I know something else too. *What yuh lose inna de bend, yuh mek it up in de straight.*'

'But who was it?'

'Babe,' said Scully, low and level. If there was any

anger in him, I couldn't see it. 'I know you're upset. But if that's how this man behaves, what will happen in the future? He's robbed his fellows when he should have been honouring his debts. He's disrespected those he ought to treat properly. Who'll be left to do business with him?'

'Yes, but – '

'That's enough. This man is making trouble for himself. So he'll have trouble come to him. He don't need me to arrange his funeral.'

But even if what Scully said was true, I couldn't let the robbery go.

I put my ear to the ground. Pretty quickly, I had a name. A small-time dealer by the name of Winston Grey. Winston was a gambler who'd been spending his time in the basement down in Landor Road. A few weeks back, things had gone badly at the poker table. Plenty of players had been wondering how he'd find the money to pay. But now, all of a sudden, his debts had been cleared.

The gambling house was not a place for women. I knew it. But if I wanted to have a quiet word with any of the mandem, that was where I'd go. The best time was always Thursday night, when a big game was on. Late in the evening, I dressed myself up sexy in a dress with a deep ruffled neckline and strappy red slingbacks. Before I left, I packed a few small essentials in a red leather bag by Yves Saint Laurent. I headed down to Landor Road.

When I arrived, it was already after midnight. The players were taking a break. Everyone looked up when I came in. I gave them a nod, said hello to one or two, then clocked Mr Grey sitting in the corner by himself. I bought myself a cognac, sat down near him, crossed my legs and gave him an eye.

Such a very easy piece of engineering. Over he came.

'Mama J?' said Winston Grey.

'You're right about that.'

'A lady with a big reputation.' He waved his hand towards the poker table. 'But I didn't know that you had an interest here.'

I gave him a long, slow smile and drew my arms together. I saw his eyes dip into the plunging V neck of my dress.

'Well, Winston – there are lots of things round here that I find pretty interesting.'

He smiled back. He thought he'd pulled – so very confident and cool.

'And what might those be, Janice?'

I opened my pack of cigarettes and placed a black Sobranie between my lips. He reached for his lighter and I leaned in very close, holding his gaze while I gently touched the cigarette's dark tip to the flame. I took my first drag and then exhaled, blowing the smoke into his face.

'I'm interested to know why you're trying to chat me up when I know you robbed the big man.'

I'd never seen anyone's expression change so fast. He flinched and recoiled.

'What you saying?' he asked sharply.

'I'm saying you robbed Scully. In broad daylight.'

'Um – uh – '

He glanced nervously around, trying to work out if anyone else was in earshot.

'Now,' I said, 'lucky for you, the big man doesn't want to start no vibes.'

'Janice – um – this is – uh – I don't think you understa–'

'Okay then – you set me straight. What was it like, when you pushed Scully to the ground and stole his money?'

He couldn't speak a word. I placed my red Yves Saint Laurent bag in the middle of the table, and opened the clasp. My Beretta Bobcat gleamed blue-black against its blood-red lining, baring its perfect little teeth. I saw Winston Grey's body go quite still.

'Uh – Janice – so you're saying that – uh – the big man don't want no problems?'

'He doesn't.' A flicker of relief crossed Winston's face. I gave him a moment to enjoy it. 'Then again,' I continued, 'he doesn't speak for me.'

Our eyes locked together.

'There is only one reason I'll do nothing to you,' I said softly. 'And that's because the man said to leave it alone.'

Sweat was forming on his forehead.

'But if this ever happens again, I won't deal with it so lightly. You check?'

'Yeah man! Yeah man! Little misunderstanding, Jan!'

'Because . . . if you want this to be on . . . it will be on.'

Winston Grey drew back from me. He wiped his upper lip. Very gently, I closed my beautiful red bag. I got to my feet and walked away.

10

WAITING LIKE A LOADED GUN

MAY 2015

MAGDA'S WAS A FACE in the women's group that didn't seem to fit. She was an energetic woman in her forties, looking in great shape and always well turned out. She came along to meetings on her bicycle. The exercise clearly made her thirsty, so she constantly sipped from a sports flask that she carried.

I asked her what she was drinking. 'Vitamin C tablets dissolved in water,' she replied with a confident smile. She certainly seemed to be paying attention to her health.

But I quickly grew suspicious. Something about Magda wasn't right. She'd been arrested for drink-driving. Now she came along to our meetings, always sipping and sipping. The way she was drinking didn't look like the way that you drink if you are thirsty. It looked like how you drink if it's *a drink*. And her elaborate concealment told me something else – that she was struggling with shame.

When a woman is standing in the dock, a life of chaos, of drinking or drug abuse, addictions, unwise sexual decisions and failures as a partner and a parent are often brutally exposed to the court. And they are judged there far more harshly than a man's would ever be. I believe that women who have problems with drinking are shamed in the criminal justice system.

It's often the case, even now, that judges have traditional social attitudes. Older ones especially view women as the rightful keepers of the home. And the keeper is to blame, in these traditionalists' eyes, when the home falls apart. The belief of the court is very often that *she should have known better*. If she didn't – well, why not? A man in that same dock might be guilty of many awful things. He might have abandoned his family, committed dreadful violence, let many people down. But the huge expectation – that you are the one who must hold everything together – doesn't rest on him. So he is censured less, and allowed more space to fail.

I don't believe that judges see the struggle that so many women in the criminal justice system are enduring. Perhaps some do, but even they still see it without really understanding. They have no sense of what a single mother's life is like, living on very little money, perhaps in an abusive situation or with more abuse behind her in her past. Such things are invisible to privileged, educated men. But the failure of a woman to fulfil her role as anchor and carer of her family is very visible indeed.

I couldn't smell alcohol on Magda. Firing accusations when I had no proof would harm her trust in me, and trust was vital for everything I wanted to do. I always made it clear that I was there to listen and support every woman in the group, not to judge. So instead, I began to keep a very careful eye.

It didn't take long to find out what was happening. One morning, as someone else was speaking, Magda suddenly flopped over sideways and passed out. She landed on Izzie, who cried out, very startled: 'My God – is she dead?' Magda wasn't dead – she was just very, very drunk. We helped her to lie down on the floor until she came round. At our next one-to-one, she and I were going to have to have a serious talk.

'So when you told me it was vitamin C in that flask,' I said to her, 'that wasn't true, was it?'

She shifted in her seat. She put so much effort into acting as though everything was great. It upset her when reality popped up and brought her down to earth with a bump.

'Look,' I told her, 'I understand – I get it. But if you don't tell me you have problems, how can I help? That's what I'm here to do.'

'I'd just had a – a bad day,' she muttered. 'It was a silly thing to do, to drink like that. Normally I don't – I never – '

'Magda,' I said, 'I think what's normal right now is that you drink more than you should. Don't you think that's true?'

I saw that she was terribly embarrassed. But if she couldn't face what was happening, there was no chance at all she'd overcome it.

'I read your file. I think that alcohol has caused you lots of problems already.'

What I'd read had been desperately sad. Her two grown-up sons were both professional musicians – one part of a well-known band. But he had felt completely humiliated when she had turned up drunk to a perform-ance. The incident caused a rift between them – and it was only one of a number of disastrous occasions. Now Magda had lost contact with both of her boys.

'Not to mention putting you in danger,' I went on. 'Riding that bike here in the traffic when you've had too much to drink sounds pretty scary to me.'

'But I like exercise!' she said brightly. 'It's good to ride my bike – it's hardly ever a problem!'

I wanted her to know that I wasn't going to blame her. She felt awful shame already. But no matter what I said, I could see that I wasn't getting through. All she gave me was bravado – her real, darker feelings lay beneath, and the more I tried to show I understood, the more she insisted that everything was fine.

She finished her probation successfully, but right until the end, I knew she was still drinking. As long as that continued, I didn't think that anything would change. I tried to offer words of encouragement and referred her to groups that might help. She desperately needed support. What I'd seen was part of a cycle. Without the help she needed, Magda would be back at the bottom in the future, again and again.

*

JULY 1989

'Mama J – you got a problem,' said Scully.

We sometimes mixed our business with pleasure, talking and making plans in bed in the afternoon quiet after we'd made love. In the rising chaos around me, his house felt like my refuge. But even there, I couldn't relax as I usually did. A sense of deep unease was hanging over us. I lit a Sobranie and sighed, staring up at the ceiling.

'This break-in, babe,' he went on, 'it's concerning. I know you run things tight. Your security's good. But somebody somewhere thinks they can take you.'

I knew that he was right.

'So who?' Scully asked me. 'Who's got a grudge? Who's jealous? Who's upset about a problem and not say?'

'Nobody's upset. It's all good.'

'But babe – it ain't.'

'Scully – I move carefully. I always clear up trouble straightaway.'

'I know you do. But babe – this time, you missed something.'

'Or maybe,' I said with a smile, 'it's someone looking for you. Maybe they know we're together. There's no secrets in south London.'

'No secrets anywhere, darlin'.' He was silent for a moment. 'But yeah – I think you're right. From now on – we de-fi-nite-ly going to keep our distance.'

We both laughed, and Scully kissed me.

'Bit late for that, babe.'

But our discomfort lingered on, distracting us from one another. As I got ready to leave, he looked straight into my eyes.

'Dis is someone in your own camp, Janice. If word get out dat dis can happen and yuh don't do nuthin' – dat create a problem. Deal with it an' get it under control.'

'You know Mummy's doing naughty things, sweetheart?'

Nadia and I were sitting together in my bolt hole, down at Chelsea Harbour. She raised her head from her Nintendo Game & Watch. The pale blue handset bleeped and warbled distractingly.

'Yes, Mum.'

'But we live nice, don't we?'

'Yes, Mum.'

'Sometimes, baby, it's good to plan things in advance. Even if the things won't really happen.'

'Okay, Mum.'

'So I'd like to do that now. I want us to plan what you would say if anybody ever asks you where I am.'

'What would I say, Mum?'

'You tell them you don't know. It doesn't matter how many times they ask. Even if they say horrible things.'

Nadia looked at me thoughtfully.

'But I would know where you were, right?'

'Of course you would. I always come here. If you

ever can't find me and I haven't been in touch with you – don't worry. I'll be here.'

'Okay, Mum.'

'And if anybody came to the flat and told you that they'd kidnapped me, and you have to give them all our money – what would you do then?'

'Will they come, Mum?'

'No, baby. Remember – we're just planning. You would tell them to piss off. Or to shoot me.'

'I really tell them that?'

'Yes, you do.'

She was wearing her most down-to-earth expression.

'So I never ever say where you are, and if they've kidnapped you, they have to piss off or shoot you?'

'That's right. Good girl.'

Nadia was nine now. She was so sensible I'd made her my little bank clerk. I gave her all the drug money to count, and she totalled it correctly every time. She tied the takings into bundles of fives or tens or twenties, every bundle exactly a grand. Then she'd separate the dollars and stray francs and pesetas and bind them together separately. I always put some of the money in her savings account. I also sewed five grand into her teddy bear – a reserve for emergencies.

I trusted Scully with my life, teddy with my secrets, and Nadia with my heart. I felt so vulnerable in those days – I wasn't sure who else I could rely on.

I needed to find out who it was I couldn't trust. I had to know who was chatting shit about me and do something to stop them.

*

'Janice, this is my boyfriend, Big Breed,' said Sabrina. 'It's funny – he lives right next door.'

'Hey, Breed.'

The new boyfriend didn't move, just raised a hand in greeting from the sofa. He seemed to have made himself at home. He was a young guy, attractive but soft-faced. Weak-looking, I thought – he'd struggle with decisions or just leave them to others. Sabrina was a beautiful girl – she could do better. *But if my sister wants fun times with the boy next door, then that's no business of mine.*

I didn't see him much after that. Now that her place was my safe house, I didn't go there often. When I handed over cash to her, we met at Clapham High Street Sainsbury's. Then one afternoon, I saw another graze on her face. Sabrina acted normally and didn't even mention the graze. Now I came to think of it, she'd not mentioned the first one either. It wasn't like her. Suddenly, it struck me that her silence was a warning.

But I couldn't be sure – at least, not yet. Then two weeks later, she had a black eye. She'd tried to cover it with make-up. Red flag. Now I knew.

'What the fuck, Sabrina?' I demanded.

'What the fuck what?' Straightaway she was defensive.

'What the fuck you think? That's three bruises I seen on you. What's going on?'

Around us, the Clapham shoppers jostled and hurried by. A woman who'd caught part of what I said gave us both a worried glance.

'Shhhh!' said Sabrina, looking very embarrassed. 'Why you talking so loud?'

'It's him, isn't it? It's Breed. He's knocking you around.'

'Shhhh! Of course it isn't Breed!' she hissed. 'It was an accident.'

She dropped her eyes as she said it. She couldn't lie to me. I knew her too well.

'Three times you had an accident and bashed your face? My – you're getting careless!'

'Janice – it's nothing. It was just – it was stupid. It was my fault anyway.'

'I thought you said it was an accident!'

'Look – it wasn't what you think.'

Why was she defending a man who would treat her this way? Then I saw that Sabrina was trembling. I reached out my hand to reassure her, but the moment I touched her, she yanked her arm away.

'Jan – why don't you give me your stuff and leave me alone? Just because you pay me now, it doesn't mean you can run my life.'

I couldn't believe what I was hearing.

'Doing business doesn't change anything else! You're still my sister.'

'Maybe it seems that way to you. Except that now you think you own me. Well, you don't! I don't care how much money you've got.'

'Why d'you keep talking about money? Money doesn't matter! What I'm saying is that lowlife needs to keep his hands to himself!'

'It wasn't Breed!'

'Sab – I hope you don't let him see what you're keeping for me at home. I want that man to stay out of my business.'

'Jan – honestly – it's fine. I don't show him anything. It's fine. You can trust him.'

But I didn't. I was afraid for my same-birthday-sister. I was also very worried about my safe house. This situation needed very careful thinking.

I gave my new Beretta Bobcat to Krystal for safekeeping. Sabrina's place wasn't secure any more – not now that Big Breed was around. Krystal concealed the gun in her outhouse. But I only found out where she kept it after she had been arrested. The police came to raid her on a day when she was clean. They ripped her whole place apart, but there was nothing there to find. Then just as they were leaving, someone noticed the outhouse. They did Krystal for possessing an illegal firearm.

'We know it isn't yours,' they told her at the station. 'Phone Nasty Girl and tell her – come and get it.'

But my Krystal wasn't talking. She stuck to the story that the gun belonged to her. She was sentenced to nine months and served three.

So now the cops knew I carried. How much else did they know? They didn't have the whole picture about me – not yet. If they did, I would be under arrest. But one thing was for sure – they were seeing far too many connections.

*

It had been a good morning on the road. I decided there'd be no more work today. I rang Sabrina. I missed her, and we needed to talk. A lovely lunch with wine in some nice relaxing place would be the perfect chance to do it. She immediately agreed, and I felt happier than I had for quite a while. Even if we argued, we would always be sisters. As I swung the car into Acre Lane, chatting like we always used to do, my new flip phone rang.

'Janice?' I heard an anxious voice in my ear. It was Pete, my neighbour, a quiet man who lived on the opposite side of my landing.

'Hey, Pete. Everything alright?'

'You need to get home right away. Your flat is full of police.'

'Oh my goodness!'

Sabrina couldn't hear what Pete was saying, but she saw the expression on my face. She widened her eyes questioningly.

'Loads of them!' said Pete, who was terribly alarmed. 'It's like some sort of raid! Yelling and shouting! They've broken down your door! It has to be some awful mistake.'

'Oh my God, it must be. Thanks for telling me. I'll come straight away.'

'Jan – what it is?' asked Sabrina.

I pulled the car over to the kerb.

'I got problems. Police are at the house.'

'Oh Christ!' said Sabrina, immediately panicked.

'Don't worry – they won't find anything. But I must get back right now.'

My heart was pounding. I knew I must think quickly, and not let shock and alarm lead me into making a mistake. If I gave my drugs and cash to Sabrina to take home, there was a good chance that Big Breed would see them. I didn't trust him. I couldn't let that happen. No – she would have to take them somewhere else.

'Sab,' I asked, 'can you do something for me?'

But Sabrina was too freaked out to listen.

'Jesus, Jan – why are they raiding you?'

'Babe,' I said grimly, 'I don't know. But I need you to stay really calm and do just as I say.'

'Uh – sure, sure, okay.'

'Take the car to Auntie Ida's and give her this lot.' I gestured to my bag down on the floor of the car. 'She'll know what to do with it. I'll get a cab home from here.'

'Okay. Okay.' I could see her hands were shaking.

'Sab – just stay calm. It's going to be fine.'

She leaned forward and opened up the top of the bag. The takings weren't bound or counted yet, just pushed inside in rolls. There was just over sixteen thousand pounds. She looked at me in total amazement.

'My God, Jan! How much is this?'

'It doesn't matter. Close the bag. Just pretend it's not there, and drive like normal.'

'But – is this what you make in *one day*?!'

'Sabrina – please just drive the car. Go to Ida's.'

I gave her everything I had on me that morning. She drove my car away. Then I found a cab and sat breathing slowly, gathering myself as I approached my home.

It's going to be fine, I'd told Sabrina. I only wished that I could be so sure.

Three blue-light cars were drawn up close to the building. The outer door was open. As I ran up the two flights of stairs, I heard voices and the hiss and crackle of police radios. My front door was hanging off its hinges. The police had trashed my place.

Stepping into the hall, I could see that my big chest of drawers had been upended. I glanced into the kitchen where the contents of my cupboards and fridge lay strewn across the floor and on the tops of the units. Containers had been toppled on their sides and leaked their contents. The searchers had even tipped out the sugar bowl. A policewoman was standing by the window.

'I take it you are Janice?' She was clearly the officer in charge.

'Yes I am, and who are you? What's going on?'

'We are authorised to carry out a search of these premises.'

'Where's your warrant?'

She held out a sheet of paper. I glanced briefly at the document, then paused and looked again, trying to make sense of what I saw.

'Firearms?' I demanded. 'What d'you mean – fire-arms?'

The policewoman arched her eyebrows.

'Isn't that what it says?'

I knew I should casual this out, but I couldn't. My head was hot.

'Bitch,' I snarled, 'don't you get sarcastic with me.'

She saw that she'd got under my skin, and gave a satisfied smile. I cursed myself for losing control. Anger can run wild.

'Anyway – if you're searching for guns,' I went on, 'why you looking in my sugar bowl?'

I stormed down the passage. The carpet crunched with broken glass. My pictures had been wrenched off the walls. The living room looked as though a tornado had passed through – cushions slashed, chairs on their backs, soil from the plant pots scattered and smeared along the windowsills. An officer was standing in the middle of the room. As I stared at the wreckage, I could have torn his face off.

'Look what you've done!' I yelled. 'You've had the place to yourselves – you could have planted anything here!'

He lifted a heavy-booted foot and placed it contemptuously on my coffee table.

'Dirty bloody drug dealers,' he said.

Radios spitting, they started their retreat from the flat. There was nothing I could do but watch them leave.

When Nadia came home and saw the mess, she was inconsolable. I'd made a start with the tidying by then, beginning with her bedroom, to try to protect her from the worst of it. But my baby stood in the wreckage of our home, tears streaming down her face.

'Why did they do this?' she kept asking. 'Mummy – why?' I had no way to answer her.

It took us days to clear up all the mess. Although my little girl was very brave, I knew that it would be weeks before she felt secure again.

'Hey there, Lassell. Is the jeep ready?'

Nasty Girl had engine trouble, and Lassell was my mechanic. He had a shop in Barnwell Road, not far from Brixton station. I sat outside with Mikey in one of my Thornton Heath bangers. Shoes was going to drive the banger home for me, as soon as I got Nasty Girl back.

'Just smartening her up,' said Lassell's voice on the phone. 'Ten minutes. Sorry, Jan.'

'S'okay, man.' I sat back to wait.

A man came walking slowly round the corner from Railton Road behind me – a tall black guy in a dark leather jacket. I always paid attention to the street. As I watched his approach, I liked the look of the man less and less. Mikey Shoes had clocked him too. His focus zeroed in. We sat there without moving.

The man came to a stop on the pavement beside me. He bent forward and very deliberately stared into the car.

Enough already. I wound the window down.

'Do you have a problem?' I asked him.

'Hey, Janice,' he replied.

'Hey yourself. You got a name?'

'Sticks Man.'

'And what are you wanting, Sticks Man?'

He laid his hand on the roof of my car. It was a small act of aggression, pushing himself into my space.

'Godfather says you gotta pay your tax,' he told me.

'Godfather? Who's the godfather?'

'He's round the corner.'

'I thought I knew who the godfather is,' I said. 'And he's not hiding round in Railton Road this morning.'

Mikey Shoes was eyeballing Sticks Man. Sticks Man tried to tough it out, but I could see he didn't like that kind of attention one bit.

'Look, man,' Sticks muttered, 'I'm just telling you what the boss say.'

'The boss? Well now, you go back round the corner, and tell the boss he can fuck off.'

'He won't like it.'

'So he can come and tell me.'

Mikey Shoes and I sat waiting in the sunshine. A couple of minutes later, another man came around the corner. I recognised him straight away. I hadn't seen him since Janet's funeral. I certainly didn't want to see him now.

Scorcher still wore beautiful crocodile skin shoes. He had his screw face on, that look of menace that he'd been practising for a very long time. He was always wanting to be gangsta. He drew level with the car, bent his knees and crouched down. He laid two finger-tips very gently against my forehead. I shuddered, feeling nothing but pure anger. I could scarcely bear him to touch me, but I didn't flinch away.

'Janice. Mama J.' His voice was a slow, mocking drawl. 'If you want to work in Brixton, you gotta pay tax.'

So now he's tryin' extortion.

He jabbed his fingers harder into my face. I allowed my head to turn. A cold stillness possessed me. As he withdrew his hand, I turned back and looked him straight in his eye.

'Scorcher, mi nah pay yuh no tax,' I said.

He reached into the inside breast pocket of his jacket, showing me a glimpse of a Browning. He wanted me to see he was carrying. In less than a second, Mikey Shoes did the same. For a heartbeat, the three of us stayed motionless. A stand-off.

He thinks he's got me scared. But I can deal with Scorcher.

I shoved the door wide open in a sudden, violent swing, sending him sprawling on his back. Now I was out on the pavement, standing over him.

'Yes, Scorcher!' I shouted. *'Shoot me inna Barnwell Road! Yuh tink yuh big and bad! Fire!'*

Furious, he tried to scramble up. Before he could manage it, I leaned over him. I pushed two fingers hard into his cheek in the same way he had done to me. I knew a man like Scorcher would never have believed that a woman would have the strength to take him on. I imagined the London pavement stained with his blood. A slow, red pool of vengeance for Pepper.

'Scorcher! You've done more damage than you ever

could put right. If I did what I'd like to, I'd fuck you up right here.'

I straightened myself up.

'Fuck with me again,' I told him, 'and I'll pay a man to fuck with you.'

Mikey Shoes had opened his door and climbed out. But it was over. Scorcher was getting to his feet and backing off, dusting himself down. I had faced him, and won. I had my army behind me, but the victory today was mine alone.

So – could dis be Scorcher who been causin' mi dis trouble?

The more I thought, the more I wondered. The break-in at my flat. Krystal arrested. The whisper of guns that had reached the police. I remembered Scully's questions. *Someone got a grudge? Someone jealous?*

Yes. I thought – someone was jealous. And that someone might be Scorcher. He knew the word about me on the street. I used to be a shoplifter. Now I ran a whole operation that was ten times Scorcher's size. This small-time criminal envied my success. He thought he could take me down.

He was nothing but a trouble-making fool, and I'd dealt with him. I'd left him humiliated, lying on the ground in Barnwell Road. I hoped it meant the whole affair was over. I was sick of all this shit. I wanted to get on with my business and my life.

But my problems were only getting started.

The moment I picked up the phone, I knew that

something was terribly wrong. Ida was trying to sound calm, but underneath I could tell she was distraught.

'Janice? I'm sorry. I'm so sorry. You need to come here now.'

'Is there a problem, Mums? What you sorry about?'

When she told me what happened, I rushed straight round to her place in Streatham. The moment she saw me, she burst into tears. I suddenly noticed she looked older now, and smaller. I put my arms around her. As I held her, her body felt so little and frail.

'Oh, Mums. Mums, it's okay. It's not your fault. Just tell me what happened.'

'I don't know. I've been burgled. This has never happened before! Oh Janice – I'm so sorry!'

Ida's house was my belly – the place where I stored not just a large amount of money, but my treasure. A robbery there was a disaster – and both of us knew it. I looked around. The break-in didn't look like a profes-sional job at first glance – just a panel of glass in the back door smashed while Ida had been out at the shops. But this had been no opportunist.

Ida still stored money for her pardners – a couple of thousand. For me she stored many thousands more. Her house had many hiding places: the under-stairs cupboard, the wardrobe, underneath the bath. And whoever this burglar might be – he'd known where to look. He'd gone straight to my stash.

But that wasn't all I'd lost. The burglars had taken something worth far more. They had stolen the Louis

Vuitton attaché case. I thought again of the day Pepper and I first saw the case in Crocodile – how she'd doubted my plan, but she'd stepped right up to help. I remembered how the two of us had burst into peals of laughter as we made our triumphant getaway. How I'd teased her as I jimmied the lock open and uncovered our haul. It was the last time I ever saw her laugh. Just a few weeks later came the horror in New Bond Street.

Oh darlin', mi miss you so.

That case was the last link between us. Whoever stole it had taken a precious memory away from me. This was far more than business – this was personal. I swore that I would find out who had done this. *And when I do, they're going to be sorry.*

But I barely had time to think how I might do it. A few days later, still reeling from the theft of the case, I took another call. It was Sabrina. She sounded muffled, then I realised she was crying so much that I could hardly make out what she was saying.

'Sab? Sab – what's the matter? Try to slow down and tell me.'

Her breath came in gasps. She started to speak, but then there was another burst of crying. This was an emergency. I realised I would have to break my rule about not going to her house.

'Just wait. Please just hold on. I'm coming over.'

As I drove, I was seized with the awful sense of everything exploding out of my control. I pulled over and sat for a moment in the quiet of my car. I breathed deeply, pulling my inner resources together.

Control your mind, and your mind controls your face.

When she answered the door, I was shocked. Sabrina looked as though she'd been in some terrible accident. Her face was badly swollen, with one eyelid puffed and scarlet. She had a deep cut on her lip, and buttons missing from her shirt. I was enraged at the sight of her – but shouting wouldn't help.

'Okay – let's get you cleaned up. Then we'll talk.'

She sat shaking on the edge of the bath while I bathed her cuts and bruises as gently as I could. Tears were streaming down her cheeks. I kept wiping them away, but every time I did, it started off a fresh burst of weeping.

'Oh JanJan! Oh JanJan!' she whimpered, over and over. I thought that she was suffering from shock.

'Right – now we need some tea.'

I led her to the kitchen. She sat down on a chair, and tried to hide her face in her hands. But she couldn't – her gashes were too raw.

'Who did this, Sabrina?'

She drew another shuddery breath.

'Was it Big Breed?'

An awful moment's silence, then she flopped back in her chair as though all her strength had drained away. She just said, 'Yes.'

I listened while she stammered out her story.

'He's a nice guy, Jan, you know – m-m-mostly.

Honestly he – he is. He just gets into moods sometimes.' She slowly shook her head.

'It's like everything is wrong. Everything I say. I
keep on asking him what did I do, did I upset you –
but – ' More tears rolled down her cheeks.

'What happened today?' I asked her very quietly.

'Oh JanJan – it was crazy. He said that I'd been
seeing someone else, and when I said I hadn't, he said
his friend had seen me and had told him, and I told
him that's shit – who would say that? And then he said
that even if I hadn't been seeing other guys, he knew
I wanted to. And when I kept on telling him I hadn't
– he just lost it, Jan. He absolutely lost it.'

I saw how hard she was shaking.

'I was scared he'd kill me,' she whispered.

I thought of his soft, empty face. Big Breed was a
weak little boy who thought that beating up a woman
made him more of a man. Although my voice stayed
calm, my anger was murderous.

'Right. I'm glad you told me. Now we can work
out what to do. Where is he now?' I asked her.

'He went home,' she whispered, pointing towards
the house next door. 'But then I think he left. I heard
the front door.'

'You don't know where he's gone?'

She gave a hopeless shrug. It was late afternoon.
Nadia was staying at Emmanuel's tonight. I didn't
know how long it would be till Big Breed came back
– but I had time. I had all the time in the world to

deal with a lowlife like him. I sat there, waiting like a loaded gun.

It was after seven in the evening when I heard the sound of Big Breed's front door. Sabrina had arranged for her daughters to go round to a friend's house, then gone upstairs to rest.

I stepped out of Sabrina's house and rang the bell next door. Through the frosted glass, I saw a figure coming slowly down the passage. The door opened a very little way. Big Breed's face peered out at me. I shoved past him and marched straight inside. He scampered behind me, stuttering. In his messy living room, I swung round to face him.

'Uh – uh – you're Ja-Ja-Janice – Sabrina's friend, aren't you?'

'You know who I am. I'm Sabrina's sister.'

'So what's going on?'

'Don't play games with me. I've not come here to play.'

'I don't know wha–'

This man and his denials were pathetic. He filled me with scorn. I laid the flat of my hand against his chest and pushed him backwards until he was pressed against the wall.

'You will not put hands on my sister! Understand me?'

'I – I – Ja-Janice, what did she tell you?'

'Tell me! She didn't need to tell me! It's plain to see what you've done.'

He started to talk shit. How it all got out of hand. How he didn't mean to do it. How Sabrina had provoked him. He didn't know how it could have happened. As I listened to his babble, all I could see were her bruises and her blood.

There was an untidy storage unit in the corner of the room. Its shelves were crowded with football trophies and piles of old papers. On a grubby, tarnished shield: 'Lewisham Junior Boys Soccer Team, runners up 1977.' The innocence of boyhood. Half-concealed behind it was a crack pipe. *He ain't so innocent now.*

'Breed?' I demanded, 'You're a smoker?'

'No, Janice, n-no – that belongs to – to – '

He was obviously lying. Every moment, I grew angrier.

'Are you telling me my sister is going with a crackhead?'

He stuttered. 'No, no! I'm telling you – it's not mine – it's – uh – '

What was Sabrina thinking, taking up with this man? She understood that doing business safely meant keeping a clear head. I'd told her so myself. Surely she knew better than to ever trust a user.

'So, then, since the pipe's not yours, Breed, you won't have anything else in the place?'

'Uh – uh – ' he stammered. I was watching him carefully. I saw his eyes slide sideways in a quick, guilty look towards the stairs.

I marched into his bedroom. The bed was rumpled and unmade. Alongside it was a row of empty bottles of booze and overflowing ashtrays. On the low table next to them was just what I'd expected to see. The rest of his gear.

'I've seen enough,' I told him. 'I've nothing more to say. It's finished – you and Sabrina. You won't go near her no more.'

I took a final glance around the grotty little room. And then I noticed something else. Something down on the floor, jammed tightly between the side table and the wall. A black attaché case. Slowly I bent and picked it up. I felt the smooth, expensive leather. Then I saw the letters 'LV' and 'Made in France' were inscribed on its heavy gold clasp. As I recognised the case, it seemed as though my heart stood still.

I had to be sure. I pushed the clasp open, and lifted the lid. And there it was, that tiny little stain on the golden-brown lining – a mark shaped like a heart. Now I was certain. This was my case. The case that had been stolen, weeks ago, from Ida's house in Streatham. How did it get here, in Big Breed's filthy bedroom?

I reached in my pocket for my phone.

'Shoes? I need you all to come as quickly as you can.'

'Sure. Where are you?' I gave him the address.

I wondered if Big Breed might try to make a run, but he didn't. He knew my boys would find him wherever he went. He sat there on the sofa with his head in his hands, muttering to himself. The three of them were with me in ten minutes – Mikey Shoes, Sharp Man and Leggy. Their heavy feet came swiftly down the hall. When Big Breed saw them, he jumped up and backed nervously into the corner. No one touched him – not yet.

'You having trouble, Mama J?' said Mikey Shoes.

'Shoes – I found the guy that dissed my programme.'

'You're lying!' Shoes was astonished. 'What d'you mean – you found the guy?'

'He's right here.' I pointed to Big Breed.

Big Breed's eyes were bulging. I held the Louis Vuitton case in my hands.

'So, Breed,' I asked him, 'where did you get this?'

'I – I – ' He could barely speak with fright.

'Lost your voice?'

'I – I can't remember. Ha-had it months. Maybe I – '

More useless, stupid lies. I cut him short.

'Big Breed – this case belongs to me. And I would like to know where you got it.'

He stared at me wild-eyed. I saw that he was struggling to grasp what I meant.

'This is my property,' I said to him. 'And somebody stole it. Now it's turned up here. I want to know how that happened.'

'Yours?'

I pointed to Shoes, Sharp Man and Leggy.

'Big Breed – these guys ain't ballerinas. They've come to do a job. You can tell me where you got the case, and how you came to find it. Or they can go to work.'

He was sweating. He licked his dry lips. His eyes darted round the room.

'Uh – uh – I went on a work!'

'Where was the house?'

'Streatham.'

'Do you know whose house it was?'

'No! Ju-just some d-d-dealer's place.'

'And when you got there – you knew just where to look. How did you know?'

'I got a d-description of the house.'

'A good description, was it? From someone who must have been inside?'

'Yes! But Janice! I didn't know the place was yours!'

'I get that, Breed. I believe you. Now all I want to know is this: who gave you the address?'

Twenty minutes later, I was driving the Cosworth through south London.

Mikey Shoes was up alongside me. As we moved through the streets, I watched Big Breed in the rear-view mirror. He stunk of sweat. His eyes darted nervously from side to side. But he was surprisingly stubborn. He hadn't told – so far. So we needed to find a quiet place to talk. Sharp Man and Leggy were one on either side of him, keeping him pinned down.

I pulled off the road onto some waste ground. The place was deserted. The car came to a stop.

'The address. Who gave it you?' I asked.

Big Breed was breathing quickly. He didn't reply.

'This is the last time I'm askin'. There's no one around these parts to hear you. Who gave you the address?'

When he spoke, his voice was shrill with panic.

'I can't tell you, man! I can't say!'

I drummed my fingers lightly on the steering wheel. I sighed and looked ahead.

'If you don't,' I said to him, 'I have no choice. I'll leave you to the mandem. Who was it?'

He still didn't answer. I said to the boys behind: 'Okay.' Sharp Man grabbed him in a neck-hold and squeezed. It only took two seconds for the name to squeal right out. But when he said it, I couldn't believe what I'd heard.

'Who?' I demanded.

Big Breed screamed the name again, thrashing around, trying to relieve the pressure on his throat. I sat frozen to the spot.

After a few seconds, I waved my hand. The boys let him go and his panting filled the car. I knew he was shit scared, so he wasn't lying. But I still needed to be sure – really sure – I'd heard him right.

'Why you bringing that name into this?'

'Cos it was! That's who set it up! That's who told me the address!'

'I don't believe you.'

'Said the house was some drug dealer's belly.' Now he was whimpering. 'And where to look. But I didn't know it was your place! Nobody never told me that!'

When I first heard the name, a bolt of pain had run through me. It couldn't be. I didn't want to believe it. Now I just felt cold. I accepted what he had told me. My world had changed.

'Alright,' I say to the boys. 'Get him out of my car.'

Big Breed howled.

He wouldn't climb out on his own, so they dragged him. Then Sharp Man and Leggy pinned his arms back. Mikey Shoes got to work. I sat there and waited until he'd finished. The three of them returned to the Cosworth. Big Breed slumped on the ground in the fading evening light. I turned the key and drove away.

Very late that night, I headed for home. Beneath the copper midnight sky, I was gripped with a loneliness so dark and deep it felt like terror. When Big Breed finally told me who'd arranged for my belly to be robbed, all I wanted was to cover my ears.

Scully had been right. *Someone jealous. Someone with a grudge but they won't say it.* But that someone wasn't Scorcher. If only it could have been Scorcher. How much easier it would be to have that snake betray me than –

I could still hear Big Breed screaming her name.

'Sabrina!'

Sabrina. I closed my eyes and lowered my head. The traffic lights changed. From behind me came the irritable blare of a horn.

'Sabrina! She told me where to go! She said there was drug money!'

My same-birthday-sister knew that I had cash. But she didn't know how much – not until the day of the police raid. The day I gave her all my takings. I remembered her amazement in the car as she peeped into my bag.

'But – is this what you make in *one day*?!'

Now I imagined her arrival at Ida's that panicky afternoon – their anxiety, their haste to put the money safely away. Ida was always very careful, but she knew Sabrina well. She trusted her. Sabrina would have a chance to see the hiding places – of course she would.

She knew my story, my secrets, my heart. When did she turn against me? I searched for answers, for warnings. But I found only grief.

My sister, my sister. I can't believe that you would do this to me.

But who could be trusted in this world built out of lies? I looked at the lights of south London, and I wept.

11

IN THE DOCK IN GUCCI

2015

THERE WAS A LOT of domestic violence in the women's probation group.

Physical abuse was very common. So was what has recently been named as coercive control – a kind of mental force which is exerted on a person by their partner to subjugate, humiliate and crush them. Women in the group lived with partners who beat and kicked and punched them, bullied them, raped them, used the threat of rape and threatened the same to their children. Too often they became involved with men in a lot of pain themselves: alcoholics, drug addicts, those who'd been hurt or abandoned as children and were raging at the mothers who had failed to keep them safe.

Many of these abusers were triggered off by drinking. Others were more unpredictable than that – a word out of place or a minor disagreement was enough to cause an outburst of anger and violence. Some would go for weeks being pleasant and loving, then suddenly explode. Some would lose their tempers if their team lost at football, or a child broke an object in the house. All of them were men who didn't know any other way to feel in control – except by force.

At first, Naomi seemed quite different. She acted like the girl who had it all. She looked confident and smart. In her first few weeks' attendance, there were members of the group who thought that she was my assistant – and she liked it that way. She had fashionable clothes and shoes and handbags. They were gifts, she told us, from her wealthy and generous boyfriend. She was keen to describe how he would often take her shopping. He wanted to make sure that she looked nice for all the parties and dinners they attended with his friends. When we asked his name, Naomi talked a lot but never really answered. She just said he was important, a businessman, someone who knew influential people – so she had to be discreet at all times.

He certainly had money. His car arrived one day to pick her up at the end of the group – an S-Class Merc with a private number plate. I watched him standing smoking as he waited. Naomi went rushing out so that she wouldn't keep him hanging around. She apologised the moment she saw him, even though she hadn't come out late. He gave her a very slight nod. She jumped nervously into the front seat, taking another little glance in his direction. That was when I knew that he was trouble.

Naomi was on probation for drunk and disorderly behaviour. But she was deeply in denial about her drinking, and wouldn't share much with the others. The only time she would talk more openly was in a one-to-one session. But even there, she tried to present herself as fully in control. I remembered Sabrina. Her smiles, the way she always wore nice clothes and did her hair. How she blocked out what was wrong and hid her bruises with make-up. The danger signs had been there, but so small, so very easy to miss. So I kept my eyes wide open, and my attention sharpened.

When Naomi talked about her boyfriend, it was clear she saw the whole world through his eyes. She wore the clothes he liked, did her make-up and her hair the way he liked, ate only food that he liked. They only did what he wanted to do.

He liked to go to swingers' parties, so she had to go. She didn't want to join in – but he liked watching her. She didn't want to sleep with his friends, but he got a kick from passing her around. He was degrading her, but she gave him permission to do it.

'He says it makes a special bond between us,' she told us proudly. 'He's asked other girls to do it, but they wouldn't.'

'Why wouldn't they?'

'He says they're too conventional.'

'And what do you get out of it?'

'He says it makes us closer.'

'What do you say?'

Naomi dropped her eyes. She hesitated.

'Look,' I said, 'if both of you enjoyed these kinds

of games, that would be fine. But I don't think you like it at all.'

But if she didn't please him, he punished her by cutting off all communication. Not talking, not phoning her, not texting. These silences drove Naomi into an absolute panic. The thought of him not being in her life made her terrified. It was an awful kind of mental control.

'How does it make you feel,' I asked her quietly, 'when you do things for him that you don't really want to do?'

She shook her head in confusion. She couldn't tell me what she felt, or what she liked, or what she wanted. She really didn't know. Next moment, she gave me a bright and cheerful smile. It was the smile that went with her best life – the one she always told me she was living – and she mentioned some present that he'd bought her.

I saw emotional dependence in other women too. It was as if they weren't real in their own eyes. And if you aren't real, it doesn't feel as though your body can be yours. You don't know that you have choices about who is, or who is not, allowed to touch you, or sleep with you, or be with you. You don't understand that you have rights – the right to decide how to live and where to go and what to do. Deciding means thinking and planning, judging from your past and looking forward to your future. But when you're lost and feel so hopeless that you don't care what happens to you anyway, then you're drawn, again and again, to men who make all your choices for you. Men who are looking for a woman to control.

So how do you help someone protect themselves? I wondered. *How do you teach them that their body is theirs, or that their feelings matter?* You can't fix the chaotic lives they lived when they were children, the mothers and fathers who beat them or neglected them or left them or were never there at all. You can't repair their lack of opportunity, the poor school attendance that meant they failed all their exams. You can't take away the poverty and violence and alcohol and drugs. All I could do was teach them how to love themselves more. And I could try to deal with the criminal record, because that's what was making a decent life in future much more difficult to find.

I wanted to help Naomi. And as I wondered how to start, Dorothy Johnson gave me plenty of ideas. When I first saw her tapping technique, I'd no idea at all what was happening. She'd been called in to give a demonstration on a training course I did.

'What's on earth is this?' I asked her. 'What does it do?'

'It's called acupressure.' Dorothy was tapping gently on the arm of a volunteer sitting in a chair. 'If you learn to do this, you can calm yourself down when you need to.'

I started off a sceptic, but I soon became a fan. Pretty soon, I invited Dorothy and her team – called the Ministry of Empowerment – to teach relaxation skills at the women's group.

BREAKING OUT

This wasn't pampering criminals. It wasn't indulging people whom society should punish. It was the start of the process of mending broken lives.

If you've kept yourself numb for a very long time, perhaps with alcohol or drugs, it's frightening when your feelings return. Sadness, guilt and anger can seem overwhelming. It's very important to be kind to yourself. You need to start in little ways, and then go on from there. We only had two hours a week, for twelve weeks. Sometimes it seemed like being sent to clear up after a hurricane – when all we had was a dustpan and brush. But at least we started sweeping.

Naomi joined in with the activities we offered in the group, but she didn't really listen. Then she disappeared for a while. She rang me up, months later, to tell me she was pregnant. After that, I never heard from her again. I asked her probation officer for news, but she'd heard nothing. Naomi was gone.

I hated that feeling of unfinished business, but by then I was used to it. She wasn't the only client who drifted away. I regretted every single one, and questioned myself over and over about why it had happened. Could I have done more? Could I have said something that connected? Could I have found a way?

All I could do was try harder. Use every scrap of knowledge I had gained to try to help the next one, and the next one, and the one after that.

*

NOVEMBER 1991

'You got a dress for the party, babe?'

Scully smiled at me across the dinner table. We loved to relax at Langan's in Piccadilly. That evening, as usual, the food and wine had been exquisite.

'Babe?' he said again. 'Janice? Is everything okay?'

It wasn't. For weeks I'd been listening to his plans for his fiftieth birthday, struggling not to put a downer on the whole idea. I knew he was excited, but my doubts were growing stronger every day.

'Oh yeah,' I answered. 'You just bet. I got a party dress. I'm sure you'll approve.'

He chuckled, but I knew I hadn't fooled him.

'It will be a nice evening,' he said gently. 'And I hope it's a new beginning for you too.'

'What d'you mean, babe?'

'The start of a happier time. I know how hard it's been for you since Sabrina.'

He'd held me in his arms while I screamed my loss and pain. We never bothered talking hearts and flowers – for us, there was no need. It was real.

'A new start sounds pretty good.' I tried to smile. 'No point dwelling on the past.'

When Sabrina learned that I knew what she had done, she ran away. She ran all the way to Canada, to stay with a relative in Toronto. I don't know what she thought I'd do, but she didn't need to fear me. I wouldn't have hurt her. Whatever she deserved – she had two children, and they at least were innocent. She'd made her choices. Karma will come knocking at her door. I tried to make peace with the event.

Meanwhile, Scully kept on planning his party. He'd hired a community hall in Peckham for a full sit-down dinner to celebrate his fiftieth birthday. He'd got a huge firm of caterers in. There was a champagne bar – and just in case the bar ran dry, a van on stand-by stocked with even more liquor. Hundreds of guests had been invited – major players, anyone who was anyone at all. A party for underworld royalty.

And that was the problem. Up to now, although his actions were known and his name was respected far and wide, the man himself had always worked in shadow. His party would bring him into the light. I couldn't understand why he wanted to do it. I was sure it was a terrible mistake.

'I'm going to arrive in a chauffeur-driven Rolls,' Scully told me.

We were in his office in Stockwell. As usual, his desk was inches deep in paper – invoices, receipts, scaffolding job requests.

'You are joking! Arrive in a *what*?'

'You know – a nice car. With a chauffeur.'

I took a deep breath.

'Can I just be honest with you?'

'Of course, darlin'.' He looked up from his accounts. His voice was mild and calm as always.

'It's just too much,' I told him.

'What's too much?'

'All this business with the chauffeur!'

'Why is it too much?'

'Because it's making you conspicuous. And that is something you have never been.'

He bristled. 'Well now – half a century is a conspicuous birthday.'

'Maybe for a business man. Maybe for an ordinary person. But that's not what you are.'

'I am an ordinary business man, Janice, and this is my business.' Scully gestured around his office. He was getting annoyed, which wasn't like him.

'Your business works when you stay below the radar, not when you ride round Peckham in a Rolls!'

'It's just a birthday party, babe!'

I'd made him angry. But he told the truth to me no matter what, and I would do the same.

'Scully – have your party. Just tone it down a bit, that's all. Forget the Rolls. Cut the guest list. Don't put yourself on offer.'

We fell silent for a moment. Such a serious disagreement was a shock to us both.

'Look – I didn't mean to be rude,' I said to him. 'But I am really worried and I want you to listen. You've always been a simple man – keep it that way. And what about your plans for retirement? This is not the time to draw attention.'

But Scully didn't listen. And in the end, I went along with his plans – I just couldn't bear to disappoint him. I drank a lot of champagne and I dressed up to the nines in the blingest gold-sequinned dress you ever saw. I wore gold Pinet shoes with sky-high heels and a gold baseball cap with dollar signs on it. That outfit told anyone who looked at me that I was Mama J – a boss in my own right. I knew how happy Scully was at the party, and I pushed down my feelings of unease. But by then it was too late.

One December night in 1991, the party blazed into life. The whole place was off the chain. There was fresh lobster and platters of oysters. The champagne flowed. There was live music and dancing. There were hundreds of guests – Rye Lane and Peckham High Street were rammed with Mercedes and BMW convertibles. Just around the corner was a Rolls-Royce Corniche belonging to the art dealer who'd sold Scully a piece for one of his houses.

But I spotted some other vehicles too, just up the street. I knew police surveillance when I saw it. Scully's birthday had attracted just the sort of attention that I'd feared. Mikey Shoes noticed too. He came up to me, frowning with concern.

'You realise the old bill are here?'

'Yes, I saw.'

'They're clocking every high-powered car that comes down this road. Names – faces – numberplates . . . '

'Yeah.'

'Does the big man know?'

'Maybe,' I said grimly. 'God knows what he's thinking.'

'This is not good, Janice. Not good at all.'

Just before three in the morning, I stepped outside.

The night was cold and still. The music and laughter of the party didn't carry very far. I lit a cigarette, and set out up Melon Road. My heels tapped the icy pavement. My breath hung in clouds. I came up to the first surveillance car with its two silent coppers, and tapped on the window.

A youngish, fair-haired man wound it down.

'You guys must be cold out here! And bored! You're missing the party!' I teased them.

'Not sure what you're talking about, love.'

'Wanna step inside and get a drink?' I asked them.

'That's okay, Goldie. We don't want to come.'

'So what you parked here for?'

They looked at each other.

'We like sitting in cars.'

'*Gwaan sit!*' I laughed.

'Enjoy your party night, Goldie,' he said to me.

I waved to them over my shoulder, and tapped back up the steps. I didn't realise at the time that his words had been a warning.

One week later, my mobile rang early in the morning. Sleepily, I picked it up from my side table.

'Janice?'

In a second, I was fully awake.

'Glen? What is it?'

'They've just gone with Scully.'

I felt sick. *That bloodclart party.*

The big man was under arrest. Glen and I didn't need to talk about what would happen next. We knew what we must do. Word on the street would quickly link us both to Scully – if we weren't linked already. Party time was over. We were going to be raided. We needed to prepare.

Scully knew who had informed on him. He told me this a few days later, when I visited him in Belmarsh. 'Someone dropped the 10p, Jan,' he said. He meant someone had grassed. He didn't tell me who. As always, he responded with calm.

When he was picked up, he'd had half an ounce in his pocket. He'd realised that police were approaching, and quickly dropped the half into the gutter. But the informer had given the address of a safe house in Brixton. He had work stored there. That location wasn't widely known. Whoever talked was close to him. Very close.

Scully was remanded in custody. After his arrest, the police took their time. The hammering and smashing on my door came in early February, first thing in the morning just like always. This time, Nadia knew nothing about it. She was on a sleepover with a friend – and by the time she got home from school next day, I'd got the place looking almost normal. The police found nothing. I always went home clean.

But the surveillance went on.

'Babe, mind what you're doing. They know you're on my right hand. Take a break,' said Scully on my next visit to Belmarsh. He was giving me an order.

We both knew what was coming. For a long time, we'd been on the ride – but this was time to pay. He told me to be patient and keep calm. He was facing time, and the authorities would confiscate everything of his they could find. His plan was to sit tight and do his bird. But I was in real danger. I had to lock up shop. I halted operations.

I looked out of my window next morning and saw an unmarked car parked in the road. I was uneasy as I left to do my shopping. Driving through Brixton, I felt raw and exposed.

Suddenly, my life was strange and empty. In the daytime, I could keep myself busy doing jobs around the flat. In the long, quiet evenings I drank more than I usually did, but it didn't help me sleep. Night-time was the hardest – I lay awake for hours, going over operations in my mind. Where might I have left incriminating material? We stored cash in lock-up garages right across south London. Had I checked that all the lock-ups were secure? Was it safe to do so now? How much more did the informant really know?

My sentences for stealing had been short – each one just a few weeks inside, so long I made sure that my behaviour was good. After that first dark time in Holloway, it had become just a dreary routine – a nuisance, the petty price for having what I wanted. But a stretch of many years would be – for me – a different, dreadful story. When I thought of it, fear enveloped me.

The cops were still a few steps behind. But the gap was closing fast between the things that they knew and the things that they could prove. Her Majesty was coming to collect.

Or was she?

By the middle of March, my sense of danger was fading. I'd been raided, after all – and nothing had been found. So they had nothing on me – or at least, there was nothing they could prove. Perhaps I'd been too worried, too panicked, when they made their move on Scully.

Doing business in London was still far too risky, so I stayed out of town. Shoes and I drove down to Bristol, to the Black and White cafe. Boxing carefully, we took just half a ki from one of our garage lock-ups. The sale went smoothly. When we got back to London, it was late. Just as I always did, I contacted Krystal. We met, and I left the money with her. I went home clean.

A few days later, I headed for Northampton to pick up some merchandise from Diego. Afterwards we followed the same careful routine. I went home clean as always. Everything was quiet.

By now it was late March. Two jobs had gone off without a problem. I was still uneasy, but I had things to do and people who were counting on me. A couple of weeks later, I went back to Northampton. I picked up another lot of work and headed home. On the way, I took a call from Mikey.

'Hey Janice – you been shoe shop? I want a three and a half, yeah?'

'Sure, babe. But it's going to be tomorrow now.'

'That's fine.'

I left the merchandise with Krystal that night and told her to bring it to me early in the morning. We met at Sainsbury's on Dog Kennel Hill. In the ladies', I separated out three and a half ounces and returned the rest to Krystal for safe-keeping. It was only a short drive to deliver Shoes his goods. As I pulled out of the car park in the bright morning sunshine, my mobile rang again. It was Mikey.

'Janice? It's me. Can you come round later on today? 'Bout four o'clock? Something just came up.'

I thought for a moment. It was early on a Saturday – no danger of a raid. Raids took place in the small dark hours of the morning. To keep the goods in my possession until later was a risk, but it was only a small one. And Mikey was a friend.

'Sure,' I said. 'No problem.'

I took his three and a half ounces of cocaine back to my flat. I put them in a Kurt Geiger shoe box in a cupboard in my hall. They were only going to be there until the afternoon. For the one and only time in my life, I broke the first rule. I didn't go home clean.

Once I'd put the merch away, I woke up Nadia and took her shopping in Knightsbridge. We had a lovely morning, then headed for home with her new dresses. She was happy and excited because Uncle Terry, my brother, was coming down from Leicester. He rang while we were driving to tell us he'd arrived and let himself in – he had his own set of keys to my flat. A few minutes later, Gill called, inviting me to lunch. We fixed to meet at Chelsea Harbour. I just had time to see her and still get to Mikey's later on. I called Terry back and he told me he'd take Nadia for pizza – her favourite lunch. Everyone was happy.

It was a bright, cold day in spring. The air was clear and fresh. I ran upstairs to say a quick hello to Terry. Then I kissed Nadia goodbye, stepped out of my front door and headed for Chelsea.

Suddenly, I heard the roar of engines. Screeching tyres. Three cars cornering fast, then pulling up outside.

A raid.

It can't be, I thought, *not at this time*. I stopped dead still on the first floor landing. It seemed impossible – unreal. Then I remembered – that shoebox. That Kurt Geiger shoebox.

A crackle of radios. A volley of slamming car doors. Crunching footsteps on the gravel. A shattering crash as the entry to the stairwell was shouldered open.

'Go! Go!' Men dressed in black and white came charging up the stairs. They were onto me in seconds. There was no time to run back to the flat, grab the shoebox, flush the package away or throw it out of the window.

I stepped back against the wall. It was instinctive, as though I believed that I might fade into the cream coloured paint. Perhaps the police would run right past me, playing out some other shadow story. In that story, they'd rip my flat apart but they'd find nothing. There'd be nothing there to find.

'Suspect's here!' 'We've got her!' they barked into the radios.

'Roger.'

As they grabbed me, up above I heard my front door bursting open and a terrified shriek. It was Nadia. Terry's voice yelled out, then dropped into sudden silence. 'What the fu – ?'

They marched me back upstairs, and shoved me through the front door.

'Nadia!' I shouted to her. 'Baby, it's okay!'

But it was not okay. It couldn't have been further from okay, because of what was in that shoebox.

I didn't hear Nadia reply. Perhaps her answer was drowned out by the static. It was hard to tell how many cops were in the flat – could be six or seven or more. The corridor was narrow and they jostled roughly past me as their search got under way. Right ahead I could see two of them tearing up the kitchen.

'Nadia!' I yelled again.

They marched me down the corridor and into the living room. Then I saw her and Terry, both face down on the carpet in handcuffs, their arms dragged painfully behind them. Nadia's head was on one side, her right cheek pressing hard into the carpet. Her eyes bulged with terror.

'What the fuck? Why is she in cuffs?' I screamed.

'Shut it, you dirty drug dealer!' snapped the officer who had me by the arm.

'Get the cuffs off my daughter, you bunch of cunts! Can't you see she's a child!'

They yanked open the cupboard in the corner of the living room. It was full of video cassettes. They pulled them out and threw them on the floor. I know they'd open every case. They'd open everything. Eventually, they would open the shoebox.

'She's twelve years old, you bastards! Get her out of handcuffs!' I was shrieking with fury.

Finally, the officer in charge seemed to hear me.

'How old is she?' He looked at Nadia.

'Twelve! Get my child out of handcuffs! Let her stand up!'

He spoke into the radio. There was so much background noise in the flat, and so much hissing and crackling, it was hard to hear the words. I caught something about a minor child – *confirm?*

'Confirm,' said the radio. 'Confirm. The daughter's twelve.'

He and his colleague exchanged glances.

'She doesn't look it,' he replied. He didn't really care. But they lifted Nadia to her feet and unlocked the cuffs. Her arms dropped to her sides. She stood there motionless, frozen with shock.

'It's okay, baby,' I said to her. Her blank expression scared me more than it would if she was screaming and crying.

They put me in cuffs too, and bundled the three of us into my bedroom. They pushed us onto the bed and we sat there in a row. Terry looked furious, but he wouldn't make eye contact – he just lowered his head and kept shaking it slowly. I said Nadia's name a couple of times, trying to connect with her. She wouldn't look at me either. She hadn't made a sound since that first shriek. From every room we heard the sounds of searching – scraping and clattering, objects falling to the floor. From the kitchen came the noise of breaking glass.

I knew that they would find what was in the Kurt Geiger shoebox. And when they found it, it was going to be my fault. As I waited for their discovery, the pain in my cramped arms felt almost welcome – a distraction from my all-consuming fury. I cursed myself to hell. How could I be so stupid? It was the first rule Scully ever taught me, the simplest law of safety. When he heard about all this, he wouldn't believe I broke it.

Always go home clean.

They marched into the bedroom and opened my wardrobe, throwing all my clothes onto the floor. Before they did, they checked the pockets, and rolled each garment tightly to make sure there was nothing hidden in the lining. They dragged out all my shoes and searched inside them. They opened my dressing table drawers and tossed my underwear onto the bed. 'Very nice, love. Very attractive.' Their tone of voice was mocking. They ran their hands right to the backs of the drawers to make sure that they were empty, then pulled the drawers right out and looked behind.

Keep looking in here, I thought. *Go on. Go through*

everything. Make all the mess you like. Search the kitchen and the bathroom. Just don't look in the hall.

At last I heard the hall cupboard door swinging open. The handle bumped against the wall – it had happened so many times before that there was a deep scuff in the paint. I heard the clunk of box lids falling, then shoes dropping onto the lino. The empty boxes being flung to one side. Any second now – it was coming. And it was all my own doing. I held my breath and closed my eyes.

'BINGO!' shouted a voice. It was full of triumph. I'd been caught in possession of cocaine.

3.6 ounces is not a large amount. It's large for personal use, but it doesn't prove a dealing operation. That was what my brief said. Gilles Toussaint insisted there was doubt – and doubt was all we needed. So expect a custodial sentence, he told me, but it won't be a long one. Between five and seven years, with half of it to serve with good behaviour. I began to have some hope.

The first blow came when bail was refused. The second was the news of Scully's sentence, which came through while I was on remand. He'd been given sixteen years. We had known it would be bad – but this was worse than we'd thought. The third blow was finding out how much the cops knew. They'd been following me – I had no idea how long. They were aware of the syndicate's bank accounts too – or at least aware of some of them – and knew that we held money offshore. That helped the prosecution. They would use the bank accounts to convince the jury I was a bigger player than I was admitting.

Still, the case against me, Toussaint said, wasn't likely to succeed as well as they were hoping. 'There's not enough evidence. What they've got – it's conjecture. There's not a good enough case. With the quantity of cocaine you had, there's no real proof that you're supplying.' I clung to his reassuring words. My careless mistake might also help me, he went on. 'A major dealer never keeps their drugs at home. Only lower level people do that. But that's where yours were found.' As if I needed telling.

As the trial date approached, I thought it might not be as bad as I'd been fearing. I told Nadia when she came for her next visit, but she didn't respond. She seemed detached, not looking happy to see me, or upset when it was time to leave. But if she couldn't talk to me right now, I understood. I kept smiling and tried to reassure her that my sentence wasn't going to be too long.

DECEMBER 1992

I dressed smartly for the trial at Kingston Crown Court. I wore a pinstriped Gucci suit, and carried a black Gucci handbag. To me, these were ordinary things. I intended to show the court respect with my appearance. But the judge saw things quite differently. His summing up was rough.

'You are clearly an intelligent woman,' he told me.

'I will never understand why you continue to commit crime. You come to court in your designer wear. You present yourself as a minor player. I'm not convinced by that. You have important connections in the drug dealing world. One of those connections has just received a substantial sentence. I must protect the public from your criminal activities.'

The jury found me guilty. Then the judge passed his sentence. It was much, much longer than Gilles Toussaint had told me it would be. I was completely unprepared. How could these barristers, these experts, have got all this so wrong?

I began my sentence burning with anger. I raged against my brief. I raged against the judge. I raged at the informant who'd grassed up Scully and put me in the spotlight. But most of all, I raged against myself for my bad judgement. I knew that it was I who'd brought my whole world crashing down.

**18 December 1992, Kingston upon Thames
 Crown Court.
Possessing controlled drug with intent to
 supply – Class A. Imprisonment – nine years.**

12

GREEN CHANNEL

IZZIE WAS STILL TERRIBLY thin. She thought she looked great. I thought it was time she had some dinner.

When she started coming to our women's group meetings, she took the sandwiches we gave her and put them in her bag. She told me she was going to eat them later. But it grew clearer and clearer as the weeks went by that she wasn't eating anything much. She was going to have to eat them in the meetings, where I could see her.

I thought she'd make a fuss, but she didn't. Whenever I set her a boundary, she liked it. For all her smart talk, she was young in her thinking, still in need of direction. If someone would mother her, this girl would respond.

'Izzie,' I said one afternoon at our meeting, 'where's your mum?'

'Ohhh . . . ' Izzie said with a frown. 'She never listens. She doesn't understand.'

'Does she call you?'

'Yeah, yeah, but there's no point in talking to her. She just goes on and on. And all that stuff with my stepdad – you know. That was her fault.'

'In your notes it says that when you went to court, your mum was there.'

'Yeah, yeah, she was. She turned up.'

For some people, family is everything. For others, it's nothing but a nightmare. For so many in the criminal justice system, families are where misery begins. There's abuse, there's addiction, there's violence. But Izzie's mum was trying to stay in contact. And when her daughter was in trouble, she had been there. Izzie needed to make this relationship stronger. Her mum might be a positive person in her life.

When I suggested contacting her mother on her behalf, she told me she'd never speak to me again if I did. A week later, she'd had a think. 'Okay,' she said, 'let's talk to her.' A short while after that, she was angry all over again. She wanted her mother – and yet, at the same time, she didn't. She was terribly confused.

I thought of Nadia. How much she'd been prepared to forgive me. And the difference it made to my life. I picked up the phone and I rang Izzie's mother.

JANUARY 1993

My nine-year sentence changed everything. When the judge spoke the words, I knew it meant the end of the life I had been living. It felt like the end of the world.

Facing those nine years meant big decisions – most of all, about Nadia. Emmanuel's father was American, and back in 1990, he'd moved to the States to be closer to the rest of his family. He got a good job with New York Transit. He did well for himself. But he was still a loving father – exactly as I'd known from the beginning he would be. He made regular trips to see his daughter in London, and I paid for Nadia to fly out every two or three months.

A few days after I was sentenced, he flew over again – but this time, everything was different. He came to see me in Holloway. Our conversation was blurred with stress and shock, and afterwards I barely remembered what either of us said. But Emmanuel insisted that our daughter should move to the States to live with him while I served my time. It was dangerous for her to stay in London. As my child, she was exposed out there on the street. Both her grandmothers were kind and devoted, but they couldn't keep her safe.

How could I argue? I knew he was right. I had no choice, but still I barely ate and barely slept as preparations were made for Nadia to leave. I was terrified of losing her, but even more afraid of what might happen if she didn't go away. Nadia herself said almost nothing. When she came to visit me, she stared at the floor. She seemed to have drifted to a place where I couldn't reach her.

The day she left, I lay alone on my narrow prison bed, staring through the window of my cell at a tiny square of cloudy London sky. I imagined her plane high and lonely in those clouds as it carried her away. As she flew, I felt the life-giving cord that stretched between us pulling tighter and tighter till it dragged three thousand miles.

All these years ahead, while she would be far away. A few minutes on the phone would be all that we had. The length of that time was unbearable. Daggers of pain shot through my belly. I thought my flesh would split and tear wide open. And then the cord broke. Its frayed ends went spinning through the sky, scattering drops of my blood that fell like rain on the roof of Holloway prison. My Nadia was gone.

NOVEMBER 1997

Happy birthday to you!
Happy birthday to you!
Happy birthday, dear Nadiaaaa!
Happy birthday to you!

My sentence had seemed endless, but now it was finished. There she was. I stood in front of her, holding my breath.

The face that I had pictured every day had changed. She was beautiful, a radiant and smiling young woman. It was wonderful to see the friends and love that my daughter had around her – but utterly impossible to me that she could be eighteen.

Nadia's party was in New York City – her home now, with her father. The trip was a gift from Emmanuel.

With my criminal record, I thought I might be stopped at the airport and prevented from entering the country, but everything went smoothly.

It was two weeks since my release from prison on licence. I'd been in the States for three days, staying in a nearby hotel, trying to adjust to the time zone change and the strangeness of freedom. I hadn't spoken to Nadia yet. Emmanuel had warned me to hold back.

'Janice – you need to understand what she's been through. Please give her time.'

I longed so much to see her, but what difference would it make to wait for just a few more days? Now her eighteenth birthday cake felt very heavy.

'Can you manage, Jan?' Emmanuel asked me as I picked the plate up. I nodded. Suddenly I was too nervous to speak.

Her friends had tied a blindfold on Nadia, and I was to carry the cake over to her. As the last strains of singing died away and she blew out all the candles in one go, someone loosened her blindfold. It fell from her eyes and cheers and whistles filled the room. She looked straight at me.

'Happy birthday, baby,' I whispered.

'Mommy?' Her face held disbelief. *'Mommy?'*

'Yes, baby. You didn't think I'd miss your big birthday?'

I couldn't hold the cake any longer. I lowered it carefully onto a table. My hands were trembling.

'Oh, Mommy,' she said. I held out my arms and she took two steps forward. I'd waited five years to hold her close. Carefully, as though we were trying not to break something, the two of us embraced.

Three days later I was sitting in Emmanuel's kitchen. I felt agitated and unhappy.

Once the party was over, they'd invited me round. I met Emmanuel's American wife, Nadia's stepmom, who was welcoming and kind. Whilst we all chatted, I couldn't help staring at Nadia. I stared so much, I realised I was making her uneasy.

The family had a lovely home, but my daughter's bedroom shocked me. Somehow I'd expected it to look the way it used to – full of her old things. But there was nothing in it – not one single item – that I recognised. The clothes in her closet, the pictures on the wall – all of them belonged to a person I didn't know at all. The teenage Nadia who'd done her home-work here at this desk, gone to school in these sneakers and brushed her hair in front of that mirror wasn't the south London schoolgirl I'd held in my memory every day since December 1992. That girl had grown up to be a stranger – one with a definite American accent.

A gulf of not-knowing had opened up between us. Once we had chatted without thinking, but now, as she came into the kitchen, I nervously considered what to say.

'Are you going to make some lunch, babe?'

'No. Why – are you hungry?'

'No – no. Not at all. I thought you might be, that's all.'

'I'll wait for Dad to get in, and see if he'd like a sandwich.'

'Where is he?'

'Oh – he went shopping.'

My God – this terrible formality between us. I didn't know how to make it stop. How could I get close to her again?

'Does Dad always do the shopping?' I asked, just filling silence.

'Yeah – he drives past the store on his way home from work, so . . . '

'That's nice of him.'

But it turned out there was something much worse than an awkward conversation. As I was getting ready to leave for London, I upset her. She asked if I'd like her to drive me, but it was late in the afternoon already. I said no. Our understanding of each other turned out to be so shallow that we could argue about a lift to the airport.

'I'll get a taxi,' I said. 'I don't want you taking risks like that.'

My words touched off something in Nadia. She stood still in the middle of the room.

'Mom – really? Oh my God. Are we going to go there? *You don't want me taking risks?* Did you just say that?'

'Baby, I mean – it's quite far. It'll be dark before you're driving back.'

'And you don't think I can manage it? You do know I drive every day?'

'Yes, yes, I know. I just thought – '

'No, you didn't. You didn't think. Not ever. Not about me. If you had – '

Her voice died away.

'Nadia, sweetheart. I didn't mean to upset you.'

'You don't get to decide what I do, Mom.'

'Of course not. I was just worried. I'm your mother.'

I tried to smile, but she didn't smile back.

'Do you think so?' she said. 'Because I don't. You weren't my mother when I was sent away and you were put in prison. A voice on the phone isn't a mother. You kept on asking me – *Are you okay, baby? Are you okay?* What was I supposed to say?'

She closed her eyes and shook her head.

'I wasn't okay. But there was no point telling you. What could you have done? A mother is someone who is *there.*'

I'd already decided that when I made it home to London, I'd get straight back to business. What did I have to lose, now that Nadia was barely a part of my life? My work was all that I had left.

As my plane took off from JFK, I leaned my head against the window. We climbed up into the night, away from Emmanuel and his family, away from the new life my daughter had made without me. The million sparkling lights of Manhattan Island ended, replaced by the blackness of the sea.

*

I'd gone into prison angry. I came out angry still. And when I realised how badly I'd lost touch with business, it made me feel much worse. It was hard to take my place again when I'd been out of the game for years. There'd been a shift in the landscape of the street. Some major loyalties had been broken.

You gotta sit back, Scully's partner Glen said to me. *The street miss good people like you. But the street ain't stayed the same.* Although I didn't want to listen, I knew that he was right.

I contacted Nana, an old contact from Ghana, just to get a feel of how things were. Nothing prepared me for the hostile voice on the phone.

'One of your people robbed me two ki!'

One of my people? This had nothing at all to do with me. I had an A-grade reputation with all my working links. So who would pull a stunt like this? I tried to explain to Nana that this person had only claimed to know me, giving one or two details that anyone listening to the word on the street might have heard. It was some small-timer, bigging himself up.

But Nana wasn't the only one who'd heard bad word on me and believed it. When Scully and I vanished from the street, ambitious smaller players moved in to fill the space we'd left behind. Many of them claimed to have worked with us – whether or not it was true – and grabbed the good name we had earned. Thanks to them, my reputation had been very badly damaged.

I wondered how much longer I could carry on like this. I decided that I wanted to retire – just as soon as I could afford it. I started to look round, searching for a way to make the money that I needed to get out.

Eventually, an opportunity came up.

Not long after my release, Mummy died. She left me a small legacy. I used it to fly out to the Caribbean and talk to some contacts. I was introduced to Stedroy, an importer I'd never met before. He told me about a million-pound shipment of marijuana he would send every six to eight months from St Vincent to Southampton. Did I want in?

A million-pound deal sounded tempting. It wasn't just the money – this would be a chance to fix everything. Restore my reputation that the street had harmed so badly. Set myself up for retirement. Then go out on a high – as a winner in the game, not as a loser.

It was my final throw of the dice. It would have to be the throw of a lifetime.

Nadia told me she had no plans to return to England. She graduated from high school and started working. Then Emmanuel asked if I'd like to come back over to see her again. I was grateful to have a second chance – and we'd both had a bit of time to think. I hoped beyond hope that this time, we could make our relationship better.

We spent the time doing ordinary things – some shopping, going out for meals. Nadia showed me the places where she hung out with her friends. I met some of them. Her life seemed a little less unknowable now, and I found that a comfort.

'Let's focus on the positive,' I said to her, as we sat in a Taco Bell on Boston Road, a day or so before I was due to fly back home. 'You're doing well and my prison time is over. I know how hard it was for you, I really do. But I hope things can get better.'

Slowly, Nadia stirred her coffee. Her dark eyes were fixed on the swirling circles in the drink. She watched them going round for so long that I started to wonder if she'd heard. Then she looked up.

'Mom,' she said suddenly, urgently. 'Mom – you've got to promise.'

She sounded eight years old. Behind this sophisticated young woman with her job and her car, I heard the voice of the little girl she'd once been.

'You can't go back to that lifestyle,' she said. 'You mustn't. But every single day, I worry that you will.'

I reached out to touch her hand, but she jerked it away. She bumped her coffee mug. Coffee splashed right across the table.

'Dammit!'

I jumped up and fetched a paper tissue. As we mopped, the tissue got soaked through and began to fall apart. I had to fetch another. When my hand brushed hers, I realised she was shaking. We looked at each across a swimming brownish mess flecked with bits of disintegrating paper.

'No more jobs, Mom. No more drug deals. No more Nasty Girl business. Please stop. You've got to *promise*.'

I wanted to give her the reassurance she needed. I wanted it so much. And there was only going to be one more job. Just one last time, and I was done. Then I would keep my word forever.

'Darling,' I said to her, 'forget Mama J. I'm your mama first of all. And I promise.'

I promise, except for this one job. Except for the biggest of them all.

I knew that what I told her was a lie. But when I said it, I meant it to be true. My *grand finale*. Nadia would never need to know.

OCTOBER 2015

'Hello? Is that Janice?'

'Yes, it is. Who's speaking?'

'It's Laura. Isabelle's mum.'

'Hi there, Laura. Thanks for calling back.'

It was the third time we'd spoken. She sounded just like Izzie on the phone. She had the same lightness in her voice. But right now, I could hear that she was close to crying.

'I wanted to tell you – she came round here again,' Laura said.

'When was this?'

'It was yesterday. I'm afraid that she – '

Her voice cracked, and then the tears came.

'Laura? What happened?'

'She wasn't here for long. She said she wanted a shower. I said okay. Then after she left, I realised – '

I didn't need to hear the rest. I already knew.

'Oh, Laura. I'm sorry.'

'She'd gone into my purse! She just came round to steal!'

'Laura,' I said, 'it's awful that this happened.'

'I thought that things were better, after last time. You know – when she had that list with her? The five things she had to do.'

Izzie had showed her mum my framework for her day. It listed the tasks she had to finish – the tidying, the shopping, the shower. It was part of my plan to put structure in her life, starting in the small ways first of all.

'And she was doing it, Janice! She really was!'

'I know she was, Laura. And she does, very often.'

'So then why – '

'I feel the same as you do,' I said. 'I want her to be better. If I could press a button and make it happen faster – I would. But recovery is always up and down. She'll make progress, but then she'll slip sometimes. We need to be patient.'

Laura sighed. She knew she'd let Izzie down in the past. Her love was imperfect. What I wanted was for mother and daughter to discover that imperfect was enough.

'Janice,' she whispered, 'I think you are the only person she listens to.'

'I tell you,' I said, 'it doesn't feel that way sometimes!'

Laura gave a shaky little laugh.

'Does she argue with you too?' she asked me.

Oh, yes. Izzie argued a lot. As her trust in me was growing, I used it to push back. She was telling me the truth about the things she was doing to get herself the money for drugs. And I was giving my opinion. The danger she was putting herself into, again and again – it was crazy, self-destructive. Why was she so determined to mess up her life?

'I've got it under control, Jan,' she'd mutter, staring at the ground.

'Under control! Look in the mirror, and tell me what you see. Then tell me if you think that's what being in control looks like!'

She'd sink her head even lower.

'I know, Jan. I know.'

I didn't tell her she looked beautiful or sexy or smart. I told her that she looked a hot mess. I took away the meaningless, manipulative flattery of Leroy, Mr B and Jay, and in its place I gave her the truth. She was learning that I wasn't going to lie. It was because I wouldn't lie that we were going to get her through this, and out the other side.

'Ah, Laura,' I said. 'You know Izzie. Yes, she argues. But she's a good girl. She's making progress. On her list, every morning, she has to look at herself in the mirror and tell herself that she deserves happiness. The more she hears it, the more she'll believe it.'

I heard Laura draw a long, shaky breath.

'Janice – please tell me the truth. Is this working, what you're doing?'

'Yes, Laura,' I said. 'Yes, it is. You just need to hold on, because it's working. You're going to get her back.'

*

Stedroy used a reliable green channel from St Vincent to Southampton. 'Green channel' means an international pathway through ports or airports, docks and customs inspections, where the only checks on goods are carried out by people on the drug supplier's payroll. The shipment goes through smoothly, no questions asked.

I was the one asking questions. Stedroy reassured me that he knew what he was doing. 'Don't worry, Miss Jan,' he said to me, 'this product will be on your doorstep.' He gave me the codename of Sandra. My real identity would be nowhere near the job.

At the UK end, I used my old friend Diego. He and Mank had never let me down in the past. One of Diego's guys – yet another new name to me, Vernon – would be my contact. He would take control as soon as the consignment left the ship in Southampton. He'd done plenty of business in the old days, Diego said, back before the airports tightened their security. Vernon's mules used to bring in drugs through Heathrow and leave them in bins inside the terminal buildings. He'd had a payroll of cleaners there, doing his collections. Diego still vouched for him, though recently he seemed to have dropped out of sight. I thought that was okay. My consignment would travel from Southampton to London via a holding point in Leicester. The holding point would be a nightclub called the Apex. The Apex's owner was on board. That sounded okay too.

The consignment was a thousand ki of high quality weed. At £1,500 a ki, its total street value was a million and a half. I couldn't pay my personnel up front, so everything was going to have to wait until the goods had been sold. Then, allowing for all payments and expenses, I would clear a million. A mill was what I needed to retire. That also seemed okay.

There was just one thing that wasn't – a missing piece of vital information. On the last job, Adam, the nightclub owner in Leicester, hadn't been paid – and he was angry. He didn't know who'd robbed him, but he wanted to find out. All he knew was – it had to be the person who had set up the green channel.

All the time I was making my plans, no one told me this. If I'd known, I'd never have touched the job at all.

I presented my visiting order at the prison gate. It was late January 2001. At HMP Swaleside on the Isle of Sheppey in Kent, Scully was just over nine years into his sixteen-year sentence.

I knew I wouldn't find him too downhearted. Scully was prepared to do his time because he knew what he had. When his sentence was over, his future was worth having. He was patient. He knew how to ride the storm.

In through the two security doors with intensive checks and searches. My photo was taken. My bag and coat went into a locker. All I could take into the visiting room was the locker key and small change for drinks and snacks at the WRVS counter in the corner. I found my numbered chair. In five minutes, they would let him come and see me. I looked around and patted my hair.

The visiting room was large and noisy. Its lights were high and harsh – that endless prison glare I remembered so well. The buzz of many voices and the sound of kids crying were magnified by echoes. The sound would make a screen.

As soon as I saw Scully, I couldn't help but smile.

'Hello, princess,' he said. 'Y'alright?'

As we sat down at the table, I reached out and took his hands. He closed his eyes and smiled while he listened to me talk. When I'd been chatting for a while, he opened them and said, 'But Janice, what else?'

We had a vibe connection. He'd always sensed when I was planning something.

'What d'you mean, what else?' I said, trying not to smile.

'Janice, what you up to?'

'You're right. I'm doing one more thing. It's planned for March.'

His eyes narrowed.

'What's one more thing?'

I told him about the green channel and my set-up with Stedroy, Vernon and Adam. The longer I explained, the more deeply Scully frowned.

'I'm not good with this, Jan,' he said to me.

'It's calm, babe, it's calm. When the stuff comes off the boat, I won't even be in England. I've fixed to be abroad. I'm hands-off. There's no connection with me.'

'Hmmm,' he muttered. 'These guys. Stedroy, Vernon, the nightclub owner – what was his name – ?'

'Adam.'

'Who are they really? You don't have that information.'

'But I was out of the game for five years. Sure, I don't know all the links. But it's cool. I got personal recommendations.'

'I tell you, babe,' said Scully, 'it's not good.'

This wasn't what I'd wanted to hear. I found myself becoming defensive.

'Look, I got space between me and the job. And these guys are okay. I can trust them.'

Scully laid his hand on my arm. *I'll let you think on that,* he'd always say when he wasn't sure I was following the right course of action. But not this time. I'd never known him be so direct before.

'No, Jan. Don't go for it.'

Up to now, I'd been confident I'd made the right decision. *The grand finale – the final role of the dice.* But when Scully wasn't with me, I couldn't help but feel a shiver of unease.

'Babe,' I said again. 'It's okay. I've done my homework.'

Scully sighed.

'I know you. You'll do what you want, not what someone else says. Not even what I say. But I'm warning you – not this. This don't feel good.'

*

When I'd told Scully I was going to be hands-off on the green channel deal, I had meant it. Ten days before the shipment was due to dock in England, I caught a plane. Being out of the country reduced the risk that I'd be linked to the job even further. I'd left no paper trail, held no meetings in England, made no phone calls. I was certain there was absolutely nothing that could tie me to the goods.

The consignment arrived in Southampton. It cleared the port without a hitch. Next day, a driver took the two crates of weed, each one about the size of a two-seater sofa, up to Leicester for storage at the Apex. Payment for the transfer was £25k – danger money. Moving merchandise is always the point of highest risk. The journey went smoothly.

Once Stedroy confirmed that the consignment was in Leicester, I flew back to Heathrow. I was close to the finish line now. It was time for Vernon, my contact, to do his job.

The phone in my flat rang very early in the morning. Not the mobile. The landline.

'Is that Janice?'

'Is that *Vernon*?'

I could hardly believe it. He started to speak, but I cut in.

'So Vernon – this is my landline. Why don't you call back on the mobile?'

I hung up on him. Too late, though – the call had been made and it was traceable. It could link us together. What a stupid, unnecessary risk. *I thought this guy was meant to be sensible.*

He called me back, and things got even worse. The shipment, he told me, couldn't move today. The driver had a problem with his licence. Fair enough – I was taking no chances, so using a driver who didn't have a licence would be foolish. But why was I hearing this? Vernon was my contact – it was his job to sort these problems out. Why hadn't he arranged another driver? I asked him where the weed was being stored while we waited for the transport to London to be sorted.

'Uh – it's waiting in the Apex. In the foyer.'

Surely I hadn't heard him right.

'Uh – who's waiting in the foyer?'

'The shipment.'

'What do you mean – it's in the foyer?'

'There's two big crates. They won't fit in the store-room.'

'A thousand ki of weed and it's sitting in the front hall of some nightclub? Are you insane?' I yelled into the phone. Vernon coughed and muttered.

'And you've got no other driver – is that right?' I demanded.

More muttering. This guy just wasn't up to the job. Instantly, I made a decision. There was only one way that this problem would get fixed.

'Okay,' I said. 'I'll get the transfer done myself.'

Ninety minutes later I was ready to go. I'd rung a mate and quickly rented a van.

'I'm going up country. Should anybody visit, you don't know nothing,' I told him.

'Okay, Jan.'

The only way to run any underworld business is to be open and honest. Always tell a colleague exactly what's going down. That way, if there's a visit from the law, the colleague knows how to deal with it. And you've been on the level.

I paid my mate in cash. I took no credit cards, no driving licence, no ID at all. I left my phones at home. I picked up Vernon, who didn't have much to say for himself, and we set out to drive up to Leicester. At Watford Gap services I stopped, found a payphone and rang the Apex nightclub.

'Hello? Who's this?' said a voice that must be Adam's.

I noticed it immediately – *this guy is wired*. I could understand why – he wanted the shipment gone from his premises. Holding on to product is the biggest risk anyone can run. I'd be angry too if there'd been an unexpected delay. And I was pretty wired myself. So I didn't focus on the tension in Adam's voice.

'Adam? My name's Sandra. I understand that you have something for me.'

'Are you Stedroy's sister?' he demanded.

I thought the question was strange. No one had told me that Stedroy had a sister. I thought quickly. Most of all, I wanted Adam to trust me.

'Yes,' I said. 'I am.'

'Oh,' he said. He still sounded annoyed. 'Right then. I expected Stedroy. So it's your operation?'

BREAKING OUT

I don't like all these enquiries.

'Yeah, yeah, it's mine. You ready?'

'Yeah. I got something to collect here.'

'That's good. I'm on my way.'

'How long you going to be?'

I'd had enough of questions. I put the phone down.

Fifty minutes later we drove up to the Apex in the centre of Leicester. When Adam saw us, he was astonished. He hadn't been expecting us for hours. He seemed angry that we'd arrived so early. When I rang from Watford Gap and told him I was on my way, he'd thought that I was setting out from London. But so what? A couple of hours here or there didn't matter. Some guy's bad mood about it wasn't my problem. Being on the road, involved in transport – the riskiest part of the whole operation – made me desperately impatient to get the transfer done.

It took three of Adam's guys to load the crates into the van. While they did the lifting, I stayed behind the wheel. Adam hung around me the whole time – he kept asking if I fancied a sandwich, a coffee, a cold drink . . . he just wouldn't let me alone. All I wanted was to leave and be on my way to London. But still he kept on talking, putting questions, trying to find out who I was.

Why does he care anyway? This thing ain't personal. It's business.

'Stedroy never said his sister was in business. I thought he managed it himself,' said Adam.

I shrugged.

'We're good mates, him and me,' Adam went on, 'and he never said a word about you.' He was scowling.

'I'm not close to my brother,' I told Adam.

'But you run his operation?'

'We sometimes work together. Stedroy's based at home.'

'Right.' He still stared at me suspiciously. What was this guy's problem? I just wanted to leave Leicester. Now the van was loaded at last. This was it. Suddenly I was buzzing, hyper-aware of everything around me.

'Let's go,' I said to Vernon. The last thing I saw in the mirror as I pulled out of the alley alongside the Apex was Adam. He was standing there quite still, shoulders hunched, face grim, staring after us. I'd have thought he would be pleased that we were leaving.

Driving back south, I began to settle down. An hour went by. An hour and a half. We'd got onto the motorway at Junction 21, and now we were approaching 14, just seventy miles from London. I was still on high alert, watching carefully up front and behind. Everything seemed normal.

Just relax.

Then I glimpsed the helicopter high up in the sky, the size of an insect, following the traffic pouring south. It was very far away – but when I saw it, I clenched my hands tighter on the wheel.

Keep calm. It's nothing. It must be an accident some-where up ahead. Or maybe they're spotting for a stolen vehicle.

I looked in the wing mirror. Now the sky was empty.

Vernon hadn't noticed anything. Better not to mention what I'd seen. I turned up the radio and fixed my eyes on the vehicles in front.

Just keep driving. That chopper has nothing at all to do with us.

Dusk began to fall. The first drivers were switching on their headlights. Another five miles passed. The exit sign for Milton Keynes came up.

Suddenly, the 'copter was back. I heard its rotors' thwack-thwack-thwack before I saw it. This time it was closer and much lower. It swept past us directly overhead.

'*What's this?*' Vernon asked me, sharply.

I peered upwards. The helicopter swooped to the right, away from the road. Just for a moment I felt a small, false hope. I clutched at it. *Perhaps the 'copter's gone.*

'It's nothing,' I said. I willed it to be true. Then, as I glanced sideways at Vernon, meeting his eyes for just a second, I saw how close he was to panic. His terror spread instantly to me.

Hold on. Stay calm. Think. We don't know for sure this is a problem. The 'copter might be nothing to do with us at all.

I thought about dipping – edging up to a mark in the West End. If my heart was racing, it was as if the mark could sense an agitation in the air. I learned to slow my breathing to their rhythm – in and out, in and out – nice and easy. Always stay in control.

'*Relax, man,*' I said to Vernon. '*Not much furth–*'

CHUKACHUKACHUKACHUKACHUK.

With a pounding roar, the 'copter was back. This time it was right above our heads.

'What the fuck?' cried Vernon.

In the wing mirror, I saw a bright blue wink in the traffic behind. Then there were two winks side by side. They were the flashing lights of police cars, closing on us fast. My mouth went bone dry. The thudding of my heart seemed to shake my whole body.

'I think we've been busted,' I said flatly. Vernon let out a dreadful wail and hid his face in his hands. No use asking him what we should do. The police cars had come right up behind us. Their headlights double-flashed, ordering us to stop. A third car, an unmarked brown Volvo, suddenly crossed in front of us and slowed sharply down. They forced us to a halt in the middle of the second lane.

Pandemonium. Voices ordering us to get out of the van. We clambered out into the roar of the M1. Up above, the chopper was still circling. Around us, dusk was turning into night. Blue lights flashed in the black. As voices yelled from the darkness, I was blinded and confused.

'Stay where you are!'

'Keep still!'

'Put your hands where I can see them!'

'I said stay where you are!'

Two of them grabbed Vernon, and two grabbed me. They handcuffed my arms behind my back.

'You are under arrest for being concerned in the

supply of a class B drug to another, contrary to section 28 of the Misuse of Drugs Act 1971.'

We're busted. How did this happen? What the fuck?

The police drove us back up the M1 to Leicester in silence. In the police station, I was put in a cell on my own. Away from doors and windows, under artificial light, I lost all track of time. My brain felt hot-wired – tiny recollections of the day started sparking and jumping. Suddenly I realised, crystal clear, what I should have seen much earlier. Something had been wrong from the start. Right from that first phone call I made at Watford Gap.

There's been an informant. Someone dropped 10p.

Why weren't we arrested as soon as we left the Apex nightclub with the shipment in the van? Why did they let us get away? All that trouble and expense to chase after us, to scramble the helicopter. Why not just stop us leaving Leicester?

There could only be one reason. When we got there, they weren't ready. They thought we'd be arriving later on. Who could have told them that? It had to be Adam.

I remembered his surprise when we turned up. How he'd tried to delay me with his coffee and his chit-chat. Why would he do that? Everyone – always – moved product on as quickly as they could.

Suddenly, I saw what must have happened. He'd told the police that we were hours away from Leicester. Then we turned up early. Their plan to arrest us had gone wrong. I remembered my last glance back in the rear-view mirror – the grim, tense expression on Adam's face. I'd walked into a trap.

I remembered a question he had asked me that didn't quite make sense. In my rush and anxiety, I'd let it just go by.

'Oh,' he'd said. *'Right then. I expected Stedroy. So it's your operation?'*

Why would he ask that? The whole entire time, he'd been probing me with questions. Why would he be digging for extra information? Why did it matter so much who I was?

If Adam grassed, he must think he has a problem with me. But he doesn't! We never even did business before. Why would he do this?

Alone in my cell, my mind went on racing. How long did I have until the questioning started? How could I explain why I was driving that van?

Keep it simple. I'll say I thought the load was wooden carvings from St Vincent, imported by a friend. I picked them up as a favour. That's all I know. There's no other information I can give you.

But Nadia. Oh my God. Nadia. I thought of our last conversation, and the words I had spoken.

'No more jobs, Mom. No more drug deals. You've got to promise..'

'Darling,' I'd said to her. *'I promise.'*

As I imagined how she'd feel and what she'd say when she heard of my arrest, a wave of despair rose through my body.

'Your solicitor's arrived now, Janice.'

That meant it was already next morning. I'd had no sleep at all. I couldn't think any more. There was nothing left to do here but play dumb.

'Have you been in trouble before?' Sasha Weller-Greene asked me.

'Yes.' My solicitor was listening, making careful notes. He looked like a school headmaster, tall and distinguished, with grey swept-back hair. He sat along-side me at the table, opposite two plain-clothes policemen.

The questioning took hours. I stalled and kept on stalling. I knew it wasn't working – nobody believed me. My only hope was that maybe – just maybe – they couldn't link me directly to the shipment. I'd made so much effort to keep from leaving a trail. If they couldn't make a definite connection, perhaps they might still let me go.

'What were you in trouble for?'

'Possession of cocaine.'

'When was this?'

'It was nearly ten years ago.'

'Nothing since?'

'No.'

'What do you know about the crates in your van?'

'I had a phone call from a friend, asking me to do him a favour. To go and pick them up.'

'Did he say what they were?'

'Art. Carvings, he said. Things he had imported.'

'And you did this?'

'Yes.'

'Just like that – you drove all that way as a favour to a friend?'

'Yes.'

'And your other friend, Vernon, who came with you?'

'He's not a friend. We only just met.'

Mr Weller-Greene and one of the police officers exchanged glances.

'So you didn't know Vernon received an eighteen-year prison sentence for supplying drugs, but absconded last year? You weren't aware of that?'

'No.' And it was true. I'd known nothing about it. Now I understood Vernon's panic – his cry in the van as the police cars closed in. He'd known exactly how long he was going to be in jail.

'What were you supposed to do with these carvings, when you got them to London?' asked Mr Weller-Greene.

'Phone my friend and ask where I should take them.'

'Who were you going to phone?'

'I can't tell you.'

'Janice, you must give us a name. It's extremely important.'

'I know it's important, but I can't.'

There was a very long silence. I wondered just how obvious it was that I had no name to give. I had no story.

'I can only help you if you tell me the truth,' Mr Weller-Greene said at last.

'I am telling you the truth.'

He leaned back in his seat. Across the bridge of his nose was a frown line so sharp that it seemed to be cut into his face. I wondered suddenly how many times he'd sat here in this room, listening to clients telling stories as hopeless as the one I was giving to him now. He must have frowned each time, and that was how the line had grown so deep. All those desperate people just like me, who knew the game was up but still kept hoping that it wasn't.

'Janice,' he said with a sigh, 'you do understand that you're in very serious trouble?'

SEPTEMBER 2001 – HMP MORTON HALL, LINCOLNSHIRE

'Take off your clothes,' said the prison officer.

'Why?'

'We're doing a strip search.'

'Take off everything?'

'Yes.'

Slowly I took off the smart black suit that I'd worn for my trial. I stepped out of my shoes and peeled off my stockings. I stood there in just my bra and pants.

'Those off too. I've seen it all before, so don't worry!'

Her voice was bright and breezy. Perhaps she thought it helped.

'Bend over,' she instructed me. 'Cough. Lift your tits.'

What this was meant to tell me was that I was not a person any more. Not in there. I was not Janice any more. Not Nasty Girl. Not Mama J. I had no identity at all.

13

ALONE TIME

WHEN I FIRST MET Barbara, she was silent and closed off. A small, slight lady in her sixties, she worked as a carer. She used to keep an eye on Lynne, an elderly neighbour whose daughters lived some distance away. They'd been friends for years, and Barbara would drop round for cups of tea and do her housework and errands. Just recently, Lynne had developed mild dementia.

Despite their friendship, Barbara wasn't comfortable when Lynne asked her to withdraw £250 from her bank account. She insisted that Lynne's daughters give permission. She also asked Lynne to sign the receipt she collected when she took the money out. Despite her dementia, Lynne seemed to understand, and she signed. This was the only time that Barbara took out any of Lynne's money.

Two months later, the police knocked on Barbara's front door and told her they had come to search her flat. She was so surprised by this that one of the officers noticed it. 'You don't know why we're here, do you?' he said to her.

Barbara didn't know. But she quickly found out. In the last month, £4,000 had been drawn out of Lynne's account in daily amounts of £250 – and now Lynne's family had accused her of stealing it.

The police search of Barbara's flat found nothing. Barbara's bank statements showed no unexplained payments. On CCTV footage from Lynne's bank, Barbara appeared only once. That was on the day she had withdrawn £250 and Lynne had signed the receipt. There was no evidence at all that Barbara had committed a crime.

Nevertheless, she was arrested and questioned. Then she was advised by a solicitor to plead guilty – that way, he said, she would receive a shorter sentence. If she contested the charge, she could expect four to five years inside for fraud. When she insisted she was innocent, he didn't seem to care.

Barbara was terrified. She did as the solicitor advised her. She was given eighteen months and sent to HMP Bronzefield. There she was so anxious and distressed that she constantly cried and couldn't eat at all. Among her fellow inmates were some hard-looking cases and every single day she was convinced that she was going to be beaten up. She was too afraid to leave her cell, even for association or at mealtimes. She only stepped outside to fetch hot water in a flask to make tea.

One day as she was sitting in her cell, the hardest

of the hard cases stuck her head around the door. Barbara shrank away, convinced something violent was just about to happen. The woman walked over to Barbara, picked her up and carried her outside. She put her down at one of the lunch tables. Then to Barbara's astonishment, she said: 'You've not eaten for a week. You're going to sit here now and have some lunch.'

Barbara gave no trouble at all, and after just a few weeks she was moved to an open prison near Maidstone. She found it easier there than in the cells at Bronzefield, but the weeks of her sentence were passing very slowly. Now she felt less frightened, her anger was starting to grow. It was three very long and painful months before she was released on probation.

I held private one-to-one meetings with women who needed them as often as I was able to. In one of those meetings, Barbara spoke to me at last. She swore to me again and again that she had stolen nothing from Lynne. She thought Lynne's family must have been to blame – they had certainly had far more opportunities than she had. And she felt victimised by the police. On a low income and with access to Lynne's bank account, how could she prove that she didn't steal the money and then hide it? All the police ever wanted was to get a quick conviction. Now her guilty plea and her sentence drew a line under the case. She'd been branded a thief.

As Barbara grew more confident, she told her story to the women's group. The others were indignant, lifting her spirits by telling her that no one there thought she had done anything wrong. Being believed made such a difference. She stayed on long beyond the twelve weeks of her own attendance as our tea-maker and social secretary, helping new arrivals settle in. It was good to watch this woman, who had once sat silently staring at the floor, now greeting everyone, offering a drink, a smile and a word.

I was glad that she felt better, but it wasn't enough. There was no justice for Barbara.

'I've got a criminal record now,' she told the group. 'It's so unfair.'

'How long for, Barb?' someone asked.

Barbara looked at me enquiringly.

'Seven years,' I answered. 'After that, it becomes a spent conviction.'

Barbara stared at the ground. To her, that seven years seemed very long.

'They just decided to pin it on me,' she said bitterly. 'Criminal justice system? Don't make me laugh. They don't care much for justice, do they?'

There'd been no chance of bail following my arrest on the M1. I was remanded in custody at HMP Pucklechurch, near Bristol, in March 2001. My trial took place in Leicester Crown Court six months later.

In court I found out at last why Adam, the owner of the Apex nightclub, had informed. He hadn't been paid for storing the previous shipment of weed. That was Stedroy's fault, but Adam believed that I was in charge of the green channel. After all, when he asked me about it, I'd told him this myself.

Scully had been right. He'd warned me that I didn't know the men who'd set up that operation – their stories, their history, their dealings with each other. *Who are they really? You don't have that information,* he'd said. And Glen had been right when he told me – *the street ain't stayed the same.* I thought I could come back and take up where I'd left off. Instead, I got caught up in a drama that I didn't understand.

At my trial, I was sentenced to eight and a half years. At least this time no hotshot lawyer tried to tell me that it might not be so long. When I stood in the dock, I knew exactly what was coming. I was ready.

As I walked along the corridor underneath the court, I saw the New York skyline on the little TV above the entry desk that always showed the news. One of the tall silver towers was pouring out smoke. Suddenly a plane, far too large and fast and low, came twisting right to left across the screen then vanished in a splatter of fire. The court jailer who was walking with me stopped.

'Both towers! Oh my God!' she said.

'Isn't that the World Trade Centre?' I asked. 'Is this an accident?' The disaster seemed too massive to make sense.

'They're saying it's a terrorist attack,' replied the guard behind the desk. Other people were stopping now too. We stood in a puzzled little knot, all staring at the screen, all aghast.

Then the jailer tapped me on the arm.

'Come on now. In the cell.' The world was in flames, but I wasn't a part of that world now.

On the first night of my sentence, a nurse brought me tablets. Tamazepam, she told me. I didn't care what they were – I just took them. She said they'd help me sleep, but they didn't. I wasn't sure what the tablets really did, because I sat on my prison bed for hours and just stared into the half-light. I didn't know what I felt or what I thought. Perhaps that was what Tamazepam was for – making everything go blank.

Going blank seemed like the best way to survive.

I kept my mind locked down and accepted the routine of prison life. I couldn't look ahead, at the long stretch of time I was facing. When thoughts like that appeared, I shut them out. I shut down my feelings too. I stayed in the day.

I tried to concentrate on practical problems – like my flat, and who was looking after it. When Scully was released from Swaleside, he moved in. At least now it wasn't standing empty. In a few months' time, he said, he was planning to go home to Jamaica for a while. He'd make sure my rent would still be covered.

Before he left, he came to Morton Hall to visit me. It was good to think of him flying far away into the sun.

'I'm off to take care of some business,' he told me. 'But don't you worry about anything. Just keep your chin up, and I'll be back to see you.'

'Sure thing, babe.'

'Remember, princess – you will reach the other side,' Scully said. He fixed his gaze on me. 'You and me – we'll be there together.'

'You're getting soft!' I teased him. 'Never thought I'd hear you be romantic!'

'Never thought it myself.' He smiled his most mischievous smile. 'But times move on. Just remember what I say to you. It's not so long. Then it's you and me.'

I held on tightly to that thought.

On 3 August 2002, Scully died suddenly in Jamaica. We would never be together again.

When the news arrived, I was paralysed at first with shock and disbelief. Then I felt my grip on my emotions start to break. I struggled with the mad desire to search for him. If, somehow, I could walk the pavements of south London, I was sure that I would see him, strolling along in his paint-stained old boots, swinging his carrier bag. How could he not be there? Next came fear, as though Scully had abandoned me. I was almost angry – how could he just leave? Finally, a deadweight of grief crushed me down until I could scarcely stand.

Whenever I'd been frightened and lonely in the past, I had summoned up my strength, and that had been enough. But now it wasn't working any more. Scully was a memory. *One day,* I thought, *I will be memory too. What will that memory be?*

Who am I? said a whisper in my head. *And what am I? What kind of mother? What kind of woman? If I died tonight, what is my legacy? What message would I leave behind?*

Sometimes I'd imagine that Nadia had suddenly arrived. I longed and longed for her to come. But if I saw her one day in the visiting room – what would I say to her? When she accused me of breaking my word, of letting her down yet again – how would I answer?

A mother, she had said to me, *is someone who is there.* She was right. I hadn't been there when she needed me the most. Could she ever forgive me?

'And how are you doing, my dear?'

The woman was in her late sixties, with short, steel-grey hair. She gave a cheerful smile as she spoke. Her voice was brisk and upper middle class.

It was association time, when we were let out of our cells. I was queuing up for tea from the big prison urn. The tea was stewed for hours and there wasn't any milk, just that powder people use to whiten coffee. But tea is always tea. There was something reassuring about it.

I said to her, 'I'm fine.'

'I'm not sure about that. Last night I heard you crying.'

'Nah,' I said. 'Nah. I wasn't.'

The coldness in my voice pushed her away.

'Very well. I didn't mean to bother you.' She turned briskly to the urn, picked up a plastic cup from the table and served herself with lukewarm, dishwater-coloured tea.

As my cell door slammed shut every night, fear and panic gripped me. It was reality check time.

Who am I? What am I?

A drug dealer. A convict. A thief.

I heard voices in my head. Mummy's voice. Nadia's. I longed to see them, to hold them, to speak to them. But I was all alone.

I dreaded the crunch as the door was locked behind me. I was so afraid of the emptiness, I was close to crying out. Perhaps I sometimes did. Perhaps the woman by the tea urn heard my cries, even though I wouldn't admit it. Perhaps I wasn't so tough any more.

'Good morning, my dear.' The grey-haired woman greeted me again. Last time she'd tried to talk to me, I'd not been very friendly.

'Good morning,' I replied. She smiled at me and held out her hand.

'I'm Edna.'

'Janice,' I replied.

'Been here long?'

'Five months.'

'And what d'you think of the tea?'

I pulled a face.

'I quite agree,' she said. 'It's absolutely awful.'

'Look – thanks for asking how I was the other day,' I said to her.

'That's perfectly alright.' Edna smiled again, in her brusque manner. 'I heard you lost your husband. I'm very sorry indeed.'

When I thought of Scully, my eyes filled with tears. The heavy weight inside my chest pressed down. But I knew how he would smile if he'd heard somebody calling him my husband. Stuck between the tears and the smile, I wiped my cheeks.

'Thanks,' was all I could manage to say.

Edna reached into her pocket. She handed me a grey and tatty tissue.

'What was your husband's name?' she asked.

'His name was – ' But before I could say it, I was properly crying.

'I would love to hear all about him,' she said, 'if it would help. I think it might. I'm a widow too, you see.'

I was so touched by her kindness that I cried even more.

'Right,' she said. 'We're going to get some tea.'

I'd never had a chat quite like the one I had with Edna. She was inside because of a land dispute. Her husband had died and she was living alone in the cottage they had shared. But then her next-door neighbour built a garage which overlapped the boundary of her land. She lodged an official objection. The man's behaviour became anti-social. He began to play loud music late at night to annoy her. He clearly thought that he could bully a widow in retirement into dropping her case.

But he'd reckoned without Edna. She hired a JCB and knocked his garage down. When she told me this, I laughed so much that I spat my tea right across the cell.

'You did *whaat?*'

'Demolished it. Completely. Just a pile of bricks,' said Edna tartly. 'You should have seen his face. Dreadful chap.'

'And then you got arrested?'

'For criminal damage. The law must take its course. But that awful little man. He thought he could get away with anything. I made him think again.'

I shook my head in amazement. Respect to Edna. She might be over 60 and alone, but she wasn't taking bullshit from anyone. And she gave me the first proper laugh I'd had in ages.

But in the middle of the night – there was still only me. I stared into the emptiness. The voice in my head was unrelenting. I forced myself to listen. Here I was, face to face with myself.

Janice – you fucked up. You have made bad choices. These are the consequences. You have walked the wrong path and this is the penalty. Now it's time to pay.

Listener lives here, read the poster on the prison wall. It explained that there were inmates trained as listeners, part of a national scheme to help others in distress. Somehow, without quite knowing why, I connected with this. I asked a prison officer to tell me more about it.

'Are you serious, Janice? It's tough, you know. You have to do a course.'

'Yes,' I said. 'Oh yes, I'm serious.'

The officer was right. Listener training was a serious thing. I took a sixteen-week course run by the Samaritans. And what I learned changed my life.

Prison listeners help those at rock bottom. They learn to use body language, tone of voice and eye-contact to connect. How to recognise crisis and danger. How to be with someone in distress, what to say and what not to, and how sometimes the most important thing is to give a person time. There is no need to be uncomfortable with silence.

Although I didn't know it then, these were some of the skills I would use much later on, when I had made a new life. I couldn't have imagined that life, back then in Morton Hall. But the training the Samaritans gave me was how it all began. I will always be grateful.

I passed the course. Now I could be called on any time. Listeners carried mobile phones so that prison officers could ring us and ask if we were able to see someone at any time of day, or even in the night. Prisoners could also ask directly for help.

Not long after I started to work as a listener, I was taken in the middle of the night to the cell of a girl who was threatening to take her own life. She was new inside, a first-timer, struggling to cope. I knew how bad that could be. I was nervous as I walked along the corridor, hoping I could find the right words.

When I entered, she was sitting on her bunk with her knees drawn up to her chest. She didn't look at me. I hesitated.

'You going to be alright, Janice?' the prison officer asked.

'Yeah,' I said. 'Yeah, I'll be fine.'

The door was locked behind me. I stood there, unsure of how to start. Then the girl raised her head. The instant she saw me, she burst out crying.

'Oh my God,' I said. 'Do I really look that bad?'

Although she was still crying, she started to laugh too. Half a minute later, she was quiet again. But I noticed how that moment formed a tiny connection between us.

I sat down on the bed. Slowly, carefully, I reached out and stroked her hand.

'Right then,' I told her. 'I'm happy to stay with you. We don't have to talk. We can sit here together, if it helps.'

She gave a very small nod.

There were a few times in the night when I could tell that she thought about speaking, but she couldn't find the words. After we'd been sitting for a while side-by-side, she reached out and gripped my hand. It eased her sense of isolation. Then, as the light of dawn came into the cell, I saw her head was nodding. Very briefly, before the door was opened, she slept. I was proud I'd been her lifeline.

When women started asking to see me as a listener, I felt a new warmth, like nothing else before in my life. But my role could be gruelling at times. I discovered on the listening course just how great the distress of prisoners can be. So often, they were struggling with desperately complicated lives. Every day seemed to bring some new disaster. Over and over, I heard their shocking histories – childhood abuse, domestic violence, poverty, depression and problems with drink and with drugs. People inside are ten times more likely to kill themselves than those not in custody.

The worst pain of all was also the most common. Most female inmates are mothers, so as soon as they come into prison, it creates a crisis of separation. Again and again I heard the dreadful despair of women who were parted from their children.

For months in Morton Hall, I didn't hear a word from New York. I wanted to phone, but when I thought about how angry Nadia must be, I decided to wait and let her take her time. Eventually, though, my longing to hear her voice became too strong to resist. I saved all my money to buy phone cards, cutting down to just one cigarette a day. It was tough and I badly craved to smoke, but now I could afford to ring her at the weekend, when we were allowed to make our calls.

I spoke to Emmanuel first. I told him that I'd been sent down and had eight and half years ahead of me. He already knew, of course. As I talked, he listened in silence. I knew he was disgusted with me. For a moment I wondered if he'd even fetch Nadia to the phone.

'She's not here now. Try her on Sunday,' he answered

at last. He was making it clear that he wouldn't act as go-between. I would have to find the words to speak to Nadia myself.

I didn't dare to plan what I might say – I was too scared. I imagined her disowning me, screaming with anger, telling me she hated me, she'd never ever see me again. It frightened me so badly that I tried to shut those awful pictures from my mind. As I stood there waiting for her, clutching the receiver, my hands were cold and clammy.

'Hey, Mom.'

I almost sobbed at the sound of her voice.

'Hey, Nads.'

I talked around in circles, asking her all about her life. She kept saying she was fine. We spoke like well-intentioned strangers. How could I reach this cool, distant woman? But what right did I have to demand that she open up to me? She had every reason to feel the way she did.

'Okay,' I said at last. 'My money's nearly out. I know there's nothing I can say. Words won't fix it this time. I know that.'

There was silence.

'There's no justification for anything I did. I broke my promise. Just telling you I'm sorry won't help.'

Then I heard her start to cry.

'Don't cry, baby,' I whispered.

'I'm not,' said Nadia. 'I'm angry. I'm so angry with you.'

I started to cry too.

'Look, baby, can we talk again? Anything you want to say, however you feel.'

'Daddy said to me – whatever you've done, you're still my mother.'

It was a tiny chink of light. Yet again I was flooded with gratitude. Emmanuel had always stepped up.

Nadia was all that mattered now. I saved every penny that I could to buy the phone cards that linked us together. Then the prison allowed me to give up my visiting orders in exchange for longer on the phone – and I was fine with that. If we chatted nonsense, I didn't mind at all. Just the sound of her voice was enough.

JULY 2004 – HMP SEND, SURREY

When I got a transfer to a prison nearer London, I was pleased. As soon as I arrived, I applied to continue with my listening.

The young woman who came into the dining room one lunchtime had messy brown hair. Her face was red and swollen with crying. An officer was walking alongside her, trying to calm her, but the woman kept on pushing her away. She sat down two tables away from me, and buried her face in her hands.

'Legal visit,' someone muttered behind me. That meant she'd seen her solicitor that day. Something serious had happened.

For the next few days, I watched her. I learned her name was Claire – she'd only just arrived and been placed in a cell just a few doors down from mine. But she never spoke to anyone, too wretched and distracted to care about whether she made friends. She'd had three legal visits in a very short time. Something was wrong.

'Janice?' said the prison officer. 'You're a listener, aren't you? Can you see this new girl, Claire?'

She was in danger of losing her two children. No one in her family could look after them and her release date was a year away at least. Her local authority had started the process to take them into care. I agreed that I would listen, and was taken to her cell.

Claire was hunched up on the bed with her arms tightly wrapped around her chest. Her cheeks were chapped and peeling from the constant fall of tears. Her eyes were so puffed-up that I could barely tell their colour. As I stood there in the doorway, I wasn't sure what I could do. Could I help a person in such utter desperation?

Then I remembered the woman up at Morton who didn't want words, but just for someone to be there. I sat down next to Claire, not at all sure she would accept me. I felt her draw a deep, lurching breath. Very gently and lightly, I stroked her thin shoulder, then her hair.

'Hi, Claire.'

She raised her head and tried to wipe her wet sticky face with her forearm. Long stretchy strings of bubbling snot dripped on her shirt.

'Claire,' I said, 'I'm Janice. I'm happy to just sit here

with you, until you want to talk. And it's fine if you dribble all over my clothes.'

She burst into giggles. Something funny, even in this dreadful situation, could help us to connect.

'Sorry,' she said. 'God, sorry. There's snot everywhere.' Then her smile crumpled and her face screwed up in pain. 'Janice – they're going to take my kids.'

Her son Jaden was eighteen months old and Bethany, her daughter, was four. The children were her world. She was sick with fear that she would lose them. As I listened, I remembered when Nadia's plane was flying to America – how I lay on my bed in Holloway prison, staring at a cold grey patch of sky. As the distance between us grew greater, I'd felt a tearing pain in my belly. As I looked at Claire, I sensed the dangerous abyss of loss and fear that was opening inside her.

As gently as I could, I tried to get her to talk. But the only comfort that mattered was a promise that her children wouldn't be taken away. I couldn't give her that. No one could. That was why she was desperate.

'I can't live without Jay and Beth,' she whispered. 'And I won't. I really mean it.'

I told her she could see me any time, or another listener if that was what she wanted. 'Don't be shy – just ask,' I said. 'It's really no trouble. It's what we're here for.' I knew how bad it was. I wished that I could offer more than words. Two days later, she would have another legal visit. I was very, very scared that she was going to hear bad news.

As I left Claire's cell, Mummy's face came vividly

into my mind, a memory from my childhood that was almost too painful to recall. I sat down on my bed, barely seeing the cell walls around me. I was back in Southall, in my parents' house. Claire's agony was dreadfully familiar.

In 1957, Daddy asked Mummy to marry him. He wanted them to move to a new country to make a new life. It was a huge, exciting adventure. But Mummy had five children already. She had to make a terrible decision. She asked her friends what she should do, and they all told her the same – that she should leave her children behind. Everyone believed at the time that it was better for them to stay at home with relatives than move around the world. Lots of families were split, with children left behind on the islands and others born in England. Terry and I were those new children for a new English life.

Mummy talked to herself when she was cooking food for us. *'Mi wonder wha' dem pickney aah eat,'* she said. Their meal far away seemed to matter more to her than our dinner right there on the table. She wrote long letters that took weeks and weeks to reach them, and the replies, when she received them, had taken weeks more to get back to her. Every day she told us how she missed her children – and every time she did, I knew just what she meant. She meant that Terry and I would never be enough. We didn't comfort her for all that she had lost.

Our parents were strict with us. They did things the traditional way that they were done in Antigua. They both believed it was the right way to bring up a child – firm discipline and jobs that we must do around the house. We cleaned the stairs, emptied dustbins and washed up. Then I found out that my schoolfriends didn't have to do anything like this.

'But I'm a child!' I said to Mummy cheekily one day when she told me that I had to do my chores. 'Children don't have to do this here. My friend said . . . ' Then I noticed the horror in her eyes. Much later on, I understood. When I rejected the way I was brought up, it seemed to her that England had stolen me away. Mummy had lost her other children – now to lose me as well was just too much for her to bear.

As I lay in the darkness and listened to her crying, I wondered where her sadness could possibly be hidden in the daylight. How was something so unbearable so silent? Year after year, I felt her sadness seeping into everything, the cooking pots and tablecloths and furniture around us. Worse than her tears was the groaning sound she made, hollow and hopeless, from deep inside her body. I knew what that sound meant: the world was ending. It ended for Mummy when she left her five children far away.

Two days later, I heard Claire coming back from her legal visit. Everybody did. Her howls of agony rang along Send's empty corridors, invading every cell in the wing. I didn't have to ask what the decision had been.

The corridors were empty because Send was on

lockdown that day. There were problems with short staffing, which meant we were confined to our cells when there would normally be free association. Claire's footsteps, and those of the officer with her, passed by along the landing. As I leaned my back against the door, I was close enough to hear her catch her breath, then give a deep and dreadful groan. I'd heard that groan before, so many nights in my childhood. It was the sound my mother made.

'Claire?' I shouted. 'Claire?'

No answer.

'Claire! I'll be there soon!'

Her cell door slammed, and there was silence. I banged on my door. When I'd been banging for several minutes, I heard an officer outside. She sounded busy and distracted.

'What is it, Janice?'

'I'm a listener. I need to speak to Claire Daniels. I know it's a lockdown and it's difficult for you – but I think she's in danger.'

'Look, you know I can't move listeners around right now.'

'She's too upset to be left on her own. If you can just take me down there and put me in with her, then – '

'I'm sorry. No one's free. As soon as we have cover, I'll make sure – '

I could feel myself starting to get angry.

'Please listen,' I said. 'She's in danger. She might hurt herself.'

'She can't. Her cell's a safe place. We'll sort this out as soon as we can.'

All I could do was wait.

Send was always noisy. There were voices and footsteps, the sound of doors opening and closing and the rattle of keys. But now I stood by my cell window in a strange, sudden hush. I pressed my palms against the cold green wall. A long time went by.

There's something wrong. I know it. There's something really wrong.

Then my cell door opened. An officer looked in.

'Janice,' she said, 'the last time you saw Claire, what discussion did you have?'

'She said – look, does it matter? Can I see her?'

The officer didn't answer, just closed the cell door. I heard the crunch of the key.

'Hey!' I called out. 'Please! Let me see her! She shouldn't be alone!'

But shouting wouldn't make them let me out. All it would do was risk my trusted role as a listener. I forced myself to stay calm. There was another endless silence. Hours went by. When lunchtime came, we were taken out cell by cell to fetch our food. This restriction of movement must mean something very serious was happening in the prison. As I carried my tray back to my cell, I heard someone shouting from upstairs.

'There's an ambulance outside!'

I started to feel sick. Then there were more voices.

'It's Claire! There's something wrong with Claire!'

I heard the echo of her whisper. *I can't live without Jay and Beth. And I won't. I really mean it.*

Claire used her clothes to make a ligature. She tied it to the handle of the door, then forced the fabric tightly in the crack across the top. It was enough to take her weight. She hanged herself alone. She could have put her feet down on the floor at any time, but she didn't. When she said she'd rather die than lose her children, she had meant it.

'Do you know what?' I said. 'I'm lucky.'

Edna patted my arm. She'd been sitting there for hours, letting me just talk about Claire and how she died. She tried to help me carry the weight of my anger and my helplessness.

'Lucky?' she asked. 'What do you mean?'

'I'm lucky that I never had to worry for my daughter. When I got locked up, her dad stepped in. Like the trooper he is. There was no question about it.'

Edna smiled. 'That was very good.'

'He took her to America. I was upset, but I knew it was the right thing to do. She was safe.'

'You had a good man there, my dear,' Edna said.

'And now – my daughter's terribly angry with me. And she's right to be angry. But Nadia's alive, and so am I. There's still a chance to make things better.'

'Yes, indeed. There's always hope,' said Edna briskly. 'You are both still here, and that means things can change.'

'And I'm in prison, but my sentence will end. My life's not over. There's still time. That's lucky too.'

'Of course it is.'

'But it's too late for Claire.'

Edna sniffed.

'My dear – you did your best. You did everything you could.'

'Yes, but it wasn't enough. It shouldn't have happened. Someone should have been there.'

I was thinking of the officers' rota – the pattern of shifts that they worked, to make sure there were always enough people on duty to manage the prison safely. On the day Claire died, there was a gap in that rota. One empty square on a single sheet of paper made the space for her life to slip away. It happened because there was a shortage of staff. The more I thought about that, the more terrible it seemed.

It wasn't fair. She died because the system didn't work. It shouldn't be like this.

Edna and I sat there together and cried. We cried for Claire, and for her children, and all the terrible things that shouldn't happen but can never be put right.

FEBRUARY 2016

'And was that how it started?' Izzie asked me.

It was the end of our weekly supervision. In the last few minutes, as usual, we switched away from business and just had a little chat. She was curious, always asking questions, trying to find out more about me.

'How what started?'

'Your job. This job you do now.'

'Yeah,' I told her. 'It took a long time, though. I didn't just fall into this job. I had to really focus to get here.'

Izzie looked at me thoughtfully.

'But Janice,' she said, 'there's something I don't get.'

'What's that?'

'You know what it's like with a criminal record. How nobody trusts you so they won't employ you, or you try to keep it quiet so you have to tell lies and it gets really complicated – anyway, all that. You must have had those kinds of problems too.'

'Certainly I did,' I told her.

'Because – it's hard for people like us, right? No one believes in us.'

We sat there for a moment in silence. Izzie's words were true, and we both knew it.

'Society don't believe an ex-con can change,' she said softly.

'No,' I said. 'No. You're right about that.'

'So – all this stuff about building your new life. How did you do it? Didn't they try to stop you?'

14

POSITION OF TRUST

IN 2004, I GOT my first job. Being a listener had given me a sense that I was useful to others – that I could make a difference. It felt so good that I wanted to do more. I knew I had to start small, so I looked at the job ads in the local paper.

When I applied for the post of ward clerk at the local community hospital, I wondered if they'd even consider an applicant from prison. But I tried, with the support of the governor of Send, and they gave me a chance. Prisoners who work are taken by van to their placements each day, and dropped off close by so that their status isn't known to everyone. All the managers knew, and so did the doctors on the ward. But everyone was nice, and I loved the job from my very first day. I found a sense of purpose and belonging, working with patients and their families, helping people through bad times. It really did feel like a new start.

In April 2005, I was released from Send on licence. When I got home, I faced a horrible shock. Throughout my sentence, people I knew had moved into my flat at different times and paid rent to the council in my name. I'd also used what was left of Mummy's legacy to make some payments myself. But then I lost track of who was living there. I had to let it go. To survive a prison sentence, it's vital to condition your mind to your circumstances, not thinking or worrying too much about outside and whatever might be happening there. *This is here. This is now. Just deal with this. Don't waste energy on things which are beyond your control.*

So the flat had stood empty for months. It had been burgled, and burgled again. When I climbed the stairs at last and opened my front door, I met a scene of devastation. Not a stick of furniture was left. The carpets were gone, and the kitchen was a shell – even the cupboards had been yanked off the walls and removed. Two of the windows were broken. There was a dank and musty smell. In the living room, wires poked from the plaster where the chandelier used to be. I wandered slowly from room to room, my footsteps clattering on the bare floors. It was desolate.

In that desolation, I could easily have picked up the phone. 'You got a parcel?' 'Looking for half a pound of sugar?' All I had to do was say the words. Except that that one phone call would cost me my whole life. Everything I'd done. Everything I hoped that I might do in the future. It would all be gone.

For months I had to sleep on the floor while I saved as much money as I could to replace my possessions. It was hard, but I made up my mind that I wouldn't feel sorry for myself. After all, the situation was one I had created. And it could have been far worse. I had a home. I had a job. There was hope. If the council had been a bit more organised, they might have thrown me out of the flat altogether.

When someone goes to prison, their housing benefit is stopped after thirteen weeks. Many lose their homes as a result. When they re-apply, they are told that they have made themselves intentionally homeless. They go straight to the bottom of the list. If they have no family or friends to support them, they can end up on the street when they're released. I was lucky that this wasn't me.

Still, my first few weeks of freedom were difficult. Making even the smallest decisions for myself seemed an enormous challenge – what to have for dinner, what time to go to bed – after years when the prison had decided every detail of my life. The simplest things were overwhelming, even eating. Metal knives and forks felt strange and heavy and the prongs banged my teeth when I tried to use them. It was so awkward that I went out and bought a pack of plastic knives and forks like the ones we used inside.

Still, I had my work, and the company of people who by now were my good friends, to keep me moving forward. Gradually, my life began to find an even keel.

And I had something else as well. Nadia flew to London to see me. She brought a gift from Emmanuel – some money to help to replace my lost things. It was an act of true kindness.

It was strange to see my little girl all grown up in the room where her toys and her dolls were once piled on the bed – and more often spread across the floor. I could almost hear her footsteps as she ran about searching for some lost object she needed for school, or her giggles as she watched morning telly. So many days and years we should have spent together were wasted and gone. But now I thought of her loss, not just of mine. I remembered the day that she flew to America while I was in prison – how the pain of parting tore me up almost as much as the day she was born. But on her lonely journey, it was Nadia who suffered, so much more than I had ever done. It was Nadia's childhood that was lost in the wrong turns I took.

We stood in that empty room and talked. I told her how much my life had changed. That I would never break the law again. That the future would be completely different. But this was all just words, I said – I know that. Only time would let her truly trust me. I told her that I hoped she would give me that time. Then a better future could come in and fill this sad empty space.

When she left for New York, I went with her to Heathrow. After she had vanished through the barriers, I realised I was smiling. It was the first time I could let her go without crying. I knew that she was coming back.

After five and a half years at the community hospital, I decided to move on. I was nervous, but by then I had experience – I thought that I could get a more responsible position. And although I'd loved my role, the daily travelling was tiring. I looked for something closer to my home. Then I had a stroke of luck. I found a really good job as Patient Services Coordinator at a large hospital quite close by.

At my leaving do, in a pub just up the road from work, I decided to tell my friends the truth – that when I started the job, I'd been on day release from HMP Send, a few miles up the road. They were astonished. At first they thought that I was winding them up.

'You *what?*'

'You were in prison!'

'You're lying!'

'Why didn't you tell us?'

'Well . . . ' I began, but then Kim stopped me.

'I understand why. I think you're pretty brave to tell us now. But to get a job like that – to rebuild your life – good for you!'

'Was that why you couldn't come to drinks after work?' asked Vivian.

I smiled sheepishly.

'Yeah. I didn't mean to be unfriendly. The prison van used to drop me round the corner and pick me up at night. So I could never go out after work, or be late getting back.'

'So . . . you told us you were your dad's carer and you couldn't be home late?'

'Sorry,' I said. They'd been so kind and under-standing that I'd always felt bad about the lies I'd had to tell them. 'But if you've been in prison, it's difficult.'

'Yeah,' said Vivian. 'I bet that's really hard. People would just think . . . ' She didn't need to finish the sentence.

'I did have a problem once,' I told her with a smile. 'With Doc Walsh.'

Dr Walsh had been cold and stiff at first, glaring suspiciously at me when the drugs trolley went around. He thought I might try to steal the drugs. It took months before we managed to establish a better relationship. My first Christmas, there was a small drinks party in working hours which meant that I was able to attend. As I sipped a glass of wine with him, I noticed no one else was in earshot. I decided that I'd risk a little joke.

'About those pharmaceuticals,' I said with a grin. 'I know you're worried, but they really aren't my thing. Not enough profit selling those. Now if that drugs trolley had cocaine on it . . . '

Dr Walsh threw back his head and roared with laughter.

'Okay, Janice! Please understand. You're not quite what I'm used to.'

'That's alright.'

I'd treasured that laugh we had shared. It felt like putting the past in its place. It was there, and it would always be a part of me. But it didn't define me anymore.

JANUARY 2010

The phone on my desk rang at 9.05 a.m. The day's first mug of tea was still steaming.

'Patient Services Coordinator – good morning,' I said. It was only my third week in the post. I still wasn't used to my new title. I heard the voice of my manager, Delia Thomas.

'Janice? Would you come to my office straight away?' Her tone was stiff and remote. At once I knew that something wasn't right.

My first thought was that I must have made a serious mistake in my new job. My stomach clenched with worry. I knew I had a lot to learn – the post at a large hospital in the city was a very big step up. As quickly as I could, I made my way down the hospital corridor and tapped on Delia's office door.

'Come in!'

Inside the office, she wasn't on her own. A serious-faced man in a suit was sitting alongside her on the far side of her desk. I recognised him from the hospital's induction day when I first started: he was the Director of HR.

'Please take a seat.'

They both looked so grim that I grew even more alarmed.

'Sure,' I said. 'Is everything okay?'

'Janice,' said the Director, 'we'll come straight to the point. It's about your DBS check.'

I'd given all the information about my criminal record on the application form when I'd applied for the role. In my interview, Delia herself had asked me about it. So while I knew that the DBS check the hospital would obtain – an official report on my criminal history – wouldn't be pretty, I hadn't been worried. Until now.

'You did not disclose your criminal record when you applied for the role of Patient Services Coordinator,' the Director went on.

I was too surprised to speak.

'The – ah – issues in your past are very serious indeed. You are suspended with immediate effect.'

His words felt like a punch in the stomach – so sudden and so shocking it was hard to take them in.

'But you knew about my record!' I protested.

'Janice,' said Delia uneasily, 'we offered you the job without being aware of your criminal history. Your past is not compatible with a position of trust. We must withdraw the offer.'

'I disclosed it on the application form! And I told you at the interview!'

They glanced at one another.

'That's not the case, I'm afraid,' said the Director.

I stared at Delia. Delia looked down at the floor.

'Yes, it is!' I insisted. I was too dumbfounded to know what else to say. 'It is the case. I put it all on the form. And when you interviewed me, Delia, remember – '

The Director cut in.

'We were never made aware that you have drug dealing convictions.'

'But I worked at a hospital for five and a half years!' I cried. 'I started there while I was still in prison. Working with patients, with doctors! That was a position of trust!'

He was shaking his head.

'You're sacking me?' I asked. It didn't seem real. 'But I gave up my job at the hospital to come here! I wanted to get something better! And when I filled out the form – '

The Director rose to his feet. Clearly the discussion was over.

'Collect your possessions. You are suspended with immediate effect. You have seven days to appeal.'

I did appeal against the hospital's decision. My appeal was turned down. But one thing was certain: whatever they were saying now – they knew. When I applied for the job, I set out my entire criminal record on the confidential disclosure form. My interviewers questioned me about it. We talked it through in quite a lot of detail.

But when it came to my word against theirs – I was a criminal and nobody believed me. Just like that, my new job was gone and my life had been turned upside down.

Even in the dark days at Morton Hall, when I'd faced up to my crimes – I'd managed to find hope. I believed that I could change, and the people around me had believed in me too.

And just four weeks earlier, I'd felt a new chapter was beginning. Now I was unemployed and my future was scarily uncertain. I'd tried so hard, and come so far. But in many people's eyes, I was still the lowest of the low. It turned out that my past still defined me after all. It was crushing.

I called a friend, a wonderful community activist who had helped a lot of people, including me, prepare for release from prison. I'd always valued her advice. Now she suggested that the best thing to do was to apply for work as a carer, using her as my referee. When I did, I quickly found a post through an agency. She came to see me, and kindly took me out for a curry. As we dipped our poppadoms, she helped me make decisions and get back some control of my life.

'Janice,' she said, 'I honestly think you have a vocation.'

'What do you mean, a vocation?'

'Almost like a mission. It's something I felt from the time when I first met you. Your mission is to connect with people in bad trouble, and to help them.'

I wanted very much to make a difference. But in the face of this huge setback, what could I do?

'A person who has a vocation should always try to follow it,' she went on determinedly. 'And I think I know a way. Have you ever heard of St Giles Trust?'

To begin with, I worked for St Giles as a volunteer. The charity helps ex-offenders who are trying to overcome serious past issues and move forward in their lives, away from crime or gang violence. But many of its clients don't accept help easily, and assume – often from very bad experience – that no one understands or even cares. To get past this, some of the trust's employees have what's known as 'lived experience'. That means they've been through something criminal themselves and come out the other side. They use what they've learned to help others – which was exactly what I wanted to do.

My first role was to support women coming out of prison. I met them, took them home if they had a home to go to, or to temporary accommodation the charity had arranged. If no home could be found, I went with them to local council housing departments, to help begin the process of looking. I encouraged them to visit a GP, and above all to attend their appointments with the probation services. If they missed those meetings, they were in danger of going back inside.

My heart went out to these first clients. I knew at first hand the struggles they were facing – except that they were up against far worse than I had ever confronted. Some of them were homeless. Others were returning to chaos and crisis – poverty, violence, addictions of their own or of the people around them. Some had lost their children, or the children were severely affected by their mother's imprisonment. These fragile lives on the edges of society were far away from what most think of as 'normal'. Then being told that they had to go to meetings, fill in forms and make arrangements could all just seem too much. But if they didn't, they would end up back in prison.

I remembered my friend's words: *'I honestly think you have a vocation.'* I realised it was true. I knew what it was like to have no solid ground at all beneath your feet. More than I had ever wanted anything before, I wanted to help these women rebuild their lives.

OCTOBER 2013

I was at home with a cold. The phone rang. It was Neil from the Human Resources department at St Giles. He told me he'd come across a job I might be interested in – a role supporting ex-offenders.

'Janice,' he said, 'they're looking for people with lived experience. This really does sound perfect for you.'

'Who's they?' I wanted to know.

'The London Probation Trust.'

'You have to be kidding me.'

'No,' he said. 'Honestly, I'm not.'

'Me? Working for probation?'

'Why not? Stranger things have happened.'

'Not recently!' I joked, and we both laughed. 'But seriously, Neil – you know that I have sixteen convictions?'

'I know all about it,' Neil assured me. 'But that's your lived experience. You are exactly what they're looking for.'

Still, I remembered the terrible day when I was ordered out of my Patient Services job. It left a scar in my mind. Now it made me scared to take the risk.

'Um . . . ' I said to him. 'Let me have a think.'

'Okay,' said Neil. 'You do that.' He'd always been respectful and kind. 'But please,' he went on quickly, 'just get the form and have a look anyway. You'd make a great engagement worker – I'm absolutely sure of it.'

*

'Jan? Oh my God, Jan!'

Izzie's voice on the phone was full of terror. My stomach gave a lurch.

It was late in the evening. An hour earlier, I'd decided that I'd taken my last phone call of the day. But I hadn't switched the work mobile off. I found it difficult, knowing that however much I did for service users, there was always still so much more that I could do. When Izzie's number appeared, it worried me. I hadn't been expecting a call.

Please, I thought, *please – don't let this be some relapse. Don't let her fall back down. Not after all the work she's done.* I picked up the call.

'What is it? What happened?'

'Oh my God, Jan. Something terrible.'

'Are you okay?'

'Yeah, yeah – I'm okay. But I just found out – someone told me – oh my God.'

'What is it?'

'It's B! He's dead!'

Mr B was the dealer who told her that he loved her. But all he really wanted was for her to throw away her life smuggling drugs through Heathrow airport. He was nothing but a predator.

'What happened?'

'He was murdered!'

'Who murdered him?'

'He'd been sleeping with Angelo's girlfriend. So Angelo ordered it. Somebody shot him in the face.

And now Leroy says he's going to sort out the guy who did it.'

'He'll kill him?'

'Yeah. He'll definitely kill him. B and Leroy were close.'

'Are you okay, Izzie?'

'I'm just – really shocked.'

There was a long, long silence.

'B was a bad person, Jan, wasn't he?' she said suddenly.

'Yes, baby. He was.'

'Sometimes he was kind to me. But really, he was scary. I just didn't realise. I should have been more afraid of him – of all of them.'

'Yes,' I said. 'They're scary. They were never really kind. All they cared about was getting what they wanted. Money and power.'

Izzie had glamorised these men. They'd seemed like bad boys, edgy and daring and cool. But all they were was brutish and cruel. She'd been lucky to escape from their clutches with her life.

'Jan,' she whispered. 'I get it now. I get how dangerous it is – that whole world. I didn't want to see it before.'

By the time we'd finished talking, if was very close to midnight. So much for professional boundaries. For me, that was still a work in progress. But even though I knew I'd be tired in the morning, I felt a sense of peace. I was truly starting to believe that Izzie would make it.

15

NINE TO FIVE TO NINE

IT WAS EARLY IN the morning, and I was on my way down to Westminster. In my bag I had my passport to show as my ID. I knew I'd be going through security checks to get inside the House of Commons. I was running slightly late, and when I showed the guard on the door of Portcullis House the invitation letter I had with me, he told me that I didn't have to join the queue inside. Instead, another guard took me quickly through the corridors and up in the lift to one of the committee rooms.

The room was crowded, with a large central table and rows of spectators seated all around. One of the seats at the table was mine, with my name tag in front of it. I'd been asked to give evidence to the Work and Pensions Select Committee of Parliament. They wanted to hear the real-life experience of ex-offenders when they go to seek employment, and about the support they receive both inside and outside of prison.

I was representing Revolving Doors, another voluntary agency that works with ex-offenders. Through St Giles

Trust, I'd come to be involved in their work. A member of the Revolving Doors team spotted me when I came in. She smiled and came across to say hello. Everyone around me looked so confident and smart, while I felt like a bag of nerves. But however intimidating the committee room might be, I was determined to speak.

Tentatively at first, but then with growing confidence, I answered questions from members of the committee, all of whom were MPs. Along with other witnesses, I told them how ex-offenders struggle in the workplace. It's extremely hard to get a job in the first place, and then we face grave discrimination. People who want to earn a living, to make a fresh start in society, are therefore denied the chance to do so.

'Even when ex-offenders show that we've changed our offending behaviours for years,' I said, 'the past is used against us. That's what happened to me.'

The committee asked me to explain. I told them how I'd been sacked without warning, even though I had disclosed my entire criminal record and worked successfully for five years in another role. I saw shock on the faces round the table. What had happened wasn't right – and they knew it. I wanted them to know how many more times this must have happened, and been swept under the carpet. The fear of it can make ex-offenders feel there's no point even trying.

At the end of the meeting, I went back to the Revolving Doors office. We talked about how the day had gone, and how nervous I had been. I was assured that I had done well.

'Today,' I told them, 'I felt like the giraffes bowed down their necks and listened to the turtles.'

'What do you mean?'

'Look at the giraffe,' I said. 'He only eats the top of the tree. That's the only place he sees. Why would he look down? The only way to make him look is if the little turtle comes along and bites his foot. Well – that's what I did today. I took a bite.'

That day in the committee room was scary, but it gave me a deep sense of fulfilment. I spoke truth to power. I represented those who are dismissed and denied a second chance because of their criminal record. And I tried to ensure that what happened to me should not happen to anyone else with a criminal history in the future.

In 2014, I began my new career, working for the London Probation Trust, then later for the Community Rehabilitation Company. They were years of personal change, and also of political upheaval.

In 2015, a very senior manager shadowed me for a day in court. He didn't say too much, but I knew that he was watching me closely as I engaged with service users. He followed up by email, and told me he admired what I was doing.

A few months later on, I got a letter. It told me I had won the service's Diversity and Engagement Award. There had been 134 nominations from across the service. In February 2016, I received my award at Draper's Hall in central London. It was hard to be elated at success when I knew how much more there was to do. But that day, I was so proud. I felt as though my journey was worthwhile.

JUNE 2016

'Well now, look at you!' I cried.

Izzie was standing on the pavement outside the coffee shop where I'd arranged to meet her. I'd been away on holiday, and hadn't seen her for longer than usual. But the moment I set eyes on her, I saw how much she'd changed. She wasn't quite so scraggy. Her cheekbones were losing their sharp angles. She'd brushed her hair, and it was thicker and shinier.

She gave me a nervous little smile.

'Look at what?'

'Look at *that!* You got bumper, girl!'

'I got what?'

'You got an arse!'

I jutted out my backside, and she laughed. And then she wiggled hers.

'Jan,' she said. 'Jan, I'm getting better. Aren't I?'

'You are, honey. You really are. And you look great! Now come in here with me and have a sandwich.'

I didn't tell her that the day before our meeting, I'd been reprimanded for taking my clients out to eat. I wasn't the only person doing it. More and more often, probation officers and engagement workers had started to buy food for our clients. And it wasn't just food – sometimes we bought clothing for their children, and toiletries as well. We knew how many of our service users lacked the basics of existence. There were women with no tampons, no deodorant, no soap. But if we declared what we were doing, or if senior management found out, we were told that helping clients in this way was unprofessional. It showed undue favouritism. I disagreed. I thought it showed humanity. Humanity that the system absolutely lacked.

Izzie was getting better. She was healthier and stronger. She wasn't using crack any more. I accepted the reprimand. And then I went on doing what was working.

This was not a simple matter. I understood just how important it was to set boundaries in work. Without them, the most skilled and dedicated people can burn out. I also knew how vital it was for professionals to always be transparent, for their own protection as well as for their clients. Rushing in, however generous the impulse might be, wasn't always the wisest thing to do. I thought very carefully before I took any course of action.

But I also knew that lives were saved by working out of hours. Going round to one service user's house to make sure that she was up in the morning to do what she had to do that day, I found her slumped on the floor in a diabetic coma. I called an ambulance. Left untreated, this coma might have led to her death.

If we want to turn lives around, we must be there with service users in the mornings, in the evenings, at the weekends – working where the crisis points are.

Right now, that isn't happening. Too many vulnerable people are falling through the cracks.

Nina sat in the circle of women.

She looked anxiously around at the others, cupping her hands around a mug of tea. She hadn't said a word since she arrived at our group, but it often took time to find the confidence to speak. When you're used to no one listening, it's hard to believe that you can say how you're feeling or that anyone will help you with your problems.

Her sentence was for handling stolen goods. But it was clear pretty quickly that the crimes had not been Nina's idea. She was extremely suggestible and always did what other people told her. I wasn't sure she even understood that what she'd been doing was illegal. Underneath her chair was a pile of dirty carrier bags. I didn't need to ask what was inside them – I already knew the answer. It was everything she owned. Nina was scared to leave her pitifully few belongings in the temporary hostel where she lived. In her world, nowhere felt secure.

I wanted us to have a private chat, but that was going to be impossible today. When the probation team was short of staff, as it almost always was, I ran the group on my own, although I was an engagement worker, not a fully qualified probation officer.

She was very hungry, and fell upon the plate of sandwiches I'd placed in the middle of the table. The food at our meetings was provided by Coughlan's, a chain of local bakers. When I'd approached them and asked for their leftovers, the director quickly agreed. The company was wonderfully supportive of our work. Later on, Greggs joined in as well. The food made such a difference. But it did much more than that. When the women walked through the doors and saw it there, their eyes lit up. They started helping each other – *Tea or coffee? Do you take sugar?* They lifted each other, without even realising it. It made our meetings feel alive.

Food made another difference too. It's difficult to plan when your belly is empty and you're scared. By feeding our service users, we could start to help them think about the future. We also offered showers to our clients who were homeless. It's impossible to keep yourself clean on the street. If they knew there was a chance to freshen up, even a reluctant service user was more likely to attend a meeting.

It was clear that Nina's hostel placement wasn't working. I asked her if she'd been to see the council about somewhere more permanent to live. No, she said, she hadn't. What was the point? She spoke so softly it was difficult to hear her. She was scared that the council would send her away, and tell her that she'd made herself homeless when she was sent to prison. (She was probably right about that.) But the thought of rejection was terrible for her. She'd feel even more worthless than she did to begin with.

As she started to talk, I grew more and more alarmed. Her difficulties in the hostel were worse than I had thought. Her hostel was mixed-gender. Nina behaved like an obedient little girl, not like an adult, following any direction she was given as though it was an order. The result was that male residents were openly sexually abusing her with no one to stop them.

She had no sense of herself. She would do anything that anybody told her to do – including blowjobs and full sex. If she was with a man and another came knocking on her door, she'd invite him in as well. Arguments broke out in her room about whose turn it was next to have sex with her. I saw tears in the other women's eyes as they tried to explain that men like that were only using her. But Nina didn't seem to understand.

A few weeks later, when I was introduced to her mother, Sarah, at a meeting, I began to understand Nina's struggles a little bit better. Sarah was friendly but completely remote. The two of them acted like acquaintances, not mother and daughter. I winced as I watched Nina turn towards her mother for a look or a word of approval, but receive just a strange, empty smile in return. I wondered sadly how they'd drifted so far from each other. But I couldn't put it right. All I could do was try to safeguard Nina.

If she couldn't leave the hostel, was there any way to make her safer? I'd heard about issues in the building before. But the situation was clearly far worse than I had thought. What on earth was going on? Should someone not have noticed what was happening to Nina? Where was the communication between the professionals in charge? How could such a vulnerable woman be put there in the first place?

BREAKING OUT

I approached a senior colleague. Shaking her head, she explained how overloaded the accommodation was. There was far more provision for men than for women, who were fitted in wherever there was space just to get them off the street. There were staff on site in the hostel twenty-four hours a day, but they weren't offering individual support. Their role was to make sure the lifts were working, that the toilets weren't blocked up, that the hostel was secure. Beyond those basics, the residents had no supervision. The kitchens were squalid. Pimps worked in the building. Sex workers were brought in and sent around from room to room. Staff patrolled in twos for their own protection.

And all of this was known. There was simply no money to improve things. A hostel place was better than sleeping on the street – but not by much. While she was living in these terrible conditions, it was very hard to see how Nina's life was ever going to get any better. But where else could she go?

With Soraya, nothing seemed to help. From our very first meeting, she always reeked of drink. The smell rolled in like a wave when she entered the room, a foot or two in front of her, even at ten in the morning. It was coming from the pores of her skin. Her whole body was toxified with booze. In this state, it took just a tiny amount – no more than a few sips – to put her back into the slurred-voice, stumbling, inebriated state where she already spent most of her time.

Soraya couldn't listen at all. She was frequently

aggressive, and no one else could have any space while she was there. When I asked her to wait and take her turn, she abused me. When other people asked her the same, she insulted them too. Arguments broke out. With Soraya present, the group was close to chaos and nothing could possibly get done.

I could see just how serious her problems really were. But that wasn't the time or the place for her to find the help she needed. She was making the others feel unsafe. I was going to have to ask her to leave.

I followed our procedures, hoping against hope that she might understand how important it was to keep the rules we set and comply with her order. First I gave a verbal warning. She responded by shouting and swearing. Her second warning had to be in writing, by email to her offender manager. It had just as little impact as the first. If there was any more disruption, I must tell her to leave.

I didn't want to throw Soraya out to face the trouble I knew would await her. Her probation officer would breach her for failing to comply with the terms of probation. Then she would be sent back to court. She might end up in prison. I hated pushing such a deeply damaged person away. I always remember the people in my past who didn't give up on me. They believed that no matter what had happened, I still had the potential to do better.

But I had no other option. Until Soraya could manage her drinking, she would never engage. The interests of the group had to come before one lost and struggling woman who was just too disturbed to be a part of it.

Lorraine was also extremely disruptive. She constantly talked over others in the group, interrupting the meeting and annoying other women who were waiting their turn to speak. She was breaking the rules of behaviour to which every member had signed up. Her interruptions had already caused two arguments. Again, the group's protocol required me to ask her to leave. And my life would certainly be easier. Trying to make sure that everyone was heard was taking far too much of my time and attention.

I noticed how desperate she was. Her words came bursting out, but they were always prompted by something that another woman said. That showed me she was listening and wanted to join in with the others. It was waiting her turn that seemed too hard. Sending her away wasn't going to solve her problems. I decided I was going to be flexible, and try to understand.

'Lorraine,' I said, 'can you do something for me? Next time, before you start talking, can you try to count to ten?'

She looked completely panicked.

'Only up to ten,' I reassured her.

But half a minute later, she burst in again.

'Can you please try to count to ten before you speak?' I repeated. But even that short pause was too much.

I gave her a final warning. If she couldn't manage

to do this, she was going to be excluded from the group.

'You can't!' she said frantically, terribly upset by this idea.

'Lorraine, I've tried to explain. It's unfair when someone else is – '

But she couldn't wait to speak. She interrupted me again.

'Lorraine! You must learn to respect other people.'

'But – but – what if I forget?'

'Forget what?'

'What I was going to say!'

'Is that what you're afraid of?'

She looked terribly worried.

'Yeah,' she muttered.

She was definitely the worst, but she wasn't the only interrupter in the group. There were many different reasons. Short-term memory problems make people scared of forgetting what they're saying. They get more and more desperate to speak before it happens. Stress can cause this memory loss, and so can abusing alcohol and drugs. What the sufferer really needs is understanding and help, so that they can start to feel calmer, and therefore less likely to forget what they wanted to say.

And Lorraine did start to improve. Sometimes it was very hard indeed for her to wait her turn. But the effort she was making was obvious. I had to give her credit and allow her to stay. She also made an effort to cut down on her drinking. That helped too. When she told the group that she hadn't had a drink for ten days, we had a little celebration.

'Janice, are we going to have vodka?' she asked me.

'No, darling. Just tea and coffee.'

I smiled at her, and she smiled back at me. It was nice just to have a conversation. A few weeks before, she could never have managed it. Among so many unsolved and unsolvable problems, it felt like a victory.

Miaow!

I looked around the circle. Several of the other women did the same.

Miaow!

'Whoever's left their phone on,' I said, 'please turn it off. You know we have a rule about phones.'

I gave it a moment. No one fumbled in a bag or a pocket. The miaowing had stopped. I decided I would carry on speaking.

Then a moment later: *Miaow!*

Now we all heard it quite distinctly.

I looked around the circle. 'So – who's brought a cat to the meeting?' I asked. Members of the group began to giggle.

A carrier bag by Nina's feet lurched to one side. I realised that the bag had an occupant. I peeped inside and saw a thin little tabby curled up on a folded pillow case.

Nina looked at me nervously.

'Where did she come from?' I asked.

'Dunno. I found her.'

'Have you been feeding her?'

'Yes. She's lovely.'

'But Nina,' I said, 'you can't bring a cat to the meeting.'

'I can't leave her on her own, Janice! She's only a baby.'

It was the very first time she had ever spoken up for herself. Her care for the little cat was clear. I hadn't seen her caring for anything or anyone up until then – most of all herself. I could only hope that at some point in the future, she might get the help she needed. Time and time again, I reached the limits of the support I could give. There were so many shortcomings in the system – and so many issues still unaddressed. But as I watched her lift the skinny little cat out of the bag and gently cradle it, it seemed to be a sign, however small, that something better might be possible for Nina.

Sheba was a slow starter in the women's group. She was softly spoken and gentle. She sat silently listening to the others for a very long time before she could tell her story.

Months later, she explained why she had been so cautious. She assumed, she said, that someone who was offering to help her was going to want something for themselves. That had always been her experience.

'I was wondering,' she told me in her quiet, steady voice, 'what you were wanting to gain from doing this.'

Sheba had been trafficked from Nigeria for sex. She thought that she was coming to England to study. She was young and naive, believing when a friend explained that she could take a course in London and pay for it by working. She saw it as a great opportunity – at first. There were only two things that she didn't understand about her English education: why she had to give all her personal documents to the course organiser, and why she must keep her travel plans secret from everyone she knew.

Slowly she was drawn into the traffickers' net. With a group of seven other girls, she was flown from Lagos to Italy. There the group divided; half flew on to Paris, and half to London. In London, she was taken to a large private home. It was the first clue she had that there was something wrong – she'd been expecting official student accommodation. A woman in charge of the house took the girls to different places to do cleaning, and told them that their proper jobs weren't ready for them to begin.

One day, at one of her cleaning sessions, she was introduced to a man and told that she must sit on his knee. Sheba said she wouldn't. The man and woman exchanged glances and the woman remarked that, 'This one is going to be a problem.' Sheba said indignantly that she had come to London to work and to study, not to sit on men's knees – and the woman laughed and laughed.

'You don't know what you're into at all here, do you?' she said.

That was how the nightmare began. Men were invited to the house to have sex with Sheba and the others. When she said no and tried to fight back, she was chained to a bed. She bit one of the men, and the woman gave her a vicious beating. She was told that she could only leave her room if she was nice to the men and let them do whatever they wanted. She had no other choice.

Once she was co-operating, she would sometimes be taken out shopping. In the street, she would stare hard at passers-by, hoping she could raise the alarm. But everyone looked through her. One day she saw a policeman and wondered what would happen if she made a dash towards him and tried to explain her situation. But she was too scared to do it. By now she understood that the people who had brought her to London were unlikely to have filled out the proper documentation. She was probably in the country illegally – so if she drew attention to herself, she would end up in even more trouble. The more she thought about this, the more desperate she felt. There seemed to be no way out.

'So then – what happened?' Izzie asked. Sheba had told her story to the group at last, and everybody listened in horror. 'How did you get away?'

'I was lucky,' Sheba said. 'I was taken to a house to do some cleaning – it really was cleaning that time. There were other people working there, and somebody slipped me an envelope. It had some cash – I'd never even seen British money before – and an address in Manchester. And there was a note saying if I could get there, somebody would help me.'

'Manchester?' Izzie asked. 'How did you get all the way up there?'

'I kept the money on me all the time, and kept looking for a moment when nobody was paying attention. And when I saw a chance – I slipped outside and ran.'

Sheba had no idea at all where she was, how far Manchester was, or who might come after her. A man in the local newsagent helped her – he told her how to get a ticket on the train in London, and then how to travel to Manchester. As she described her escape, the only sign she was upset was a shudder that would pass through her body every few minutes. I wondered how far down inside her she'd pushed her awful trauma. I was deeply worried about her.

She found the house in Manchester. For a little while, she was looked after there. She was provided with meals and could relax, instead of being confined to one room. She saw the news and tried to get a sense of what was happening in England. She was given a Nokia phone and a number to call if she needed any help. But she was still completely trapped, illegal, with almost no money and no way to get home. She was warned to stay close to the place where she was living, and not to trust anybody else who might approach her. The traffickers would certainly be trying to find her. She was absolutely terrified, every single day.

'My God – so what happened?'

'They did find me,' Sheba explained. 'By now I'd had a baby. He was just a few weeks old. They threatened me with everything – they'd call the police, they'd take away my son . . . I was out of my mind with worry all the time. I said I'd work for them, do anything but not sex work, and pay back the money it had cost them to bring me to England. I was desperate to be free of them. I thought that if I gave them all the money I could, they might let me go.'

'Did it work?'

'I never found out. One day I was arrested. I got a suspended sentence. That's why I'm here.'

The group sat there in silence.

'But,' said Izzie, frowning, 'you're not a criminal. You didn't even mean to be illegally in England. The traffickers – they broke the law. It wasn't you.'

Sheba looked at her sadly.

'They told me in court that I could have tried to contact the police much sooner than I did. They thought I didn't because I wanted to stay in England illegally. But all along, I wanted to go home.'

'They blamed you?' Izzie said angrily, 'because you were too scared to run away?'

Sheba sighed.

'Yes,' she answered. 'Yes, they did. They said I should have done more to get away. But I couldn't. I just don't think they knew what it was like.'

And sometimes, when I'd tried to teach everyone to set their own boundaries, I found that I was struggling with my own. I'd leave the work phone on after hours so that my service users could ring me, and answer when they did. I knew that I should switch off from work. If I was exhausted, I couldn't do my job properly anyway. But to be there for my clients was my passion.

Sometimes the phone would ring after hours and I wouldn't be able to answer. I left a voice message, telling the callers I would get back to them tomorrow. Then when I checked, I'd find long rambling messages. Sometimes the messages were from people who'd been drinking, or taking drugs, their thoughts so scrambled that the messages made very little sense. I found one left at 1 a.m. by a girl who was just about to take heroin. It was harrowing to listen. But I tried to play the messages back so that I could respond. For some service users, even to say how they were feeling was a breakthrough.

One morning, when I turned on my phone, I found a message from Carla, an Italian woman on probation for drink driving.

'I know you're not going to answer,' said Carla's voice, 'but it really helps just talking. Is there any way that you can change the phone? Could there be longer for me to leave a message, before I get the beep?'

For Carla, an automated message was the only comfort that she had.

16

CLEARING UP A HURRICANE WITH A DUSTPAN AND BRUSH

AS I SETTLED IN to my new job with London Probation, my skills for engaging with service users, and especially with women, were spotted by senior management. They felt that I could represent exactly what the service was trying to achieve. I became one of eleven engagement workers within the organisation, part of a 'lived experience' project. I also became a member of the Pan-London Strategy Group. The goals of the group were to develop services for female offenders and ex-offenders across the city.

The constant talk of funding streams confused me initially. This political language was difficult to understand at times. I don't have that managerial background, but the knowledge I have gained on my journey has provided me with insight.

As the years have gone by, based on everything I have seen, I have developed a vision for change in the way that the criminal justice system deals with offenders – in particular, the way it deals with women.

I understand the struggle of change – I've been there. I believe that a great deal can be done to reduce offending and support those who have offended in the past.

These are the changes I would really like to see:

Men do far more offending than women. Only 5 per cent of prisoners in the United Kingdom are female. But in that 5 per cent is a quarter of all cases of suicide and self-harming in British prisons. Women prisoners need much more attention and help.

Many are mothers. I believe that the whole of society is damaged by their sentences. Women who have suffered from violence and abuse are often traumatised when they go into prison. But the system doesn't notice. The way that they are treated makes their problems far worse. The results are anxiety, depression, self-harm and suicide.

I also worry about what happens to boys when their mothers go to prison. They feel terror, abandonment and rage. They can't cope with it. As men, they close their feelings off to allow them to cope. This is the anger that drives so much violent offending later on.

So I'd like to see female minor offenders dealt with very differently. In many cases, this would mean not putting vulnerable people into the criminal justice system in the first place.

Right now, when they leave prison, many of these women will face homelessness, lost jobs and broken families. Their children's lives are thrown into chaos. The costs of trying to solve all these problems are enormous. If we did things differently, I think we could avoid them in the first place.

The prison system is bursting at the seams. Serious mental health problems get missed. So I believe that assessments of a person's mental health should be presented before they get to court. This vital work shouldn't have to wait until someone has breached their probation.

I'd also like to change the expectations of the courts and probation service. Right now, when a court hands down an order, a woman's circumstances can get overlooked. I have worked with a client who was heavily pregnant, then later on, breast-feeding. She had no one to leave her baby with, and could not comply with her order. I had to breach her and return her to court. She was put through awful stress, and so was her baby. It could have been avoided.

I feel particularly strongly about the women recruited as mules to smuggle drugs into Britain. To them, the payments can seem large. They've no idea what's waiting for them when they land at Gatwick or Heathrow – the checks, the trained eyes watching as they step off the plane, the experienced customs staff who know the signs to look for. For the people who organise the mules, it's a numbers game. If many mules are sent, enough of them get through to keep the profits flowing.

I will never forget one service user who was recruited as a mule. She was told that her journey to England and back would take three days. She left her thirteen-year-old daughter in the care of a neighbour and boarded a plane with cocaine in the lining of her suitcase. She was caught. Her sentence was ten years. There are many others like her.

I also think the Disclosure and Barring Service (DBS) should be re-assessed. It produces reports on the criminal backgrounds of people applying for work. Of course, there are serious crimes which can never be omitted. But my own DBS illustrates the problem with the way the system works right now.

A check run on me in July 2019 contains six pages of offences. Any employer would freak out when they saw that. But I started work at the community hospital in 2004. I believe that my career since then counts for more than my previous history.

I've never lied about my criminal record. But I would like society to understand how offenders feel when they are trying so hard to give their best in the future. They know their history puts employers off. But if they try to keep some details back, and then the DBS is carried out, they look like liars.

Due to cuts in government funding, our probation service women's group sadly came to an end. I believe it should have been expanded. I believe safe spaces should be offered in place of the rushed appointments too many probation service users experience now.

Instead of sending people to prison, I'd like to see far more opportunity for community resolution for women. The police could then record a resolved crime, but these women would not spiral off through the criminal justice system, getting more and more hurt at every stage.

Right now, we have services strained almost to breaking point, and never-ending cutbacks. I wish I could offer so much more. I'd like to see a joined-up approach to turning people's lives around: help with housing, mental health, debt management, childcare, education and work.

My dream is to run a proper residential unit where women on probation could live while they were getting back on their feet. While they were there, they would be supported, trained and equipped with the tools to move successfully on with their lives. I would provide wholesome meals and good surroundings to give them their dignity back. There would be therapy and coun-selling for those who needed it, along with education and advice about interviews and jobs.

There would be help with addictions and substance abuse. There would be someone to talk to, not just in office hours, but 24/7. There would be massage, relax-ation and music in the evenings. A play room and a garden would keep their children happy when they came to see them on visits. Family rooms would let them spend time together, allowing them to rebuild their trust with their kids.

This isn't pampering criminals. This isn't rewarding crime. This is peeling back layers of damage that have happened over many years. If you have nothing and nobody helps you, if you're released from prison to live on the streets, you'll quickly fall back into the problems and the crimes that put you in prison in the first place.

If, as a society, we really wanted to cut offending, this is what we'd do. In place of sabre-rattling, vengeful policies, we'd help people turn their lives around.

So I would like to connect the powers at the top – the politicians who run our country – to the people on the ground who understand what needs to be done. If I could say one thing to those in charge, it would be this. We are each others' keepers. We are sisters and brothers. If we could run this system in this way, I profoundly believe that we could change the outcomes for the better.

On 2 May 2017, my role changed again. The change was due to political decisions. The probation service split into two: the National Probation Service (NPS) and the privatised Community Rehabilitation Company (CRC), owned by MTCnovo.

My new role was that of Community Payback Officer. It was significantly different. I was no longer hands-on, able to go out into the community, visit homes and intervene actively to support my service users. Instead, I answered phones, recorded issues and directed service users to their projects.

I didn't like the changes. From my seat behind a desk, I found it was much harder to hold people's hands. The careful, sometimes slow process of building up trust until a vulnerable person would confide in me could no longer happen. I saw clients hesitating to talk openly to anyone, knowing that the next phone call they made would very likely be taken by someone else who knew nothing about them. It was difficult and painful for traumatised people to keep going through what had happened with a different professional, each time starting over again from the beginning.

I felt a real sense of loss, and deep frustration. I worried about the clients I had left behind when I moved on. They had been left hanging, and to me, this seemed very wrong. But there were only so many hours in the day, and a limit to what I or my colleagues could manage to do.

Probation is a lifeline. Our job is to keep offenders out of prison. Help them to make changes before it's too late. Support them as they try to turn things round. Far too often, this lifeline comes very close to breaking, and the situation's growing worse, not better. The political changes that have happened have not, in my opinion, made the service's vital work easier. Sadly, I believe that in recent years, the opposite has happened.

Right now, far too often, we are trying to clear up after a hurricane with a dustpan and brush.

'It was sad of me, really,' said Izzie with a grin, 'to enjoy being on probation. But I did. I was so lonely before.'

The women's group grew in size until we had around fifteen regulars – all different ages, facing different charges, but finding support from each other. Izzie became a central member. Instead of the skinny, fidgeting girl with the dealer hanging around for her outside, she shared her story and listened to others, offering them feedback and advice. I saw her kindness blossom. She made friends. And every day, her own recovery grew stronger.

In the summer of 2016, the women's group was closed down. The women we had worked with were bereft. Many of them wrote to protest at the closure of their group. Izzie was one.

'I am writing to explain what the women's probation group has done for me', she wrote. *'I was depressed, using heroin and crack every day, lonely and breaking the law to fund my habit. I had no motivation to change. But when I met Janice, she told me her story and showed me there is a way out of drugs and crime. She was someone I could turn to for support and advice.*

'The group has helped me in so many ways, to have female company and friends and to share anything that's on our mind or issues or worries, or anything that's going well. At first I thought I didn't need to go, but I now look forward to coming and have close relationships with the girls and the staff.

'I cannot put into words what Janice has done for me. I am forever grateful for her support. It's vital that other women in the criminal justice system get the help and support they need.'

The women's appeals were unsuccessful. Cuts always seem to be unstoppable – no matter what anyone tries to say. The havoc that they bring goes unseen by the hand that hacks the services away.

Izzie and I had talked so much. At the end of our last meeting, we'd said everything we needed to say. She walked across the room to me and simply held my hand. I knew that she was making me a promise. There would be no going back.

I trusted her. I always knew I could. And Izzie has kept that promise to this day.

ACKNOWLEDGEMENTS

FIRSTLY, THANK YOU TO Elizabeth Sheppard for the love and dedication equal to mine towards the writing of this book. Your support has been boundless.

To David Riding and the MBA team: I am grateful to you for believing in the power of my story.

Kate Fox, aka LadyBoss at HQ: from the moment I met you, I knew you were the one! Thank you for taking *Breaking Out* to the world. And to the rest of the *Breaking Out* team at HQ for your hard work and attention to detail across the book. I'm totally in love with the book cover.

My thanks to Edward Shivmangal for bringing the writing challenge to me with a lunch date that I will never forget. Emma Parton for supporting and managing me during my time at LPT – Diversity and Engagement Award recognition would not have been possible without you. Charlotte Durnun, for the time you have taken out of your busy schedule to discuss new and innovated ideas for the women's project. Francine Knowles-Weller, my buddy, for always being the person I'd moan to in my early years as an Engagement Worker. Sharon Millington, you always believed I could do this, and I am grateful for the support while on life's journey. Ros Griffiths, for being a friend and confidante throughout my younger years.

To St Giles Trust, thank you for the opportunity to be a part of your amazing volunteering team and the HR team that signposted me to London Probation Trust.

Heather Munroe, the Probation Chief at the London Probation Trust 2014, for the opportunity you gave me to work with professionals who believed ex-service user involvement would make a significant difference in society. This would not be possible without your vision.

Sonia Flynn, thank you for the care and support you gave me as an engagement worker while you were senior lead at London Probation Trust. Paula Harriot for being the champion and voice for developing women like me, and for showing me how to shine.

Finally, Delphine Duff for being more than just a friend and colleague, thank you for the patience you took to mentor and support me in developing my gift.